NAPOLEON AND UNCLE ELBY

NAPOLEON
AND
UNCLE ELBY

by CLIFFORD McBRIDE
With an Introduction by Don Herold

COACHWHIP PUBLICATIONS
GREENVILLE, OHIO

Napoleon and Uncle Elby, by Clifford McBride
© 2025 Coachwhip Publications edition

First published 1945
Clifford McBride, 1901-1951
CoachwhipBooks.com

ISBN 1-61646-603-0
ISBN-13 978-1-61646-603-9

To "Boss" Dodge, veteran art editor of The Los Angeles Times. *The first great man of my youth and whom now, after twenty-five years, I admire even more.*

AN APOLOGY FOR
CLIFFORD McBRIDE
by DON HEROLD

I want to apologize for the work of Clifford McBride. In American daily newspapers where comic art has become, largely, tragic art, and where dope operas reign supreme, and where comedy, if any, is predominantly abdominal and almost invariably moronic, Clifford McBride produces an output of amiable pen-and-ink humor in which there is consistently gentlemanly restraint, gentlemanly drawing and gentlemanly intelligence. It is unspeakably un-American. I apologize for this outrage on our worst sensibilities.

But, strangely, the "strip" (as the trade calls 'em), *Napoleon and Uncle Elby,* which Clifford McBride draws, is eminently successful and appears regularly in scores of daily and Sunday newspapers. In its success, it is paradoxically American.

I am maddened mildly when I look at the so-called comic pages of our newspapers today and find them filled largely with lurid adventures of secret agents, spies, smugglers, narcotic peddlers, kidnappers, gyps, gangsters, jungle prowlers, or men from other worlds with magic means of locomotion—in short, with melodramatic claptrap of the yellowest hue. Either that, or with vestigial survivors of an earlier school of pig-bladder comic art which stemmed directly from the old burlesque theatres.

And surveys reveal that these are the pages which 96 per cent of our population devour avidly as a daily diet, skipping printed text as if it were poison.

I must apologize again and again for Clifford McBride's perversity in going against the tide. But, slyly, I must rejoice in his unorthodox success; it's as easy for him as floating downstream.

Maybe this Clifford McBride will, almost alone, eventually turn the tide of public taste in the contents of newspaper comic pages.

His cartoons depict the genial relationship of a rotund Uncle Elby and a big lubberly, lovable dog, Napoleon. Napoleon's antic romps bring almost daily disaster to his master, yet his canine soul is so great that we can well understand Uncle Elby's interminable tolerance.

And there is almost invariable subtlety in the humor. Imagine *that* . . . in a newspaper funny page! Some of the Napoleon strips, you have to look at twice to see the point. Whereas, you can look at most strips twenty times and find no point.

Clifford McBride handles his difficult medium, pen and ink, as well as anybody else in America of whom I can think at the moment. His technique is as good as that of some of the better pen-and-ink artists of the old *Punch*. I predict that his work will be found in libraries a hundred years from now, and I can think of the work of few other newspaper artists of today of which that can be said.

This man McBride needs further apology for working almost entirely in pantomime. He minimizes dialogue and resorts rarely to that atrocious American device, the "balloon," in which laborious inanities are strung out for the delight of our public which (if the average editor is right) consists entirely of persons who move their lips as they read.

And this brings me to newspaper editors. Somehow I blame them for the starved gauntness of the American funny-bone. They have fed it nothing but the grossest fodder. Somehow I believe there would be acceptance for a score of Clifford McBrides in this country if the editors would offer 'em, and if there were that many Clifford McBrides—which there aren't.

Incidentally, when I discussed the writing of this introduction with Clifford McBride, he said: "Be sure and tell them that I'm not related to the publisher. Most people will decide, after turning a few pages, that nobody but a relative could sell a book like this to a publisher."

I'll say that Mr. McBride, the publisher, could well be proud of having Mr. McBride, the cartoonist, for a second-cousin or something.

CONTENTS

NAPOLEON AT HOME

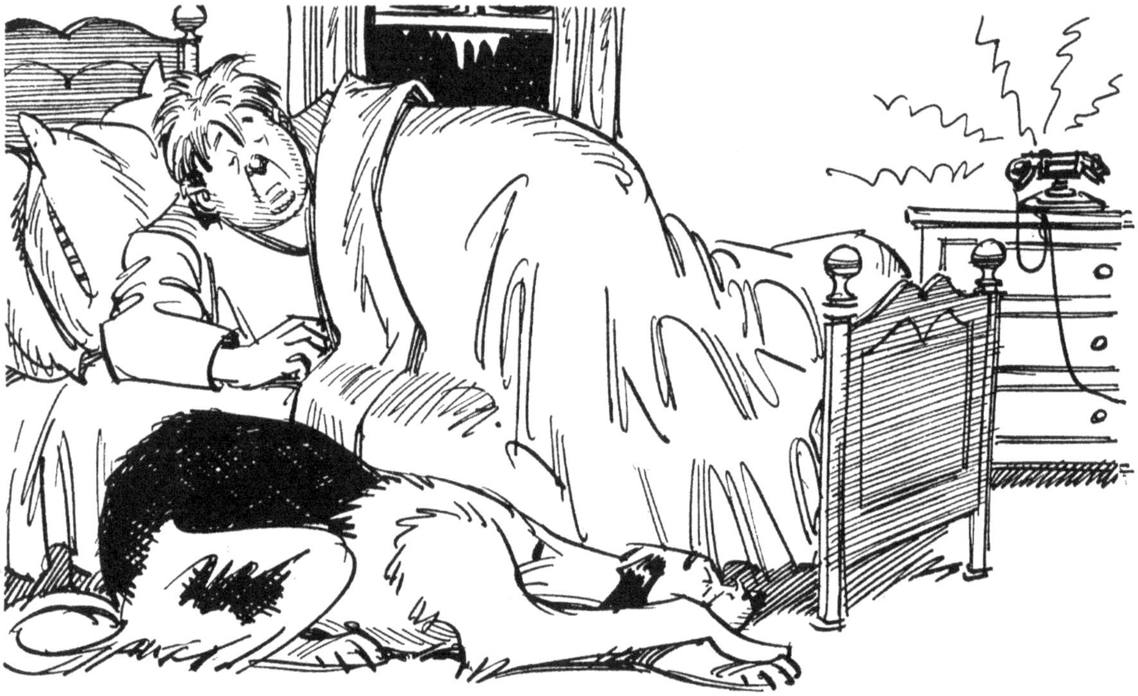

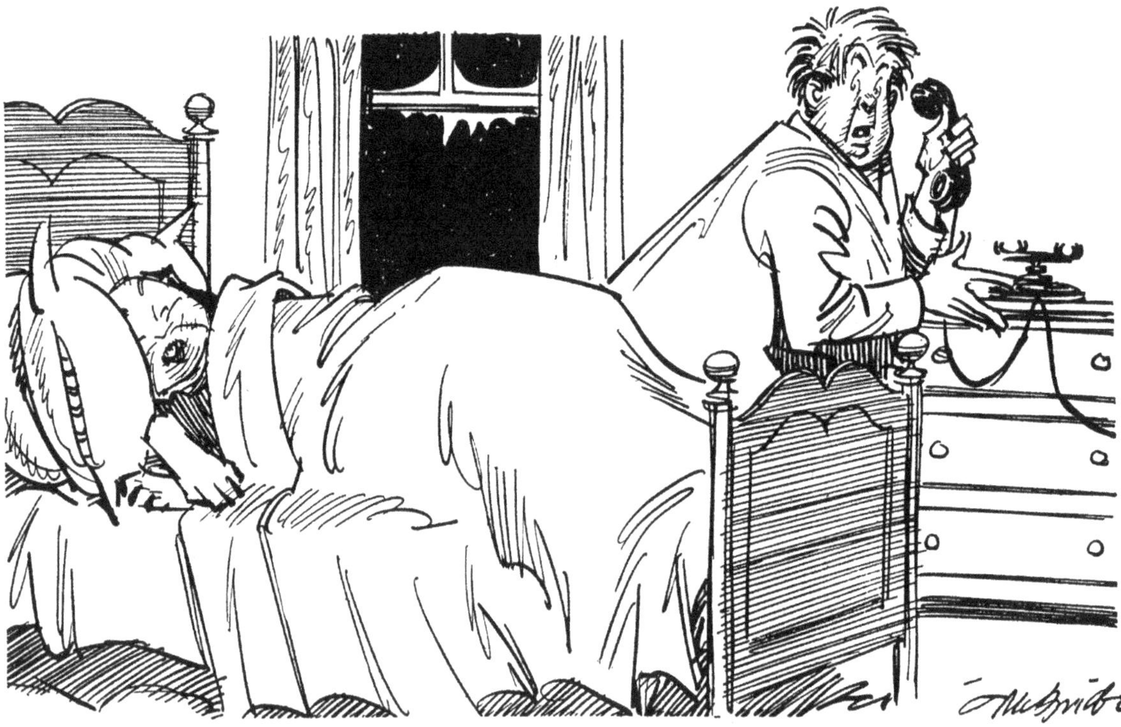

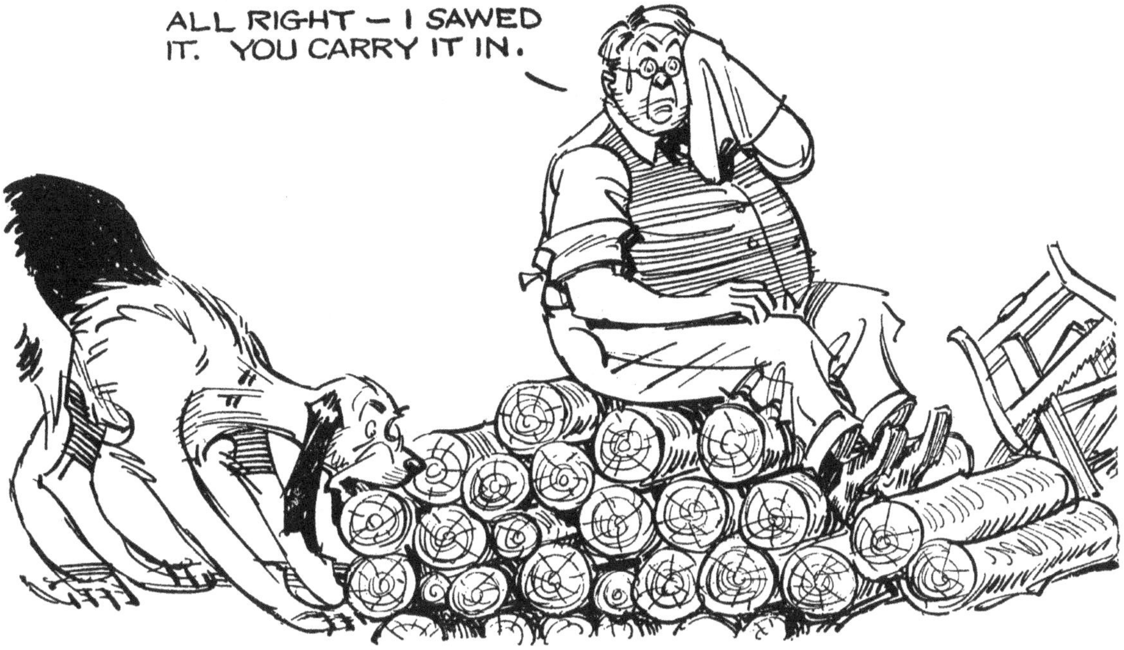
ALL RIGHT – I SAWED IT. YOU CARRY IT IN.

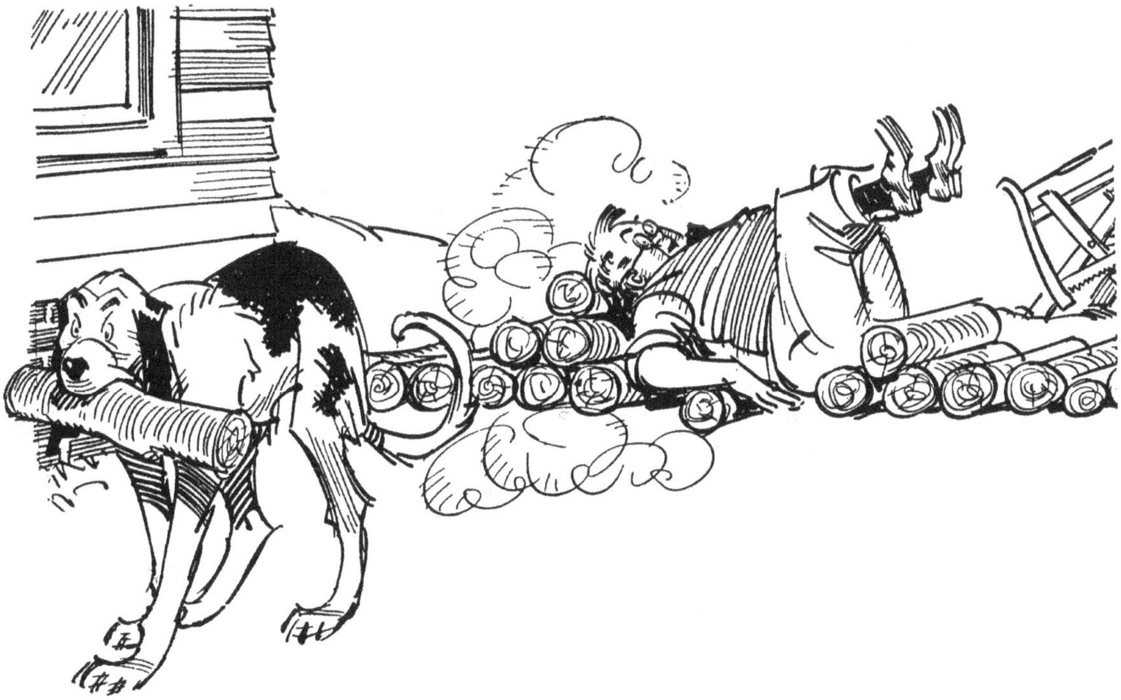

ELBY, I LOST MY UPPER PLATE WHEN I WAS UP THERE PRUNING MY APPLE TREE. IT FELL SOMEWHERE ON YOUR SIDE OF THE FENCE. MAYBE THAT STUPID BEAST OF YOURS CAN LOCATE IT.

14

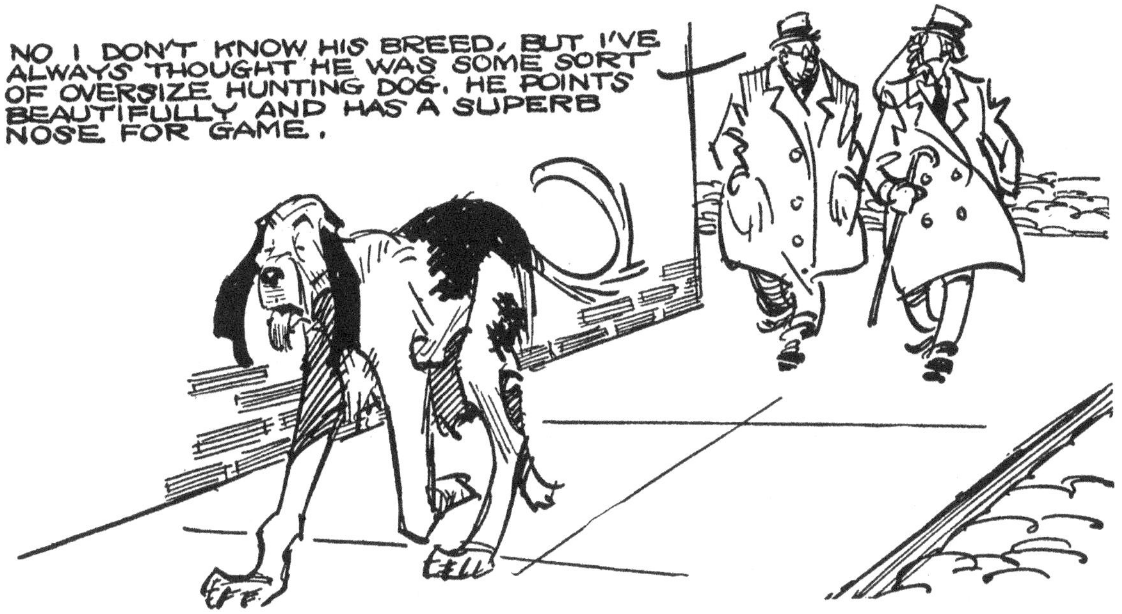
NO I DON'T KNOW HIS BREED, BUT I'VE ALWAYS THOUGHT HE WAS SOME SORT OF OVERSIZE HUNTING DOG. HE POINTS BEAUTIFULLY AND HAS A SUPERB NOSE FOR GAME.

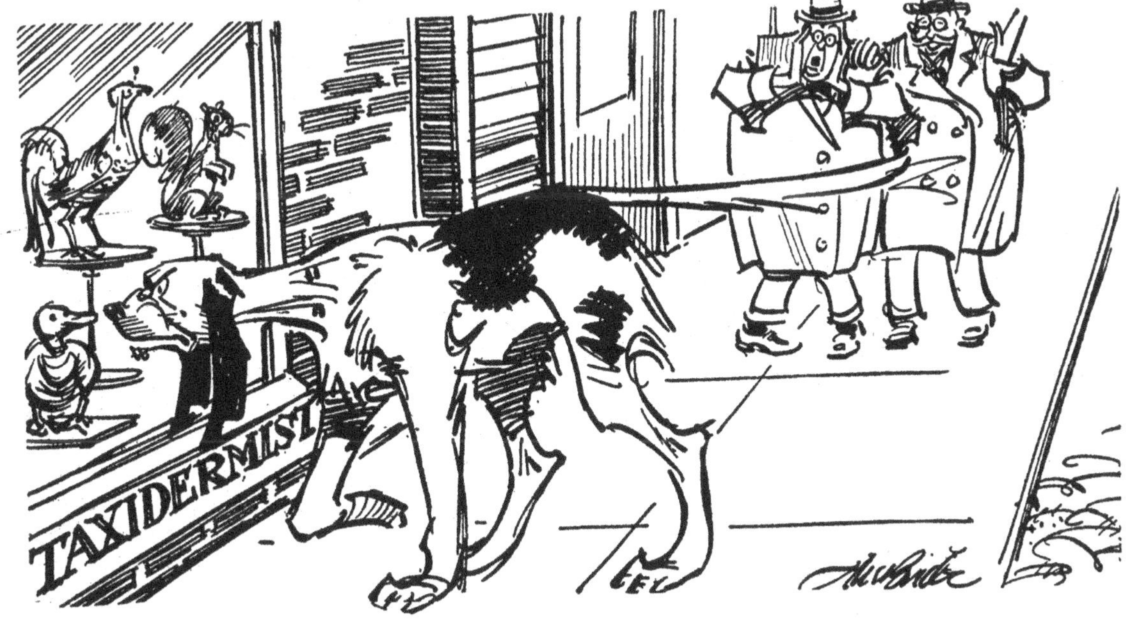
TAXIDERMIST

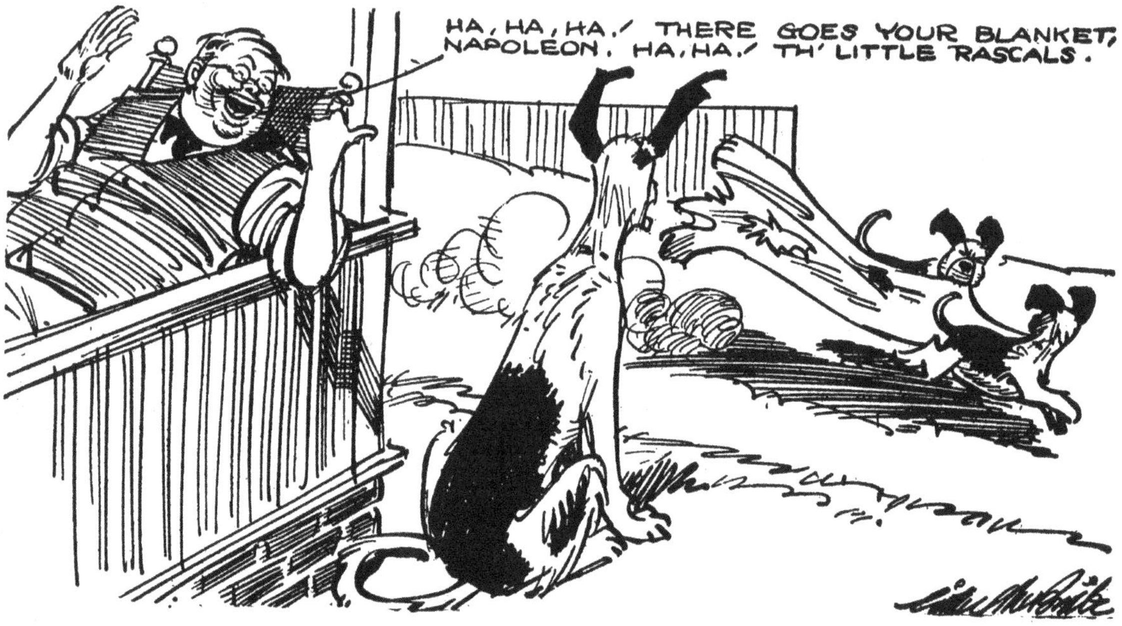
HA, HA, HA! THERE GOES YOUR BLANKET, NAPOLEON. HA, HA! TH' LITTLE RASCALS.

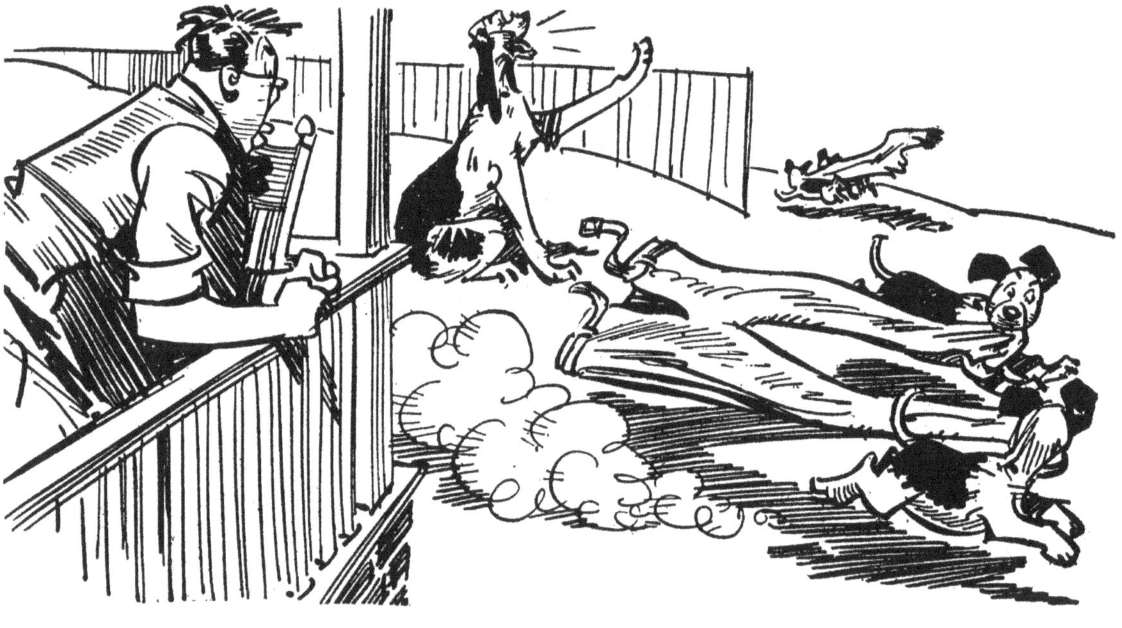

I WISH TO HEAVENS I KNEW WHERE TO HIDE THESE CHRISTMAS PACKAGES!

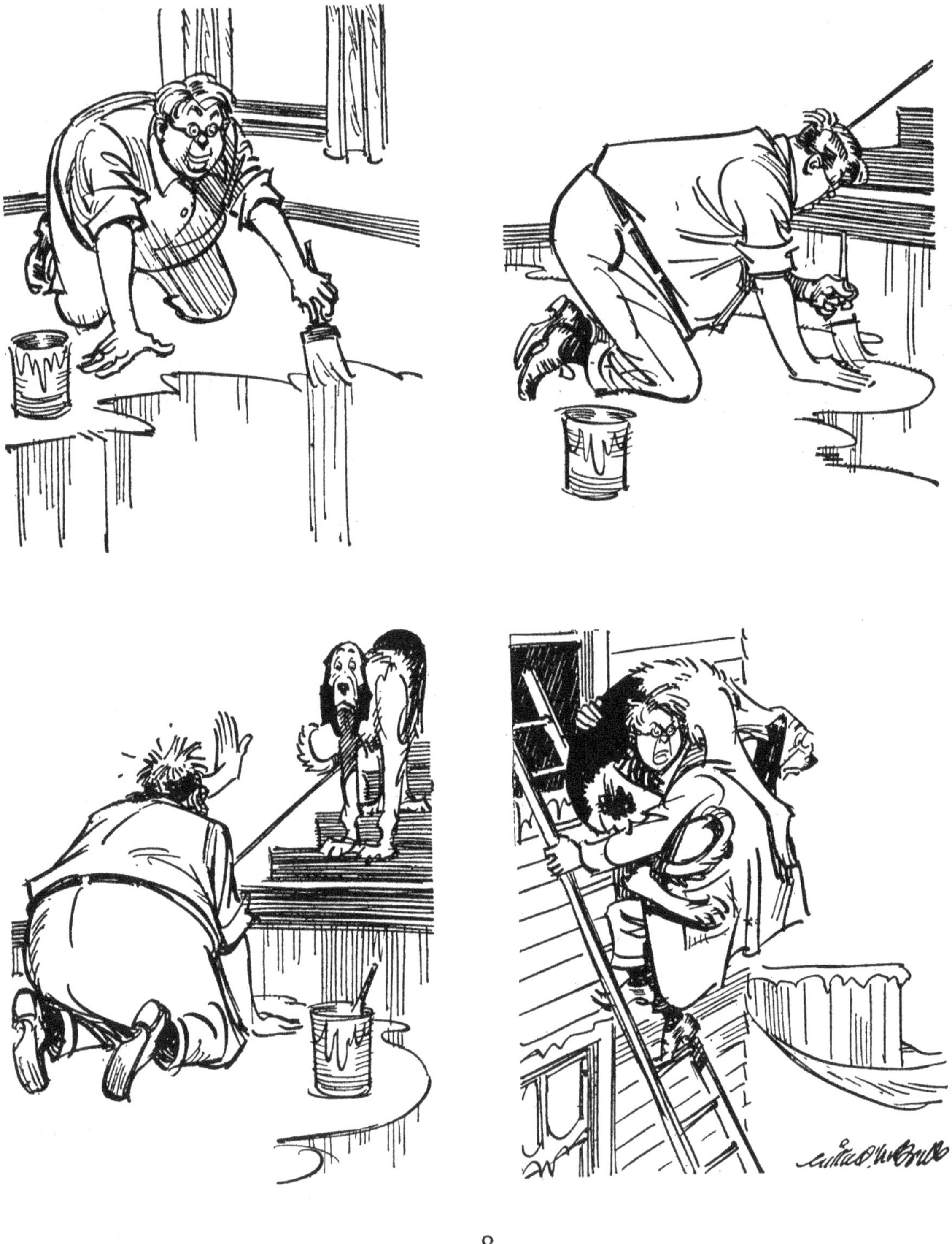

BY GOLLY, THIS BACK BENDING EXERCISE IS THE ONE TO TAKE OFF THE WEIGHT. NOW, ONE -- TWO -- BACK I GO.

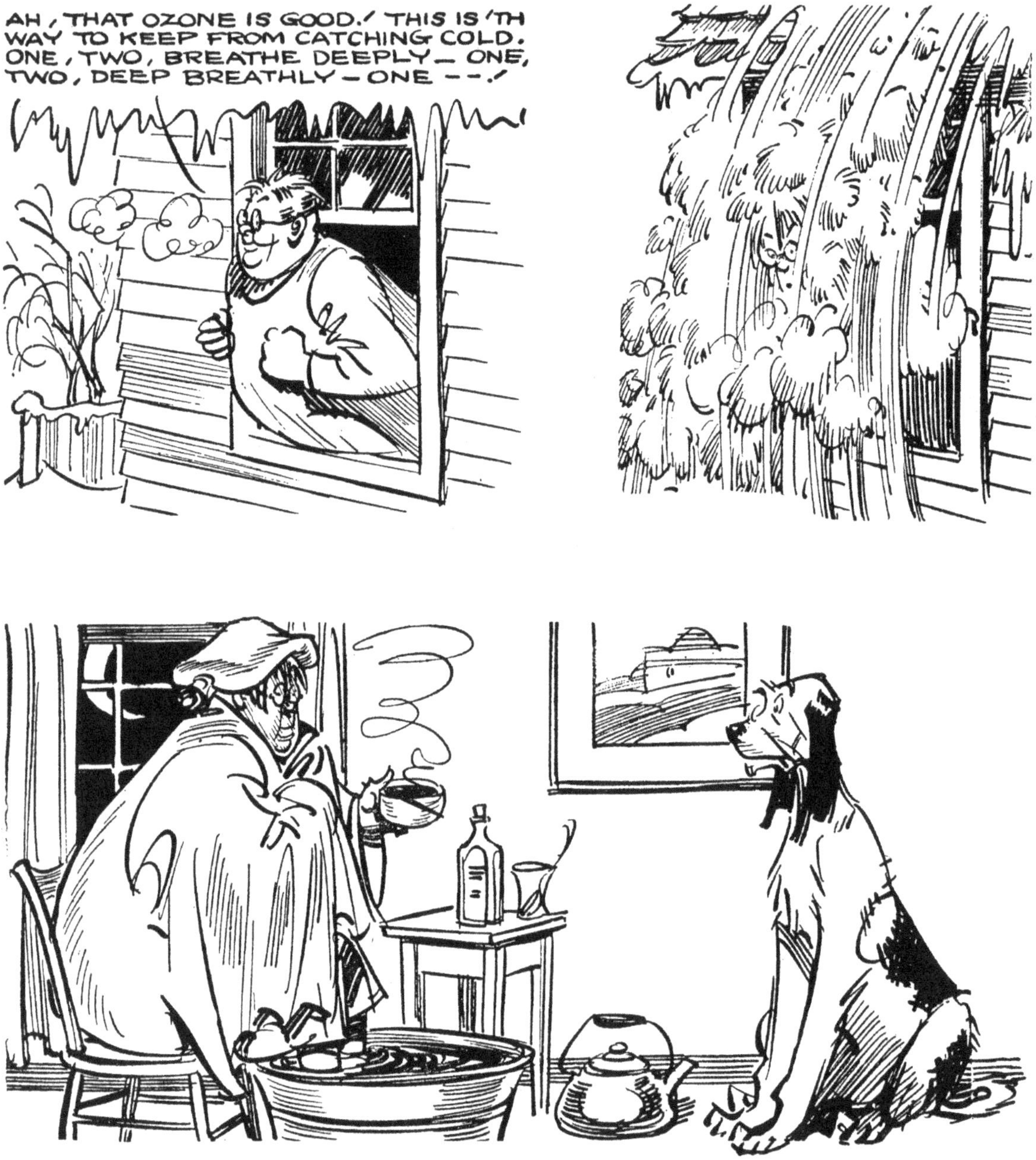
AH, THAT OZONE IS GOOD.! THIS IS 'TH WAY TO KEEP FROM CATCHING COLD. ONE, TWO, BREATHE DEEPLY— ONE, TWO, DEEP BREATHLY—ONE ——.!

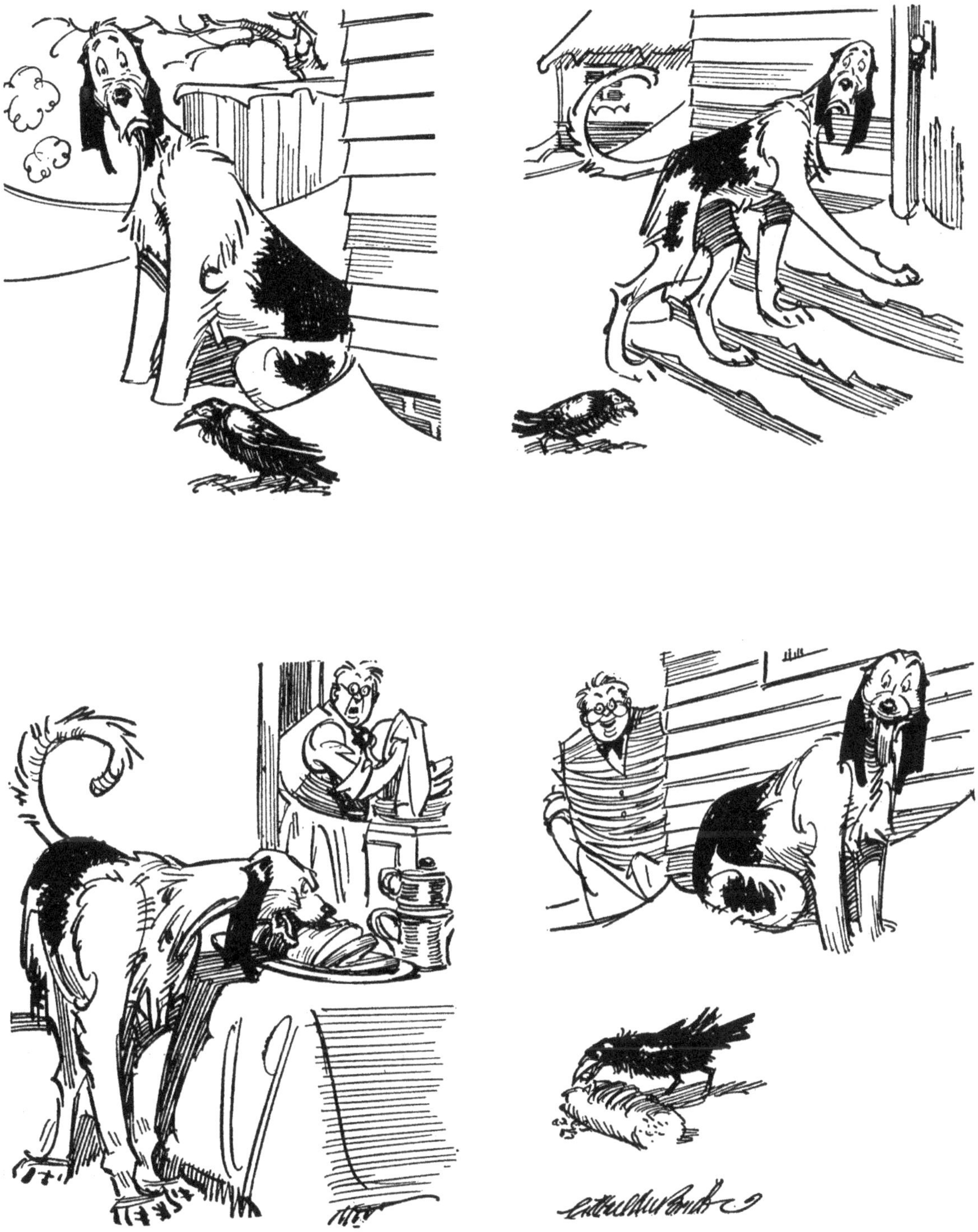

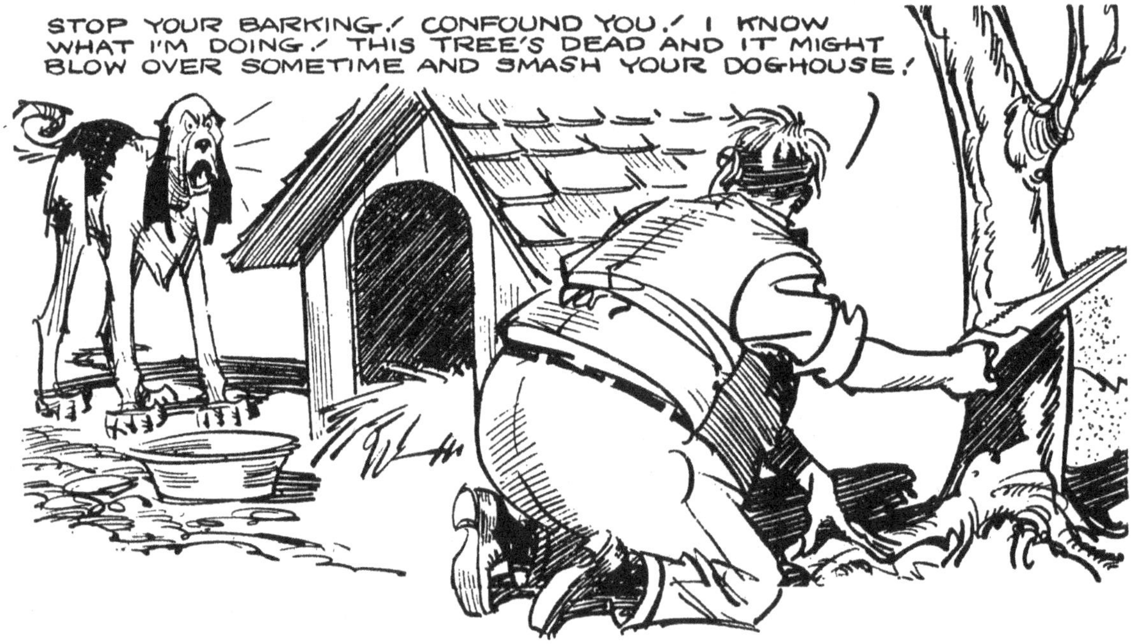
STOP YOUR BARKING! CONFOUND YOU! I KNOW WHAT I'M DOING! THIS TREE'S DEAD AND IT MIGHT BLOW OVER SOMETIME AND SMASH YOUR DOGHOUSE!

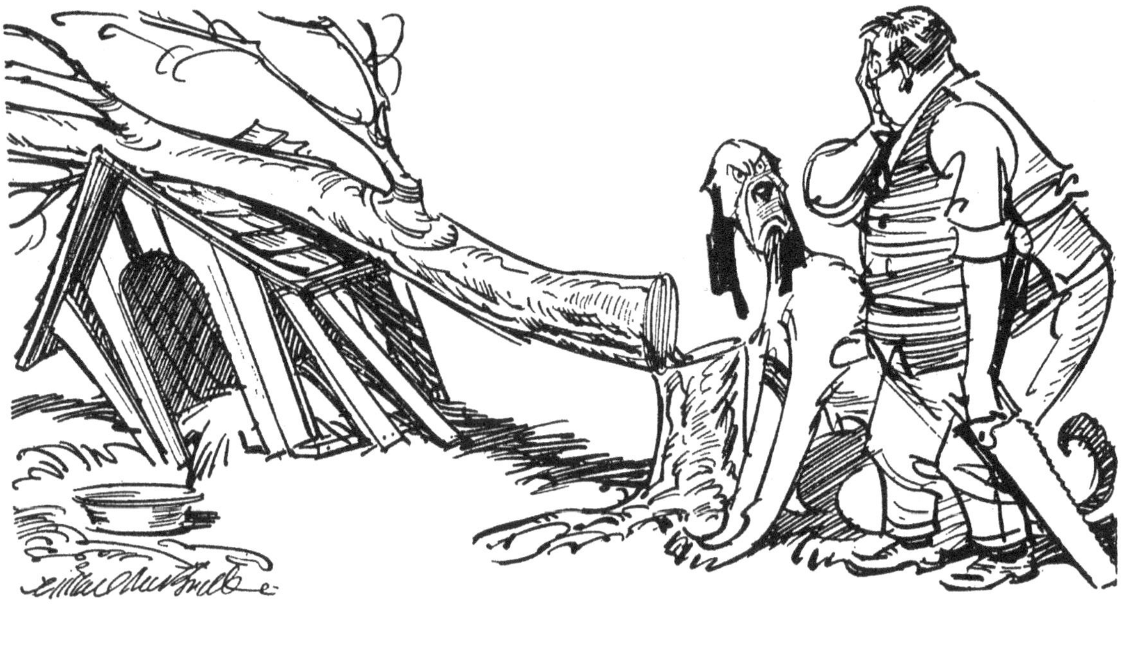

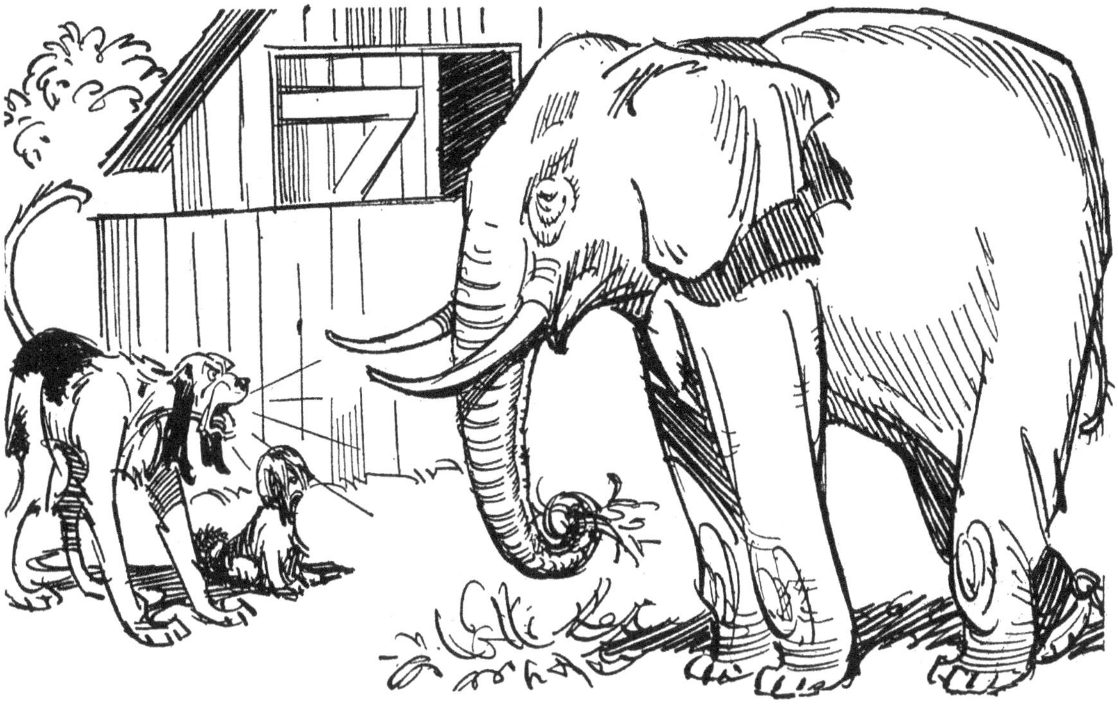

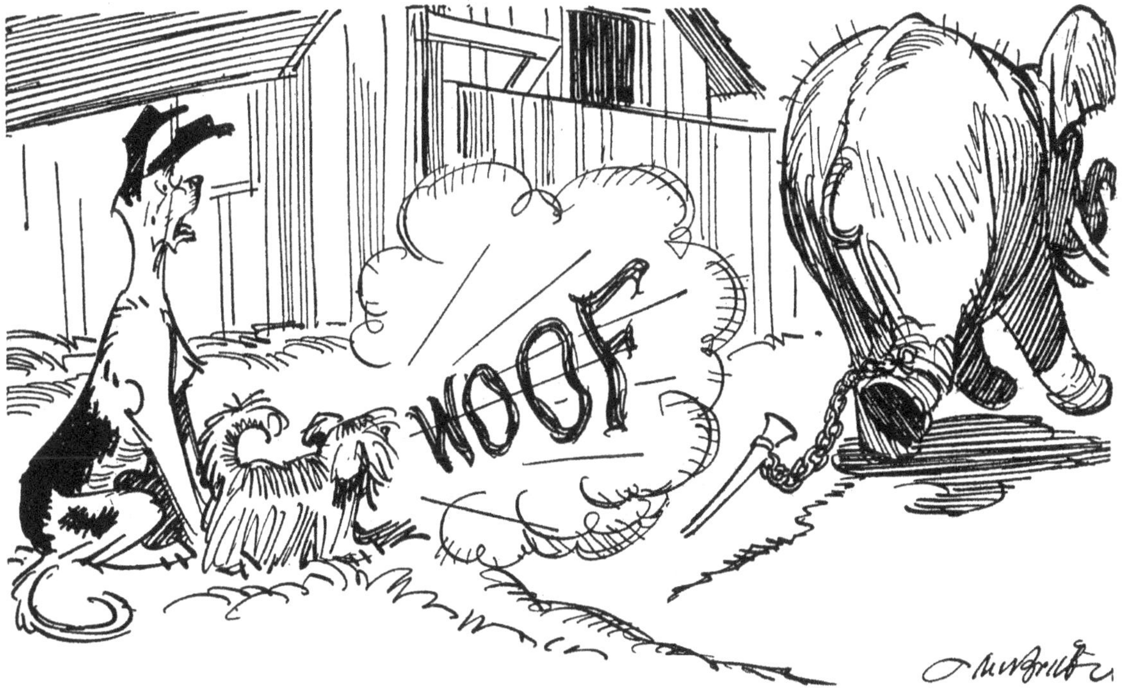
WOOF

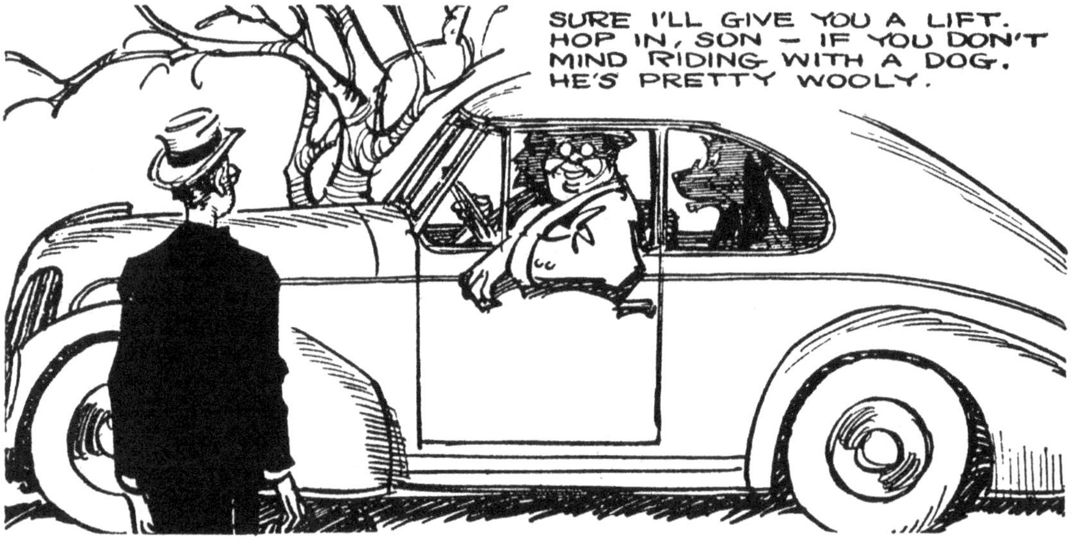
SURE I'LL GIVE YOU A LIFT. HOP IN, SON – IF YOU DON'T MIND RIDING WITH A DOG. HE'S PRETTY WOOLY.

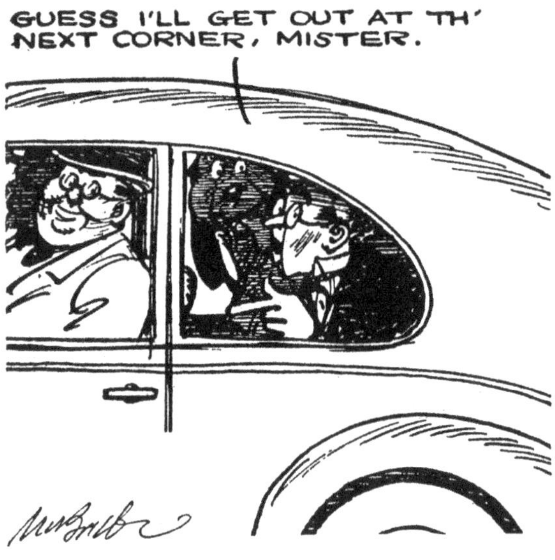
GUESS I'LL GET OUT AT TH' NEXT CORNER, MISTER.

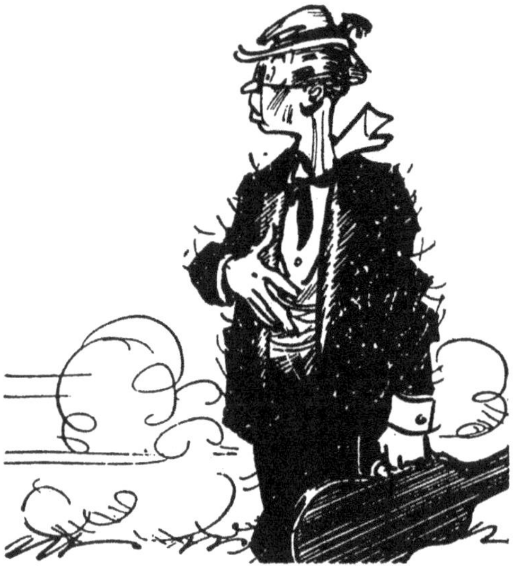

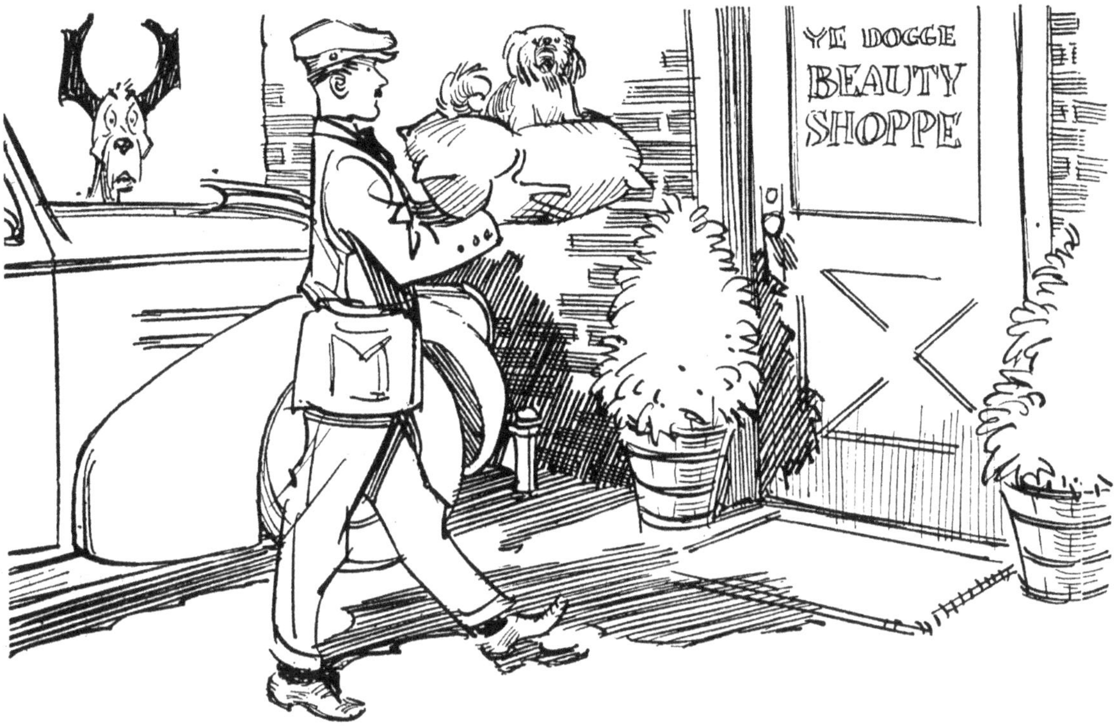
YE DOGGE
BEAUTY
SHOPPE

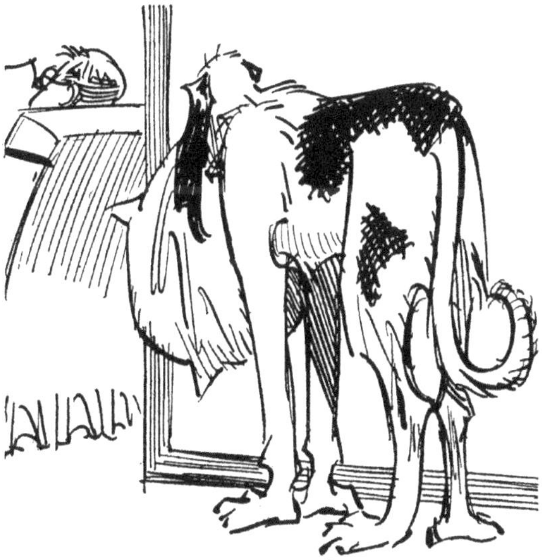

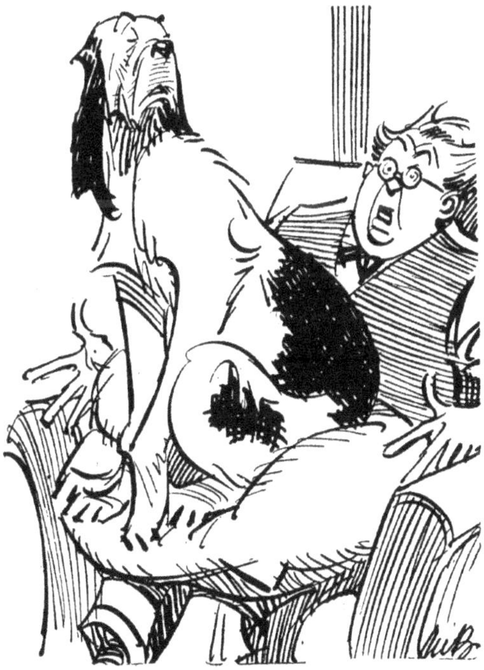

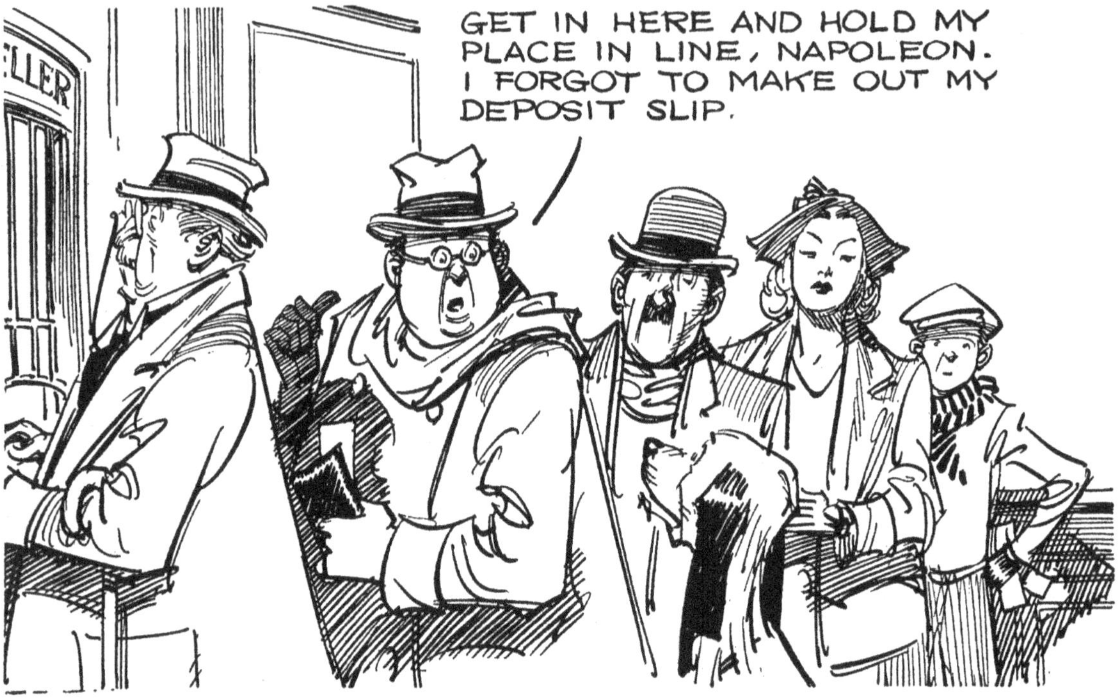
GET IN HERE AND HOLD MY PLACE IN LINE, NAPOLEON. I FORGOT TO MAKE OUT MY DEPOSIT SLIP.

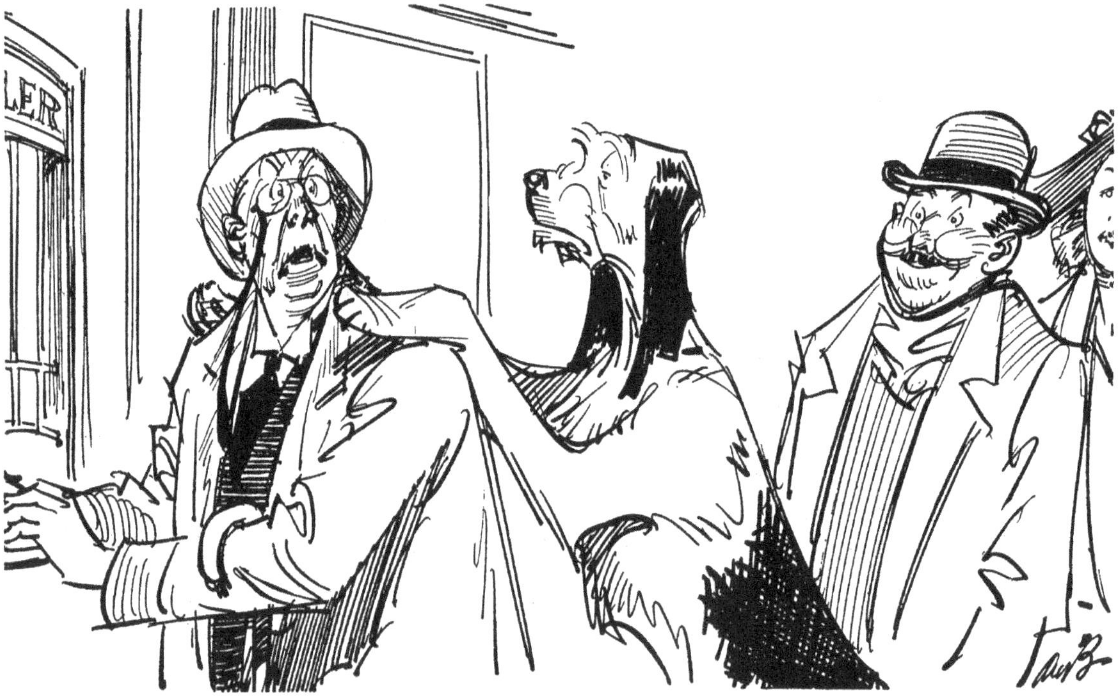

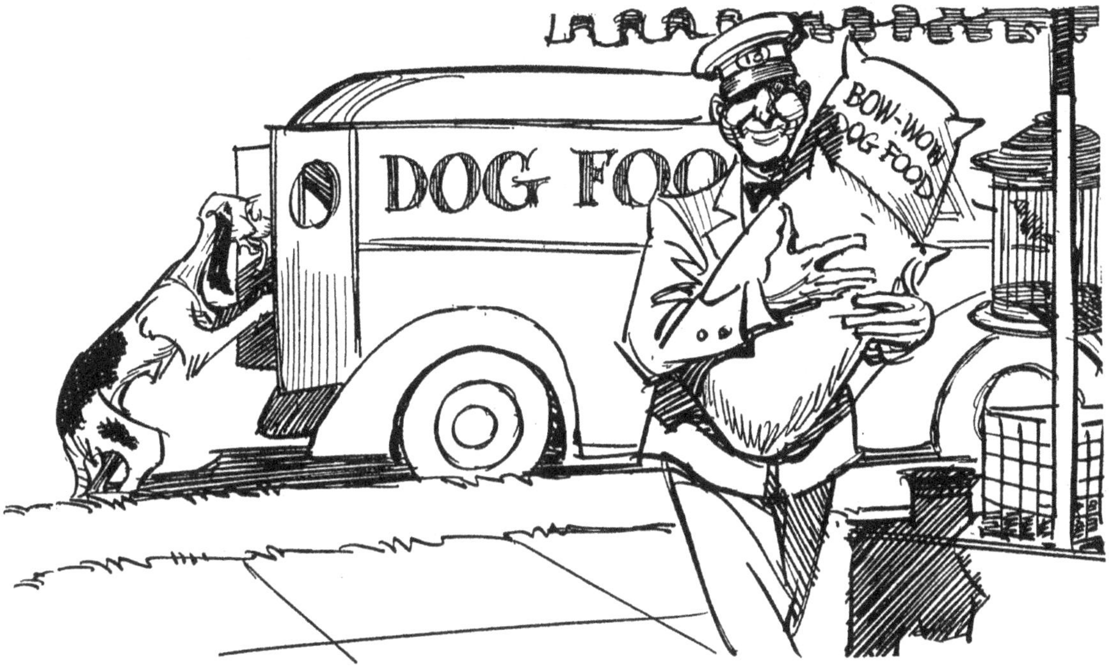
DOG FOO
BOW-WOW
DOG FOOD

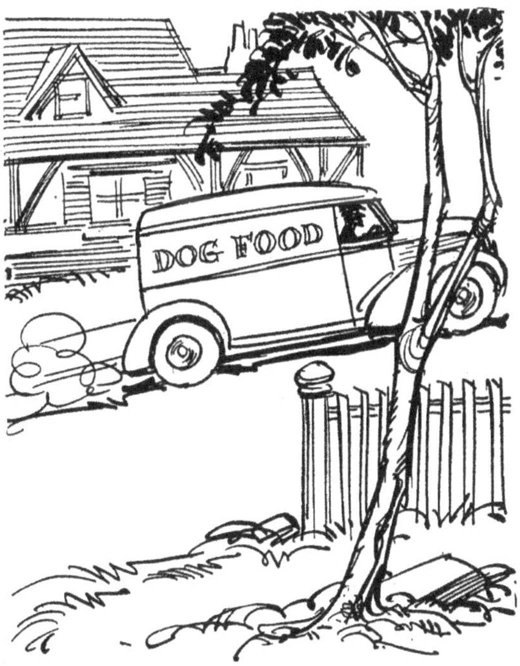
DOG FOOD

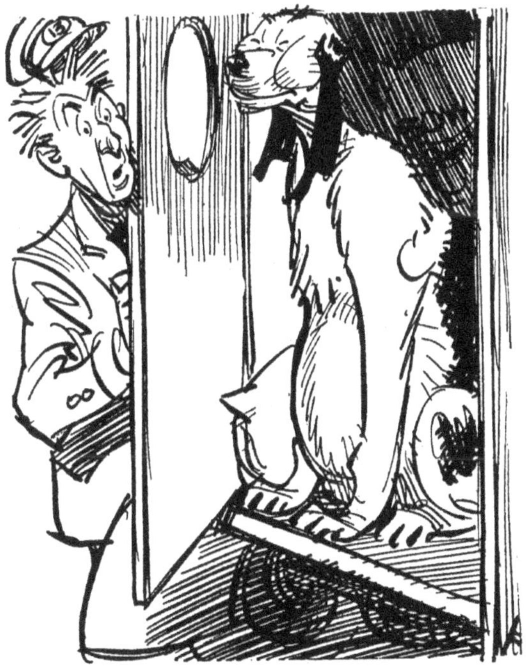

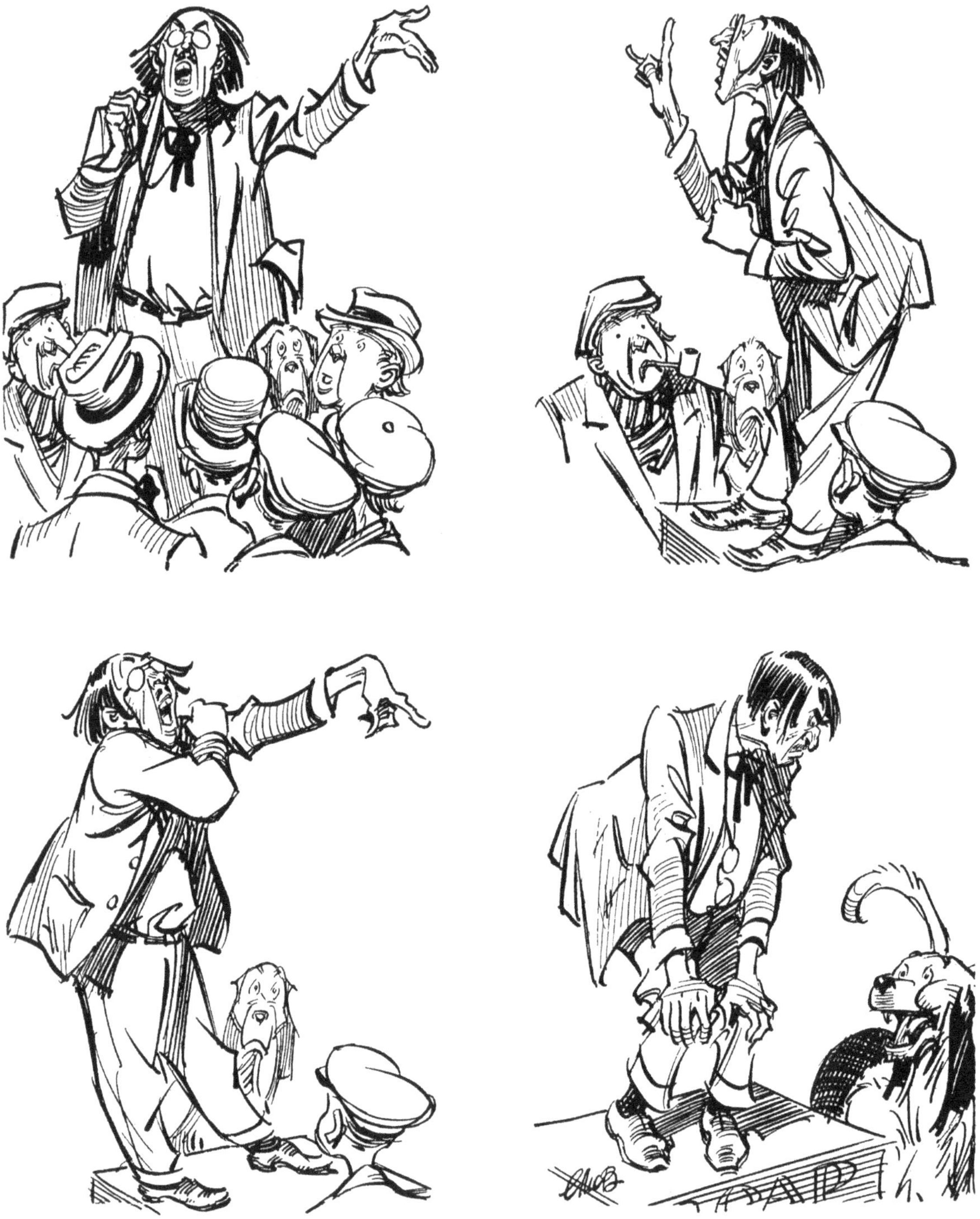

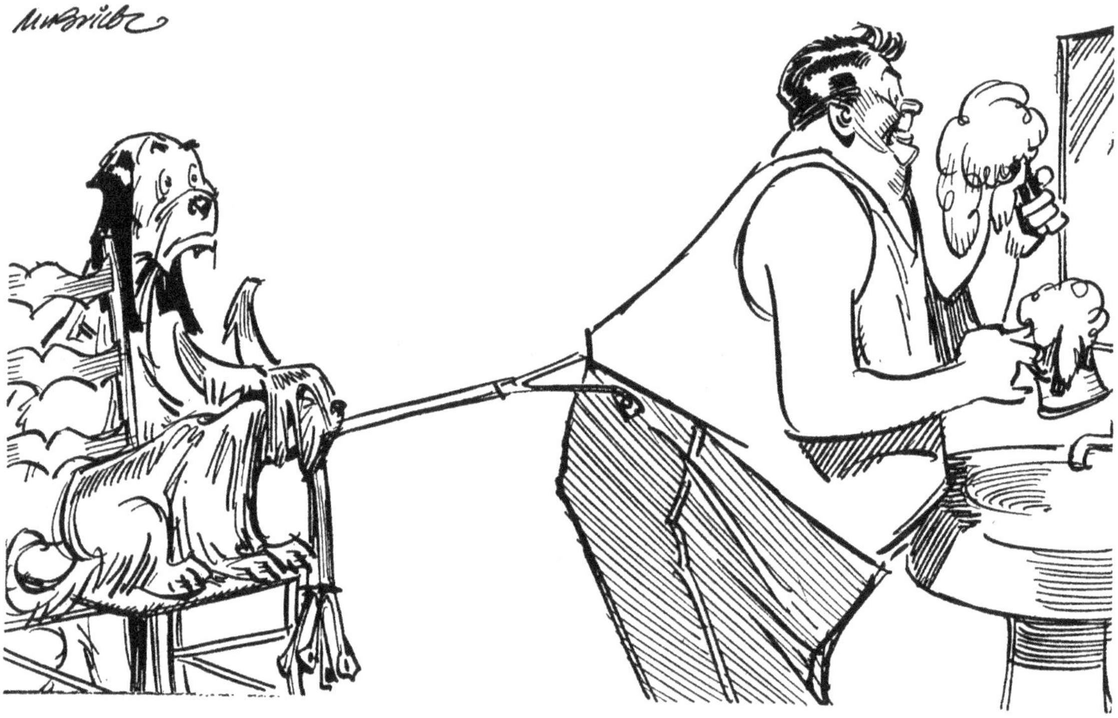

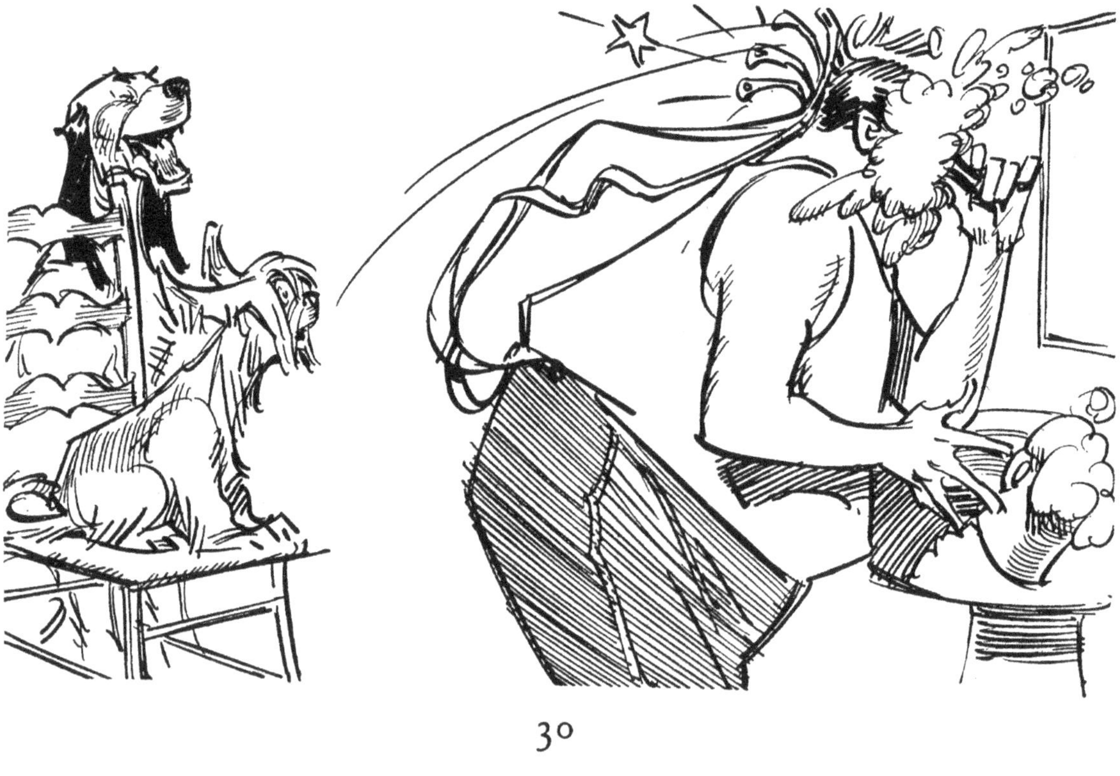

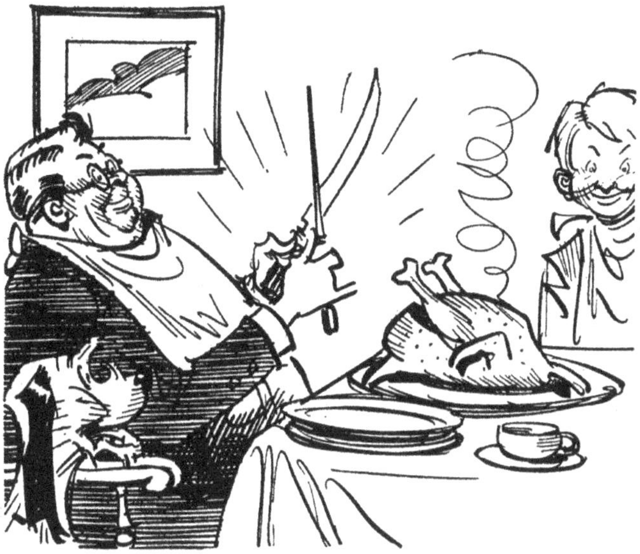

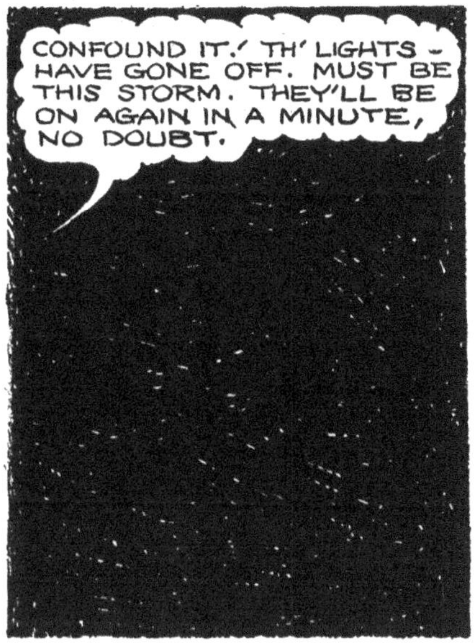
CONFOUND IT.' TH' LIGHTS - HAVE GONE OFF. MUST BE THIS STORM. THEY'LL BE ON AGAIN IN A MINUTE, NO DOUBT.

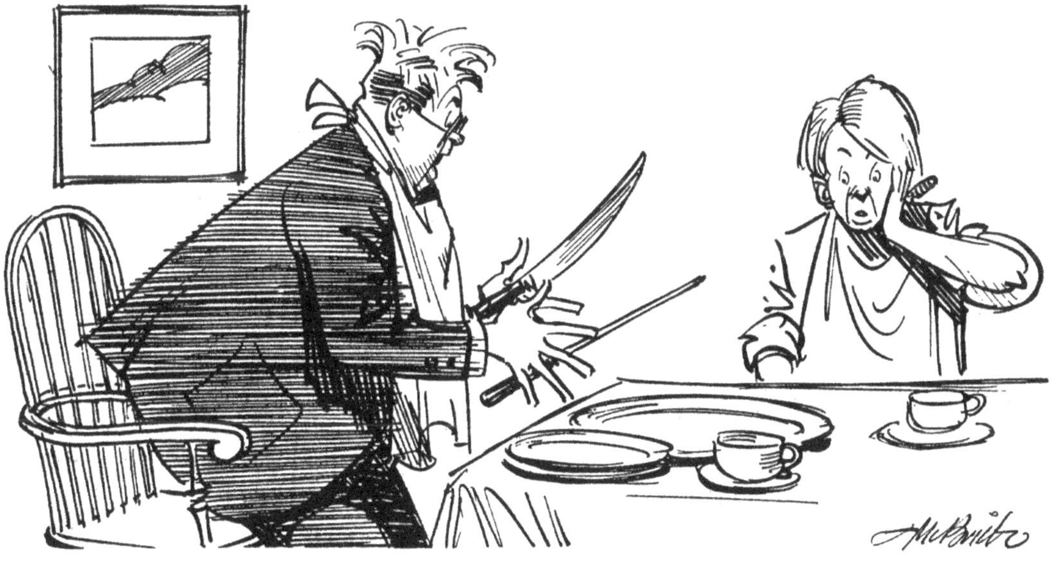

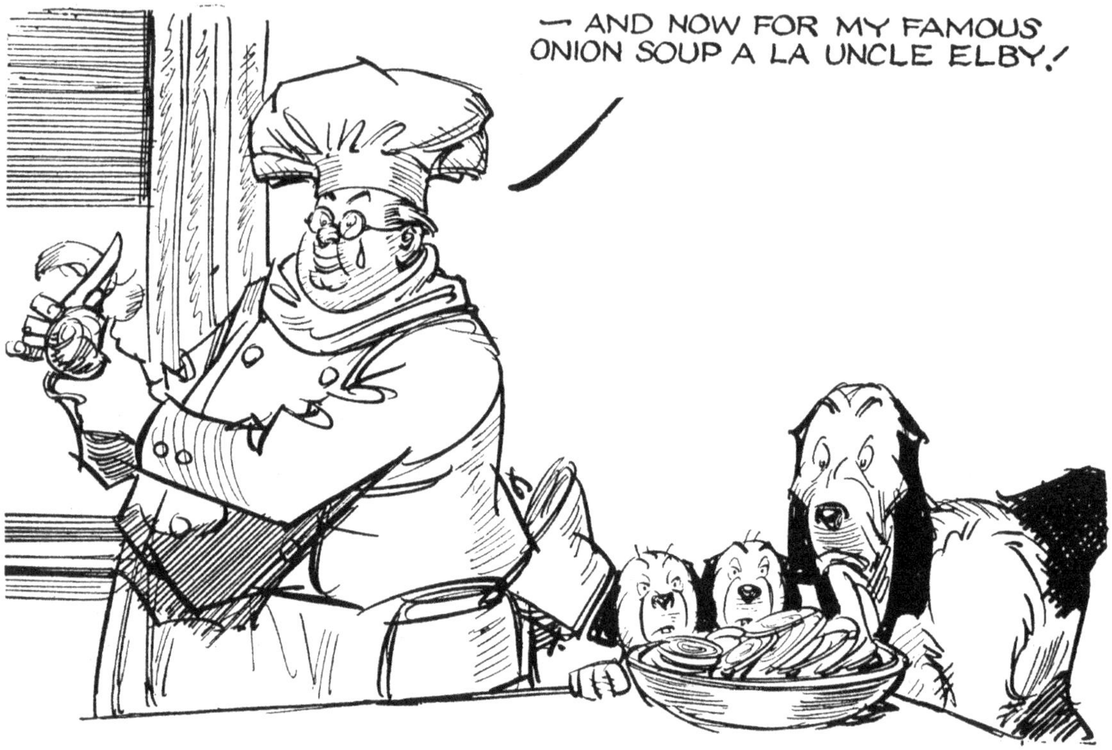
— AND NOW FOR MY FAMOUS ONION SOUP A LA UNCLE ELBY!

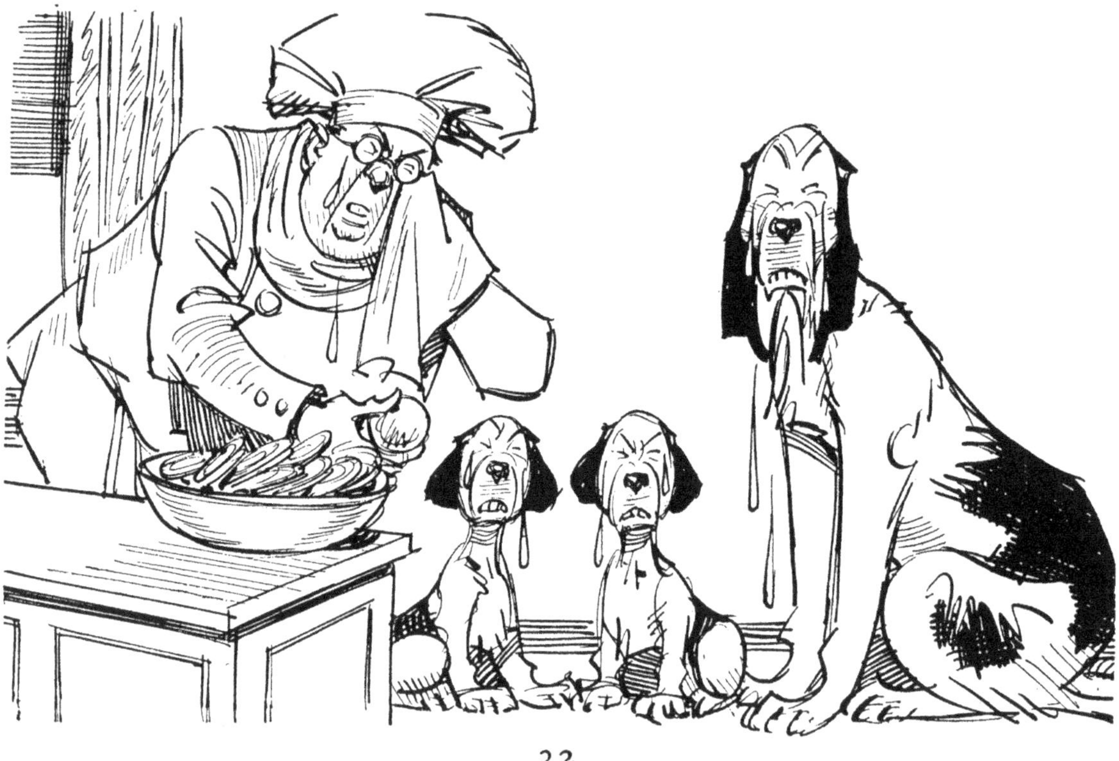

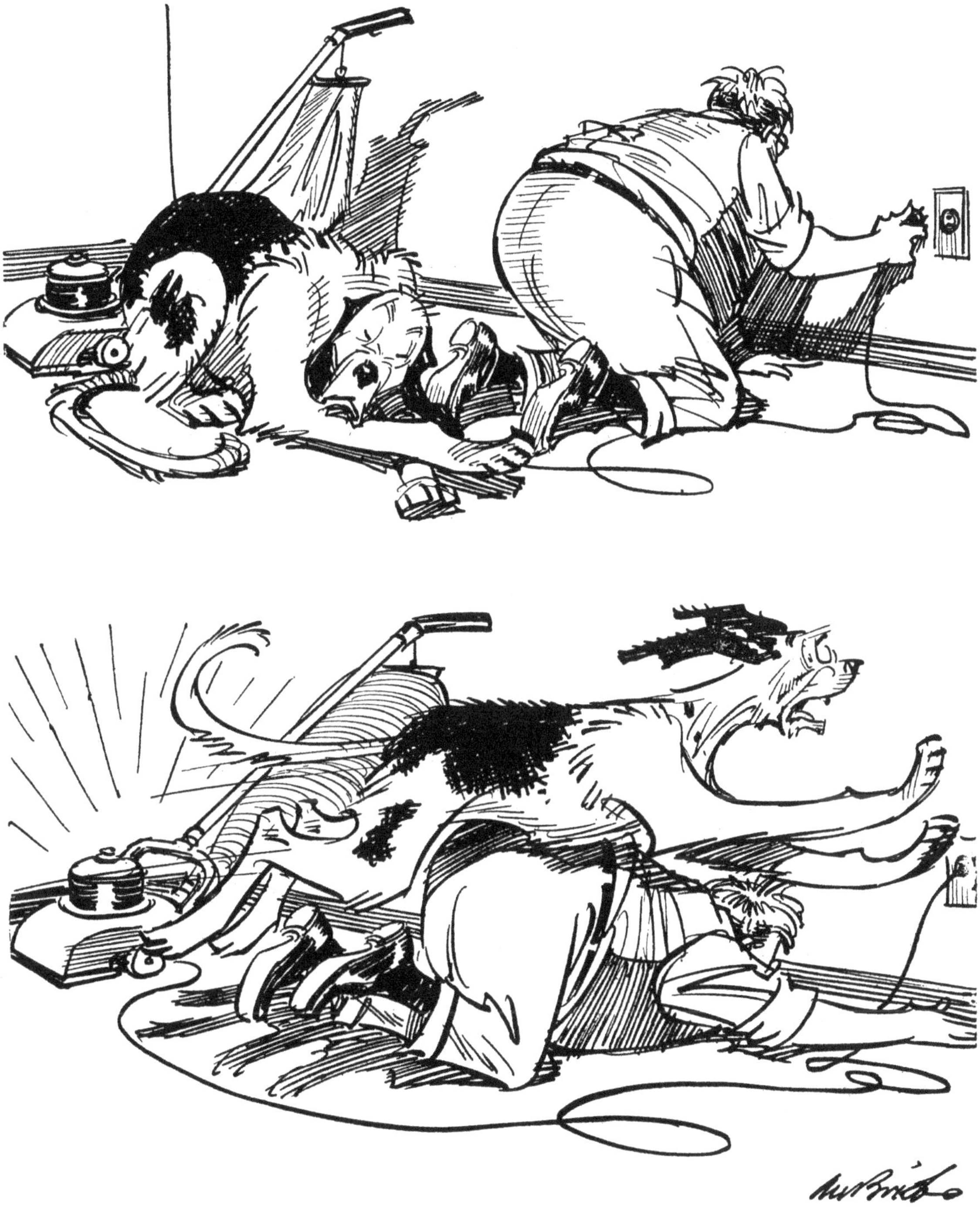

YOU SAY YOU'RE GOING TO DROP PAST WITH A PACKAGE OF NICE BONES FOR NAPOLEON ?
WELL, THAT'S MIGHTY THOUGHTFUL OF YOU
HE'D, NATURALLY, BE DELIGHTED, BUT—
I COULDN'T THINK OF ALLOWING YOU TO GO SO FAR OUT OF YOUR WAY. BETTER GIVE THEM TO SOME —
NEIGHBOR'S DOG. THANKS AGAIN FOR THINKING OF HIM.

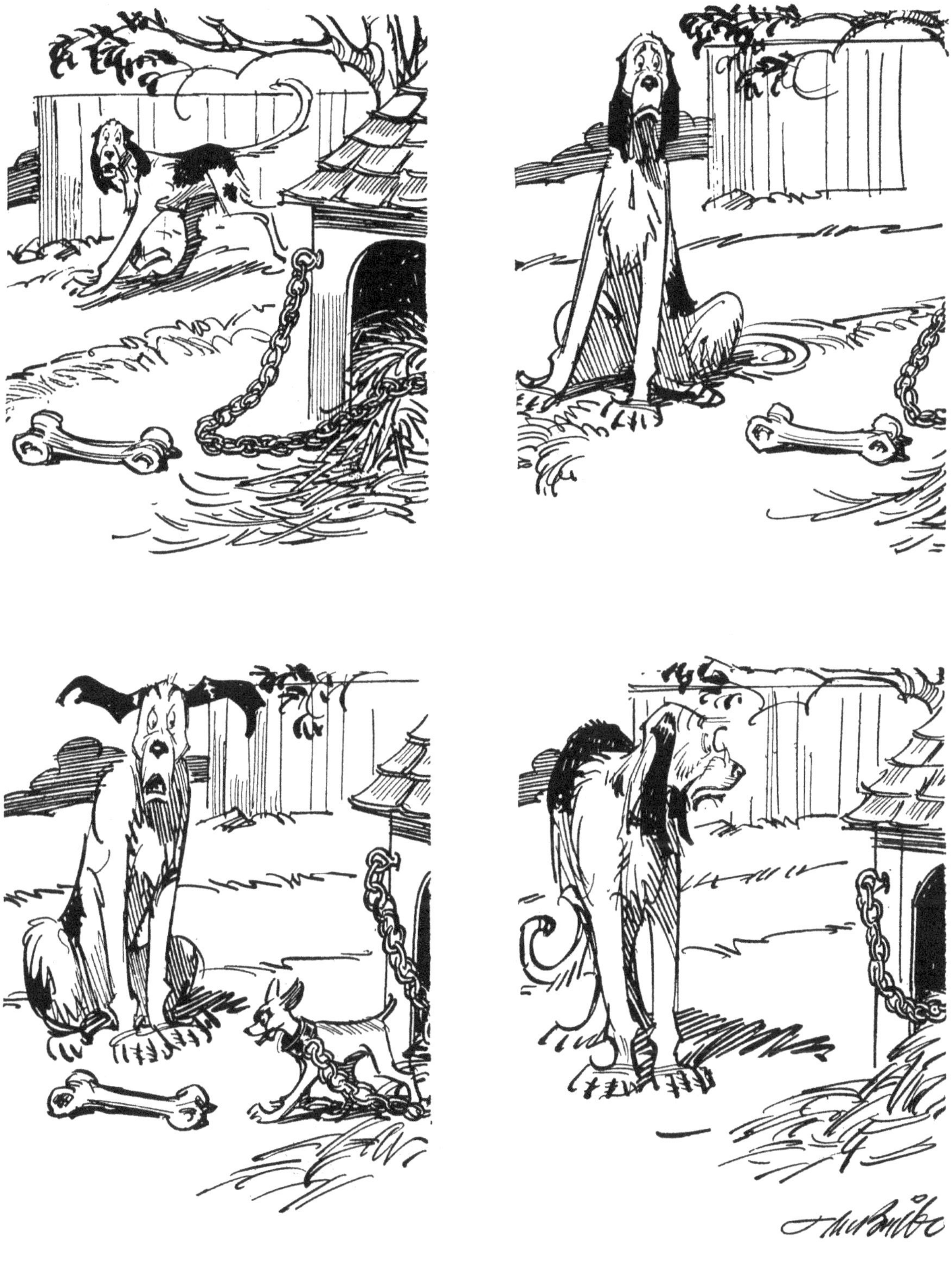

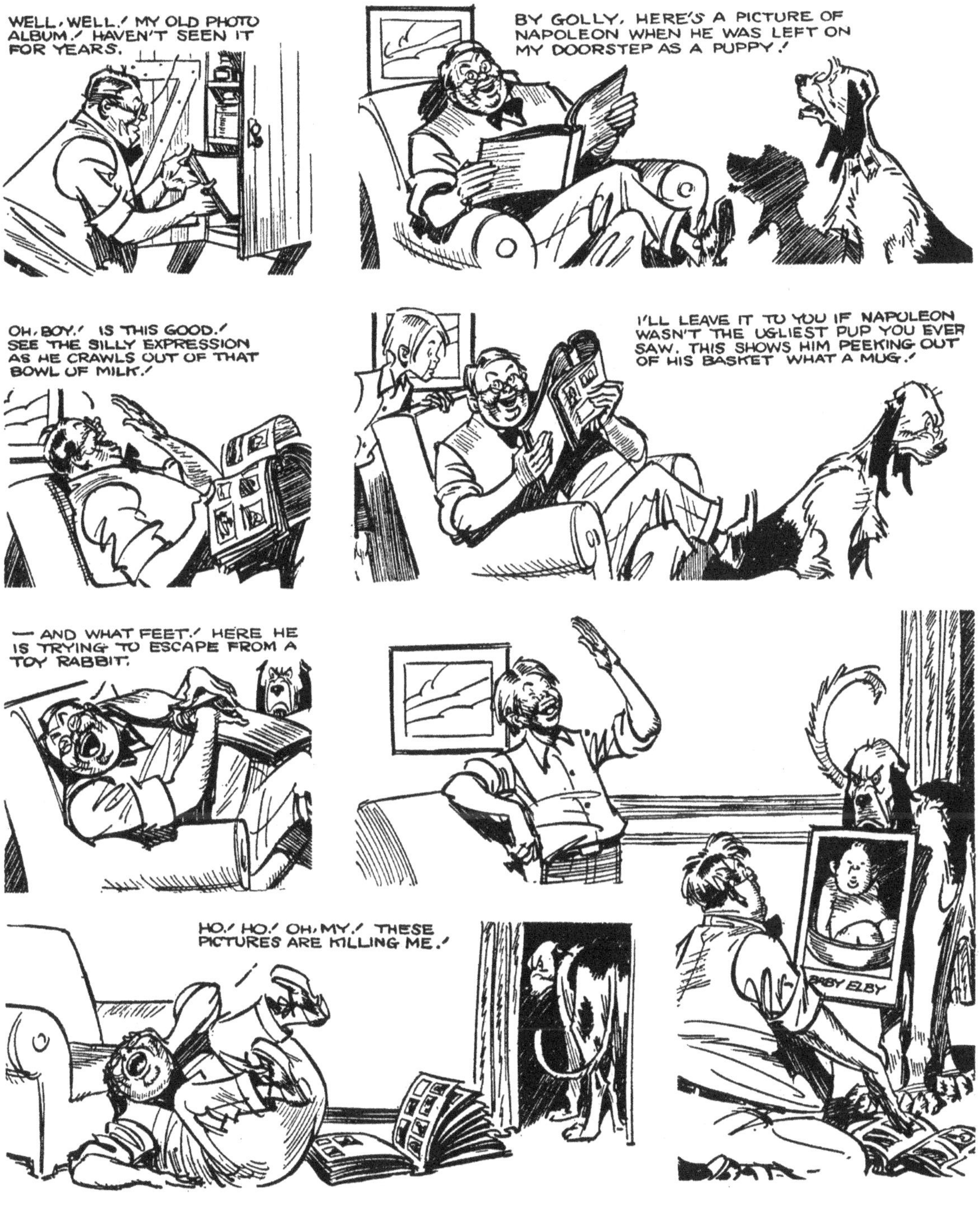

WELL, WELL! MY OLD PHOTO ALBUM! HAVEN'T SEEN IT FOR YEARS.
BY GOLLY, HERE'S A PICTURE OF NAPOLEON WHEN HE WAS LEFT ON MY DOORSTEP AS A PUPPY!
OH, BOY! IS THIS GOOD! SEE THE SILLY EXPRESSION AS HE CRAWLS OUT OF THAT BOWL OF MILK!
I'LL LEAVE IT TO YOU IF NAPOLEON WASN'T THE UGLIEST PUP YOU EVER SAW. THIS SHOWS HIM PEEKING OUT OF HIS BASKET WHAT A MUG!
— AND WHAT FEET! HERE HE IS TRYING TO ESCAPE FROM A TOY RABBIT.
HO! HO! OH, MY! THESE PICTURES ARE KILLING ME!
BABY ELBY

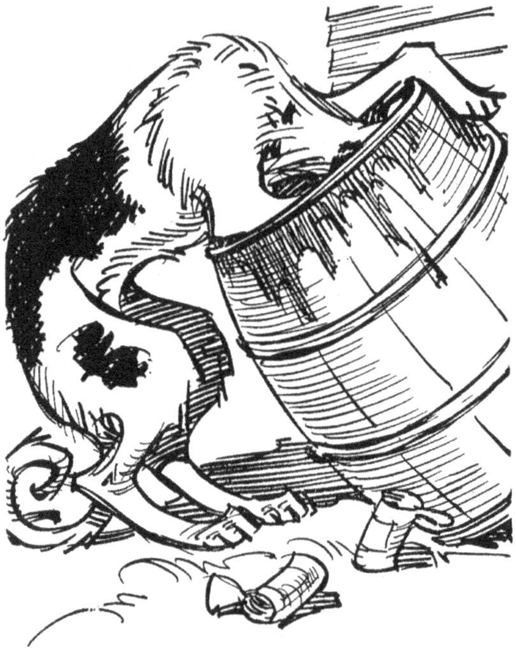

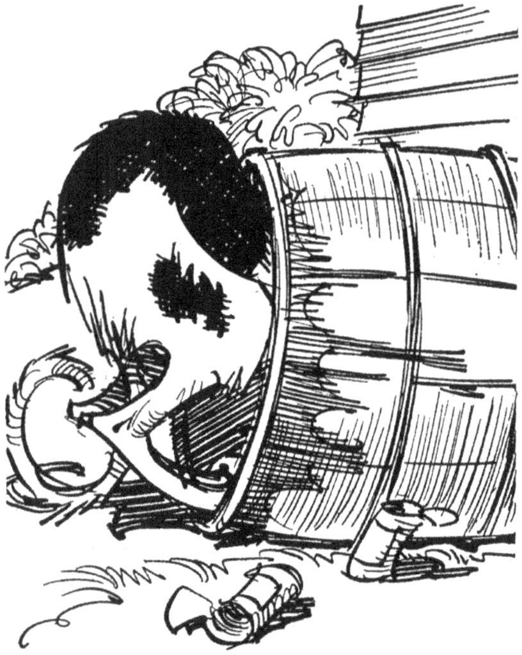

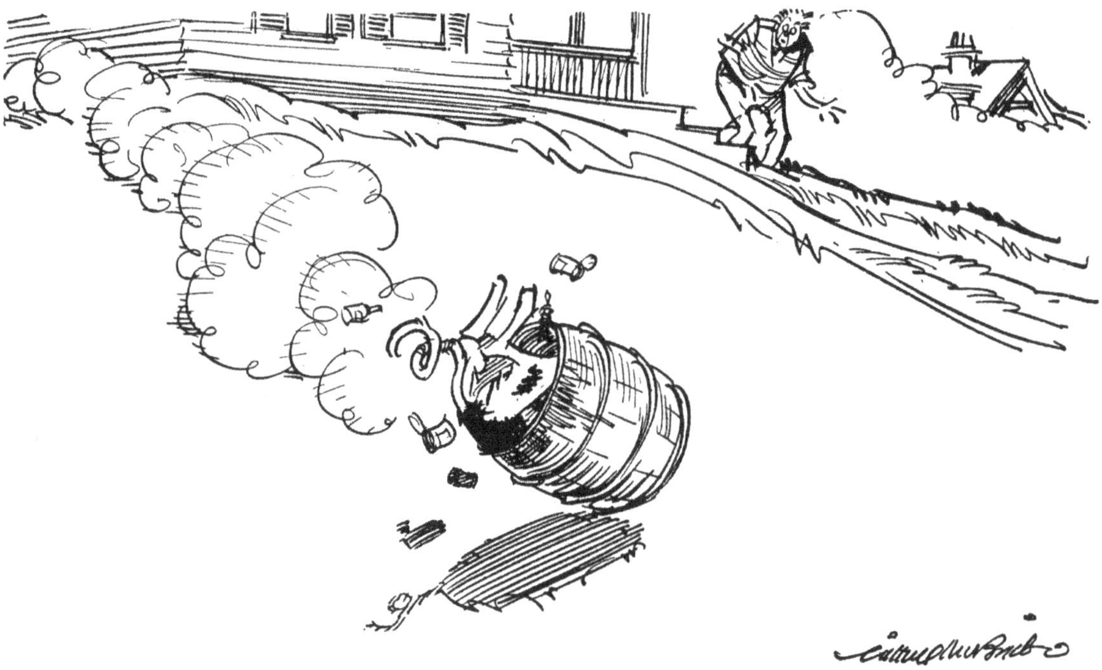

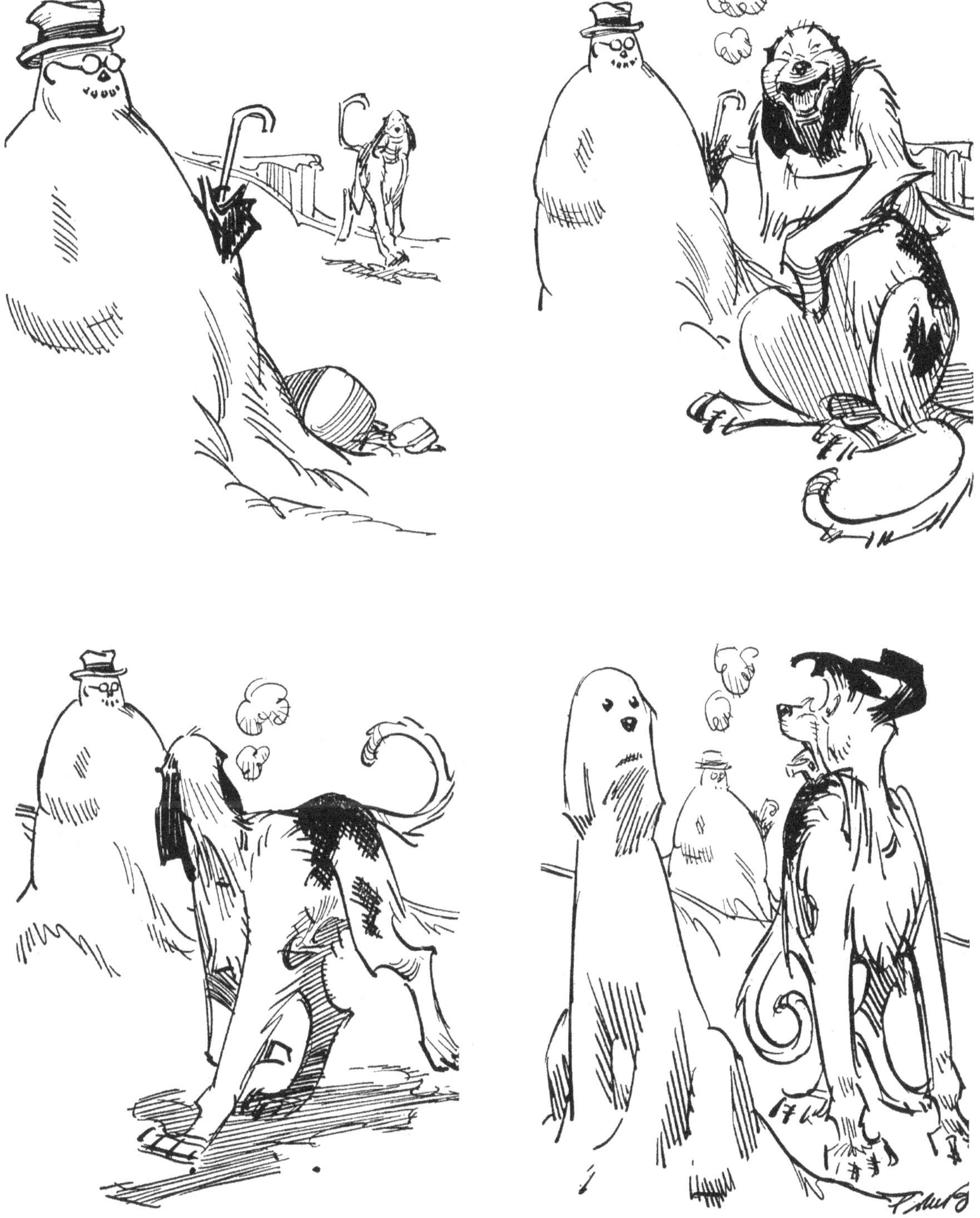

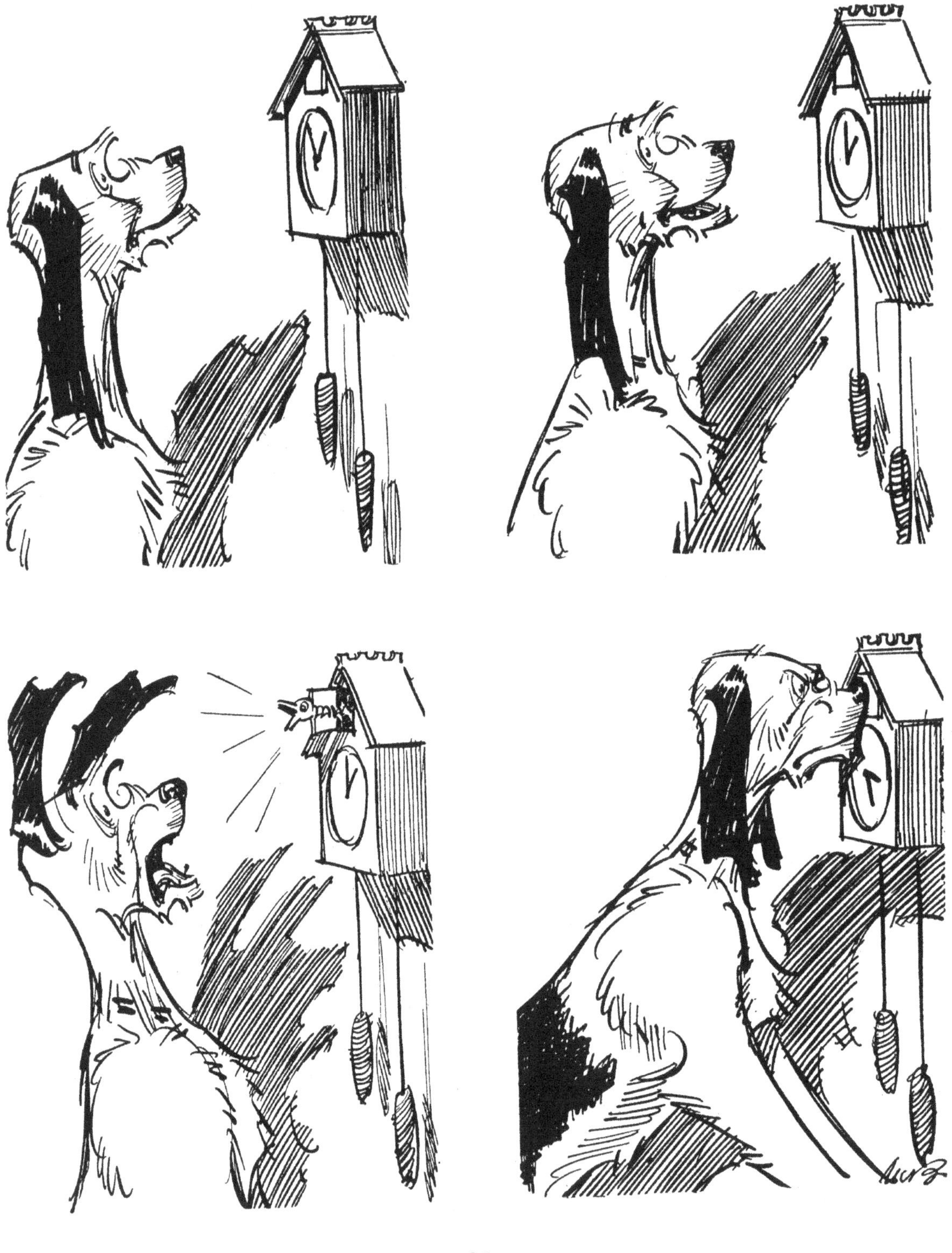

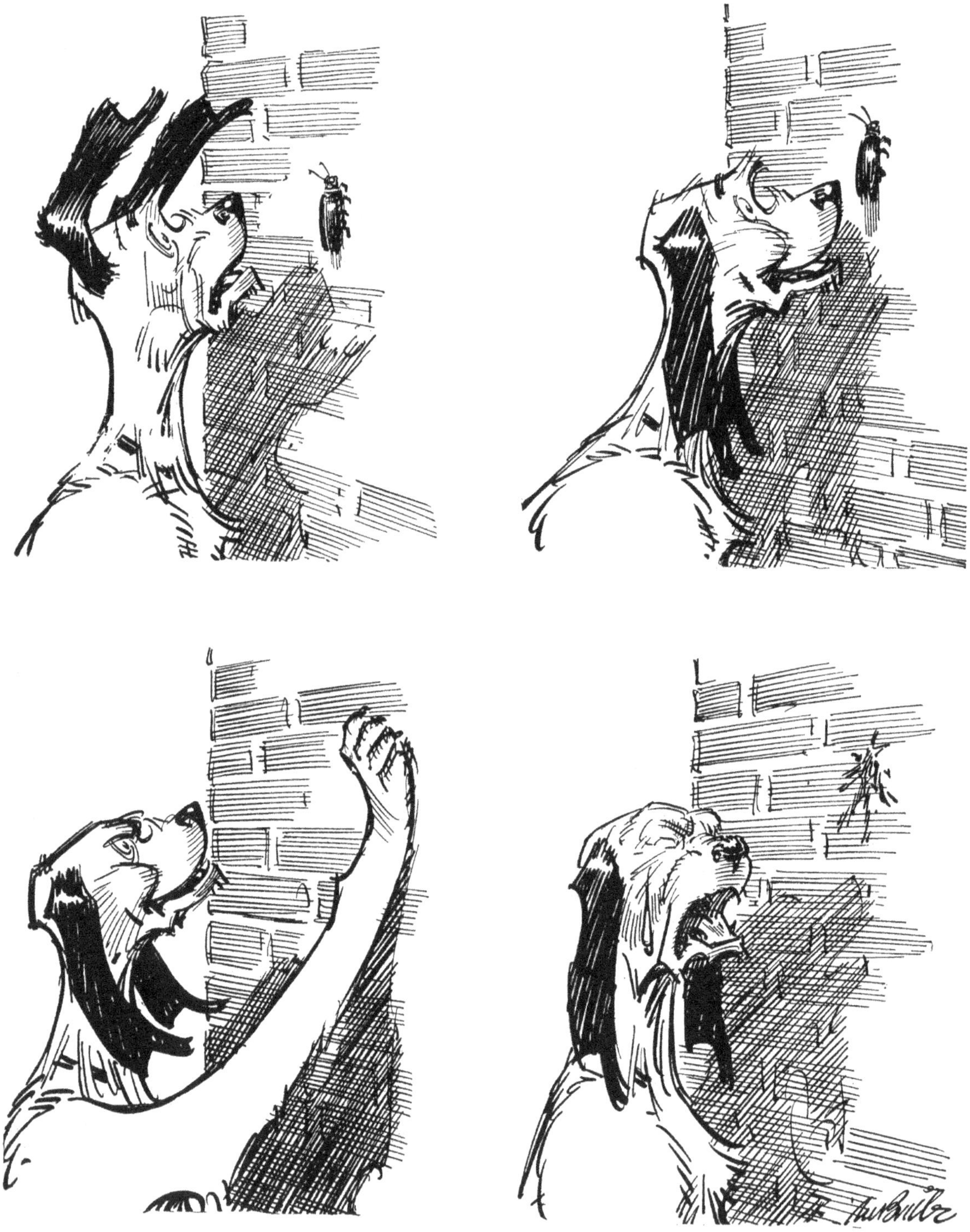

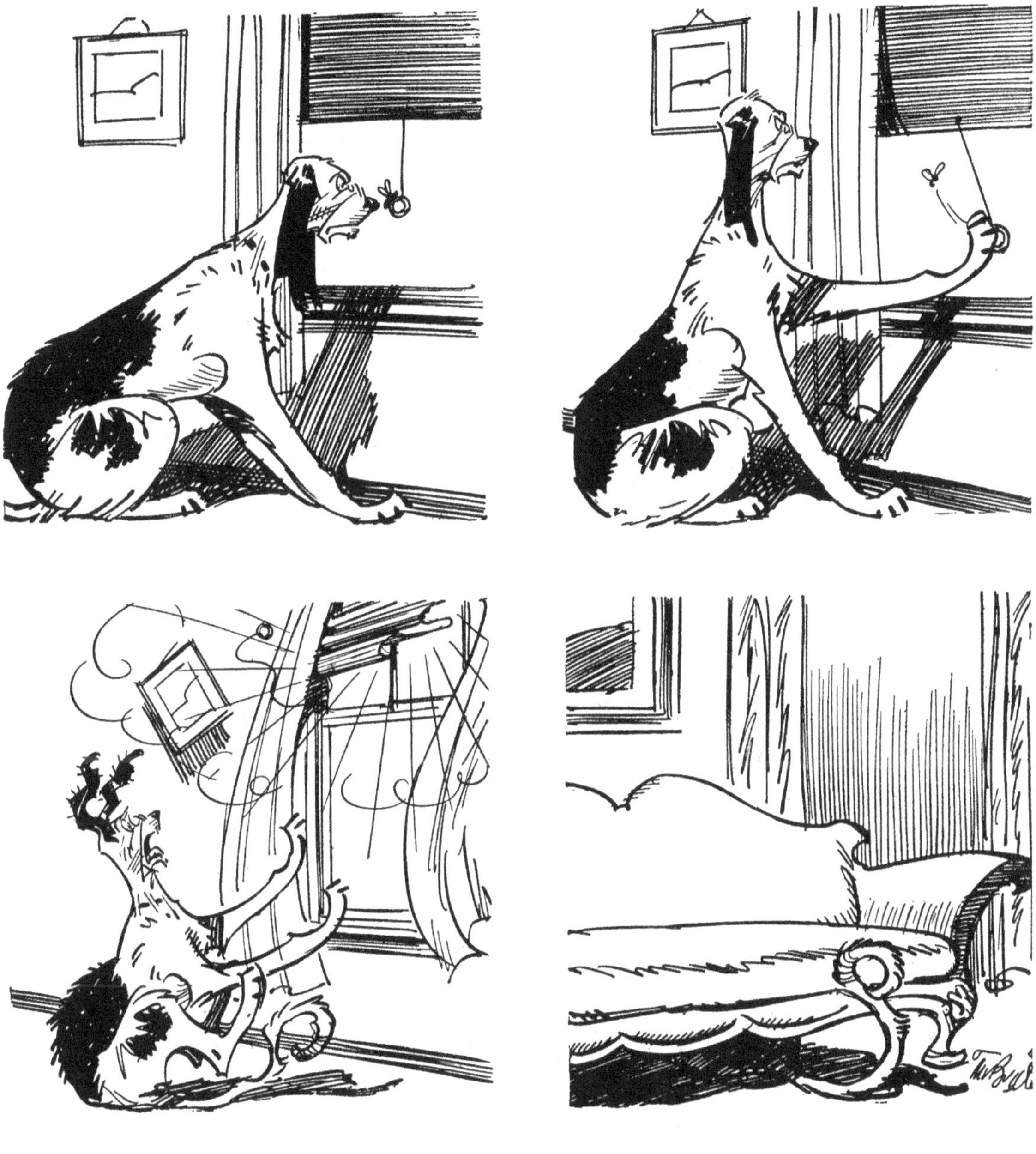

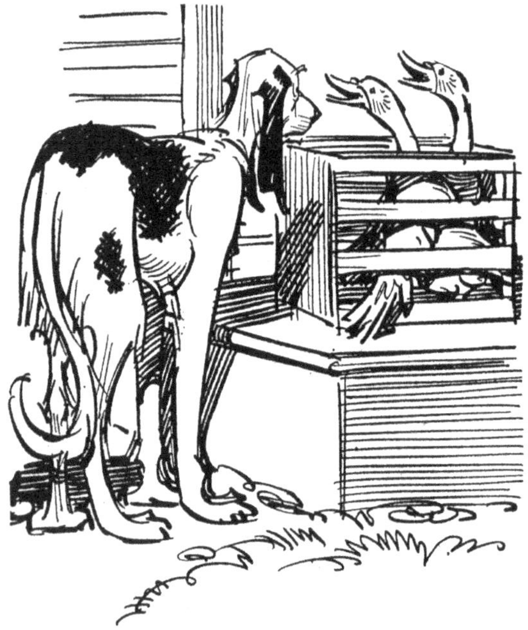

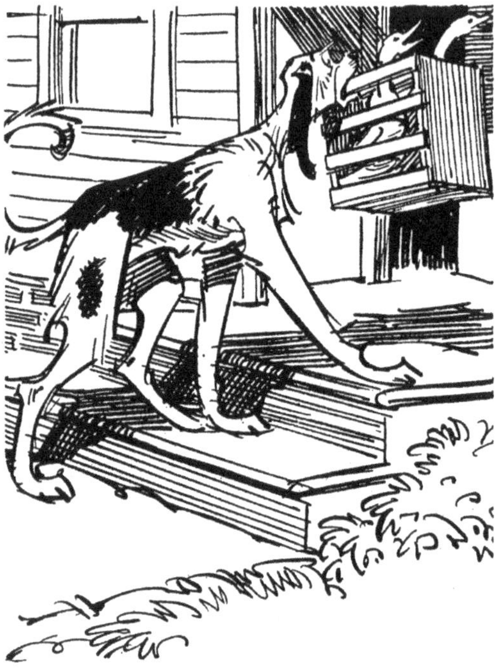

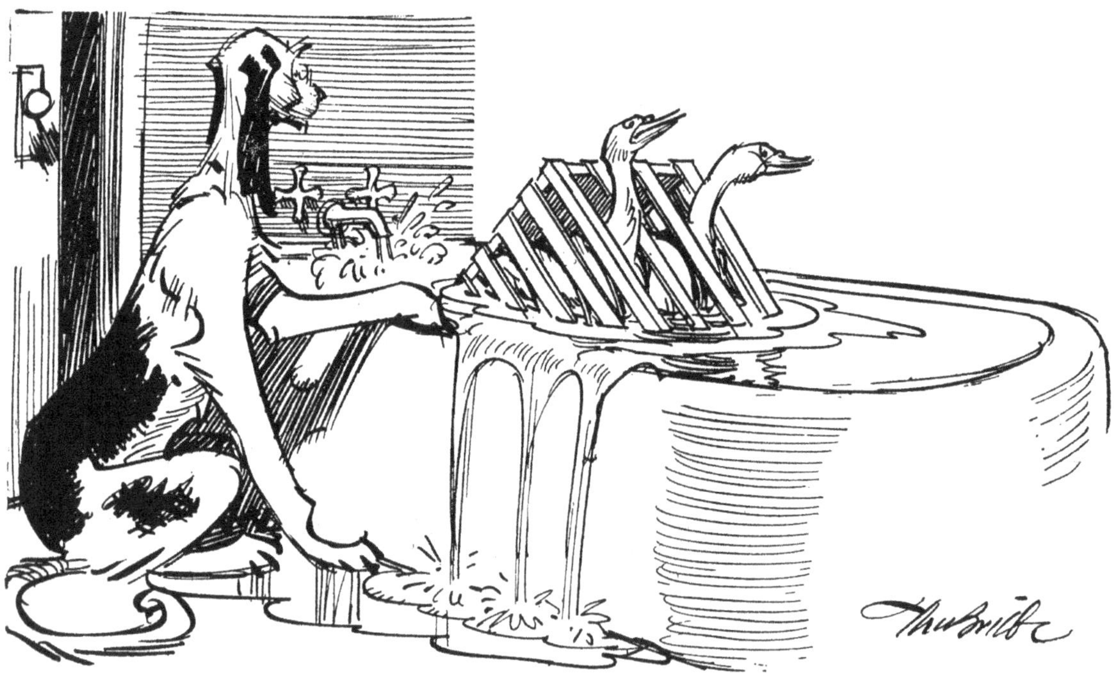

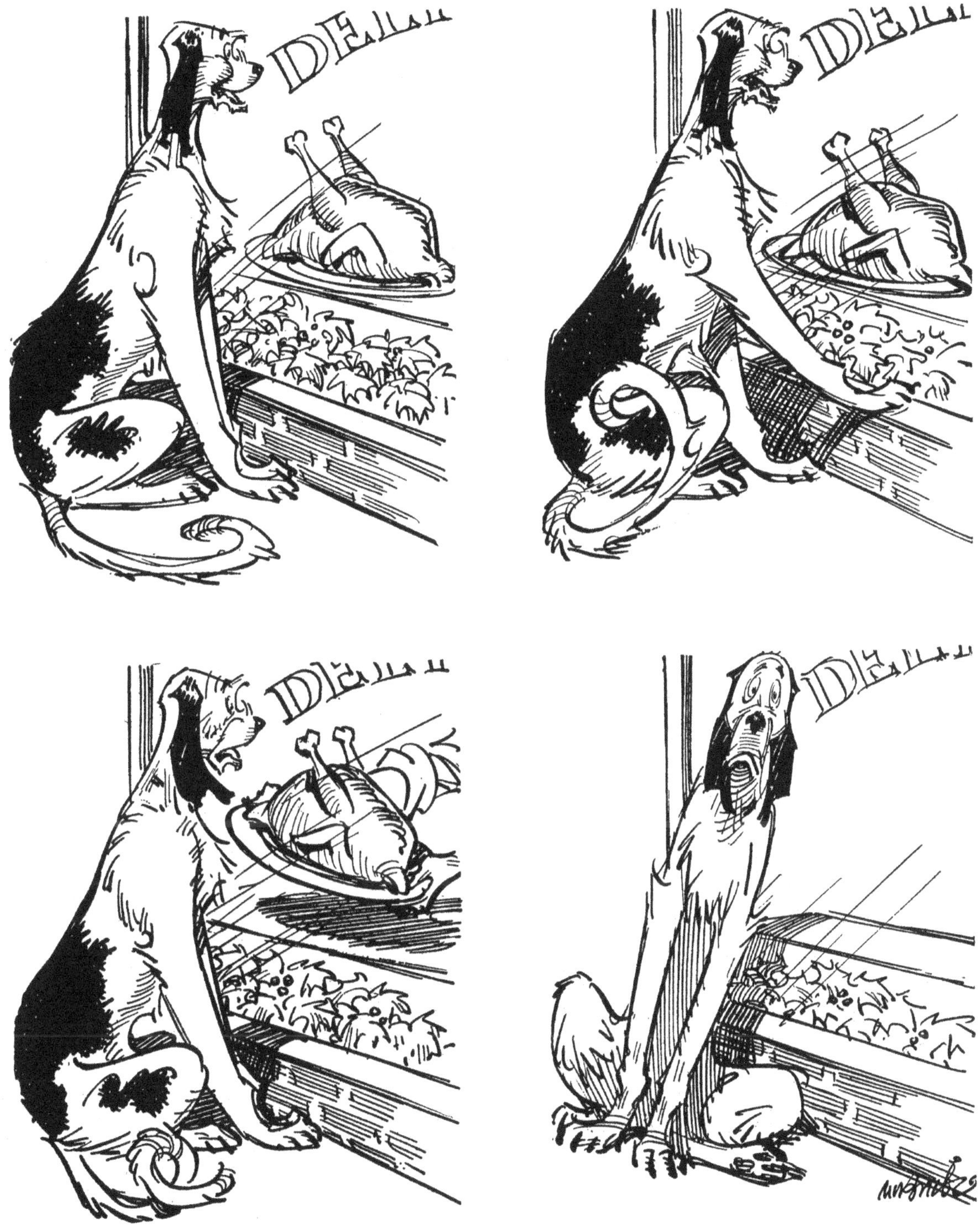

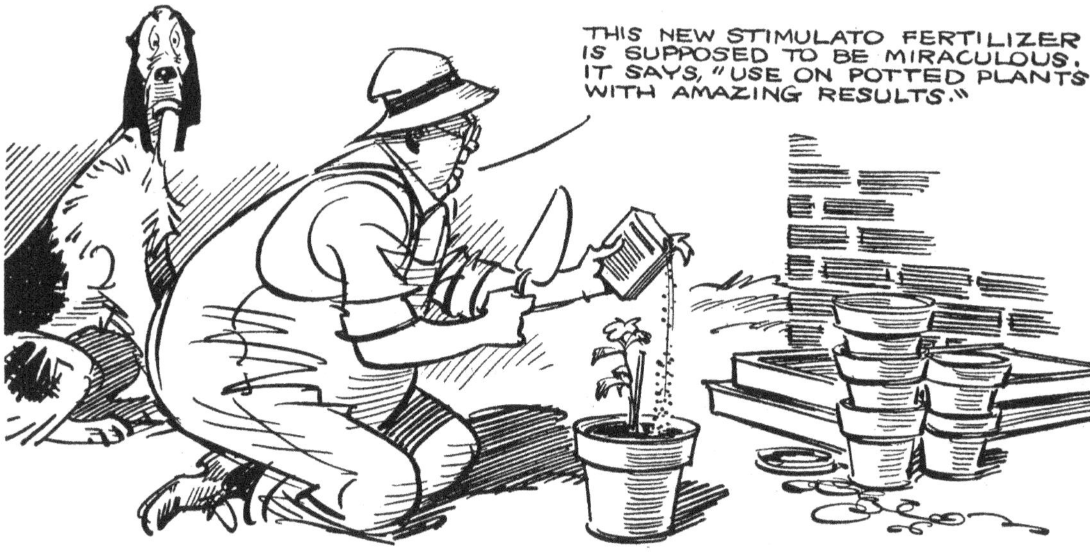
THIS NEW STIMULATO FERTILIZER IS SUPPOSED TO BE MIRACULOUS. IT SAYS, "USE ON POTTED PLANTS WITH AMAZING RESULTS."

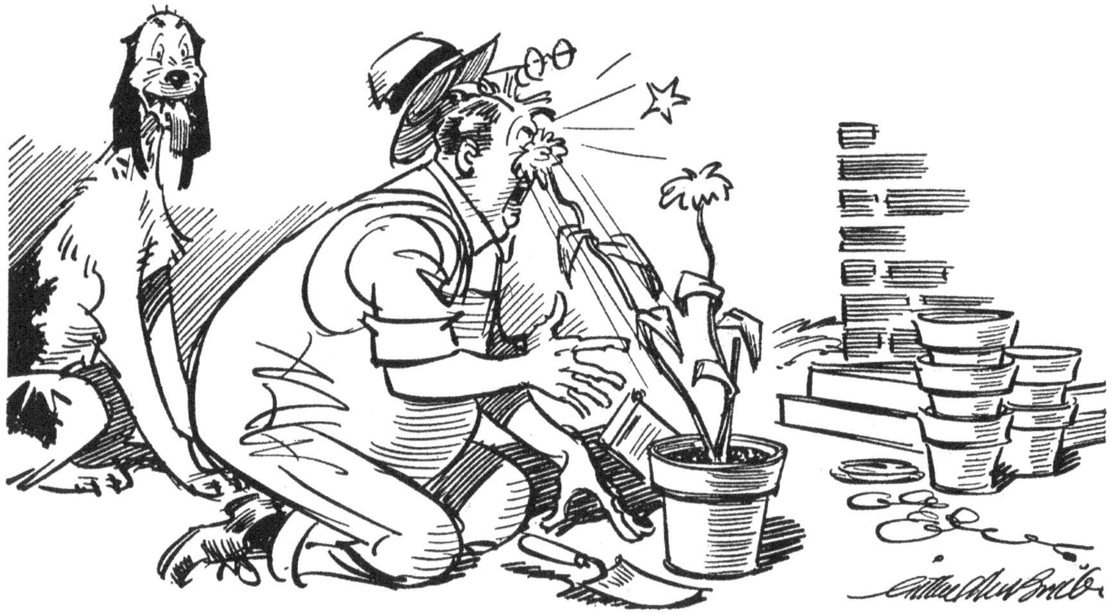

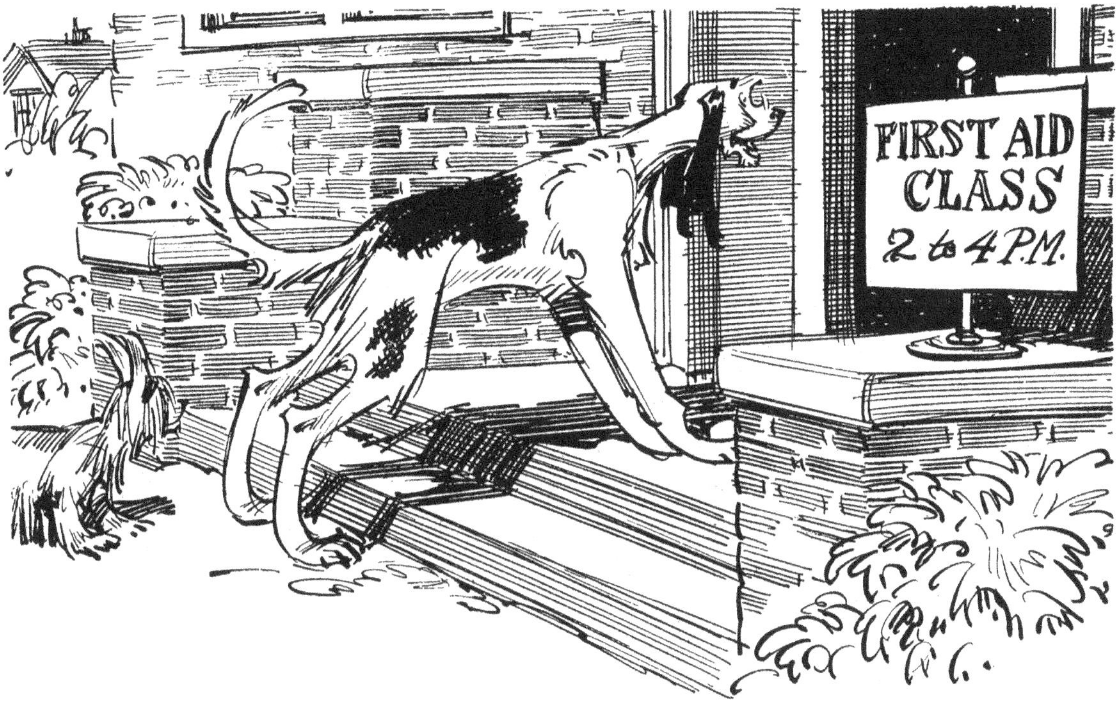
FIRST AID
CLASS
2 to 4 P.M.

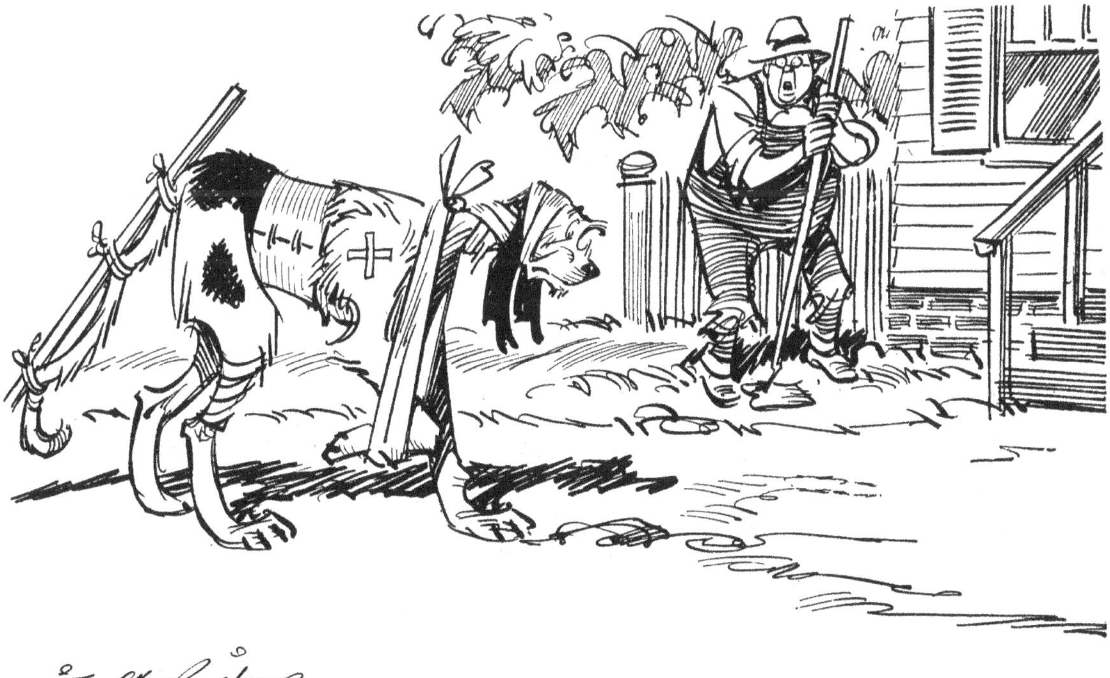

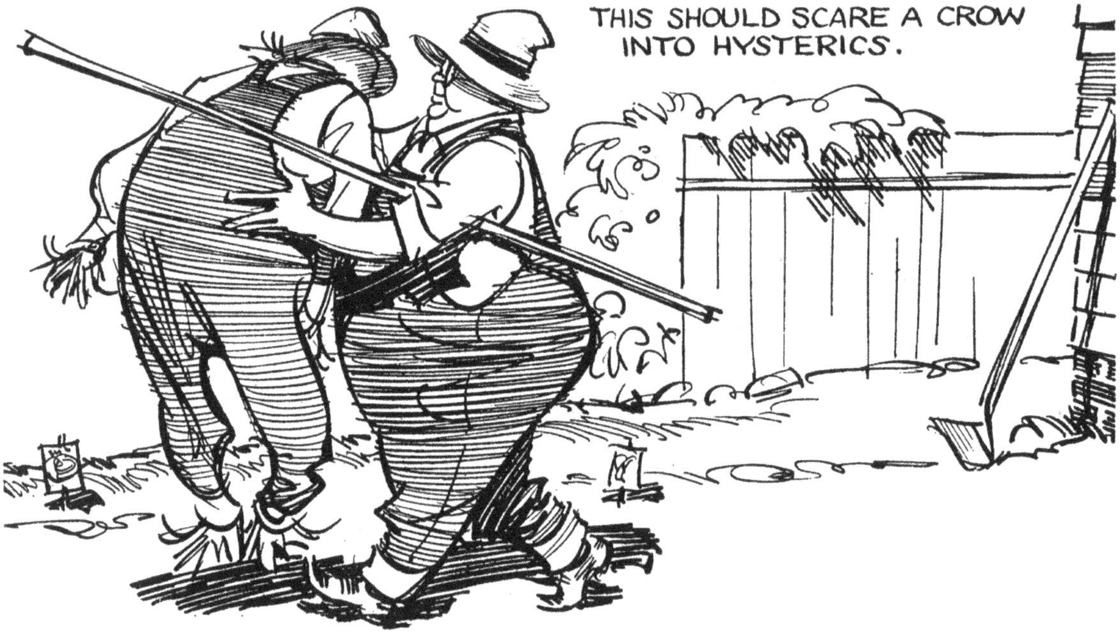
THIS SHOULD SCARE A CROW
INTO HYSTERICS.

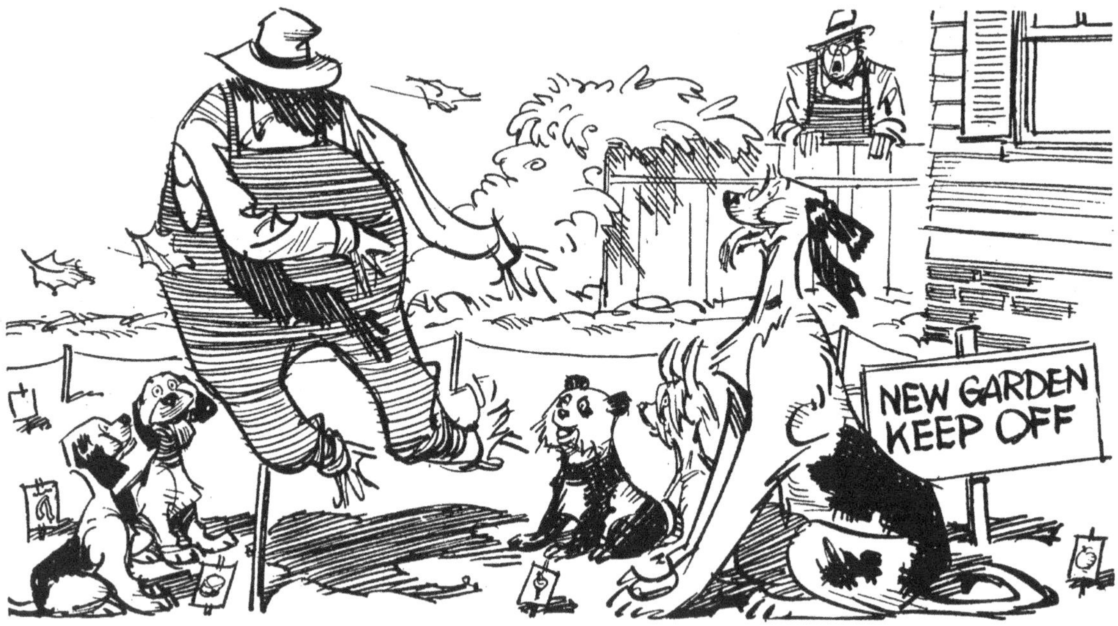
NEW GARDEN
KEEP OFF

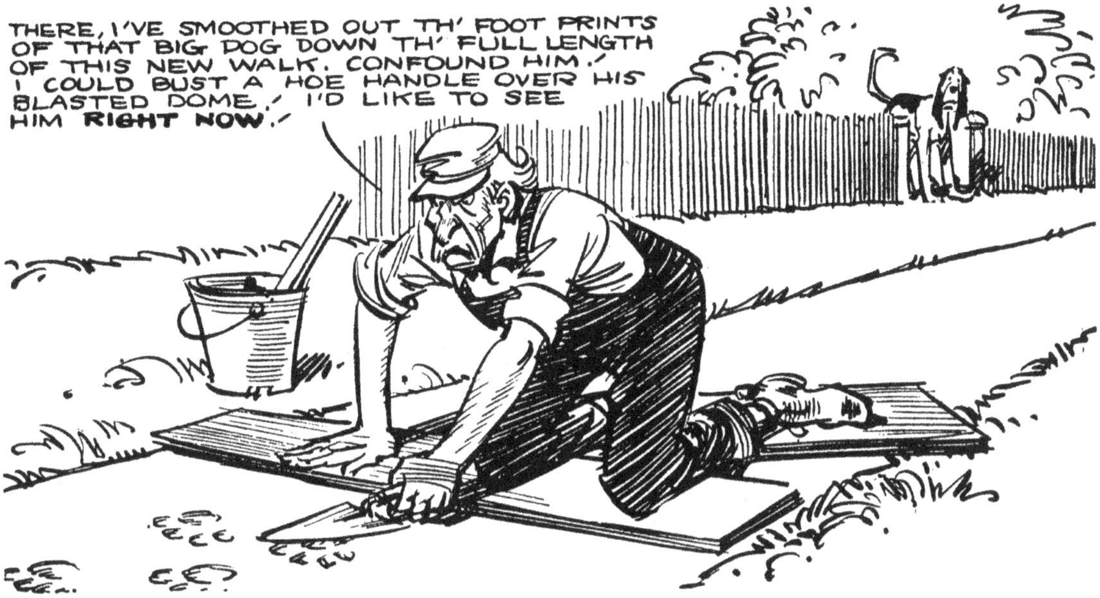
THERE, I'VE SMOOTHED OUT TH' FOOT PRINTS OF THAT BIG DOG DOWN TH' FULL LENGTH OF THIS NEW WALK. CONFOUND HIM.! I COULD BUST A HOE HANDLE OVER HIS BLASTED DOME.! I'D LIKE TO SEE HIM **RIGHT NOW**.!

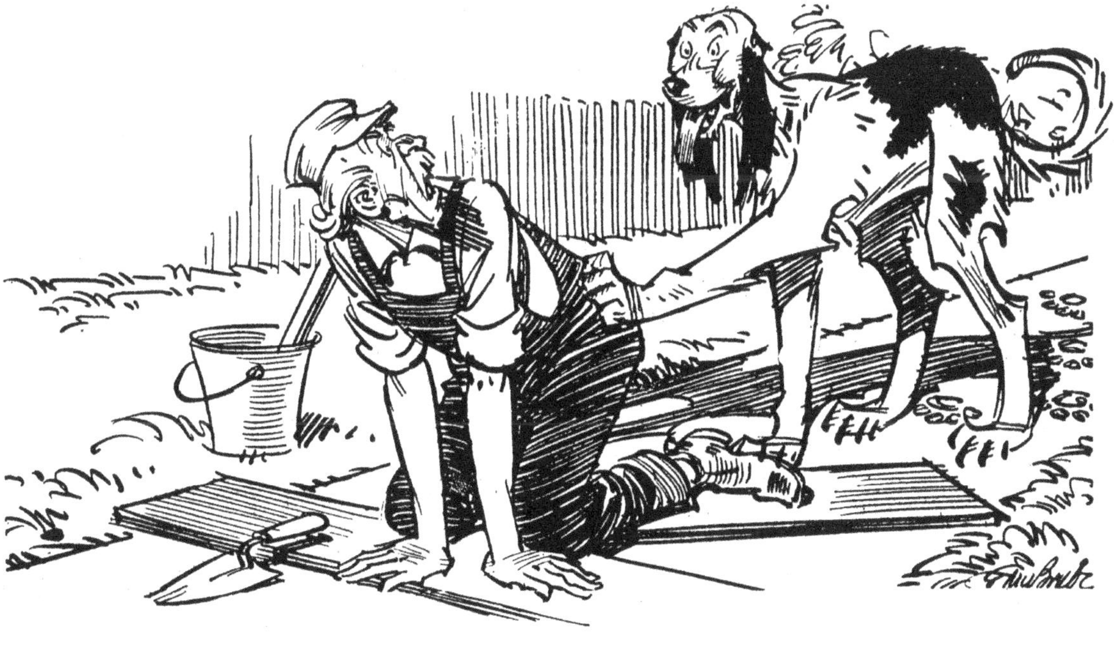

I HAVEN'T VISITED THE OLD FARM FOR YEARS. HOW MY BOYHOOD ALL COMES BACK TO ME! I REMEMBER WHEN I WAS A LAD ABOUT YOUR SIZE, WILLIE. I BURIED A PIRATE TREASURE UNDER THAT TREE — AN OLD BEAN JAR CONTAINING EIGHT CENTS AND A JACK KNIFE.

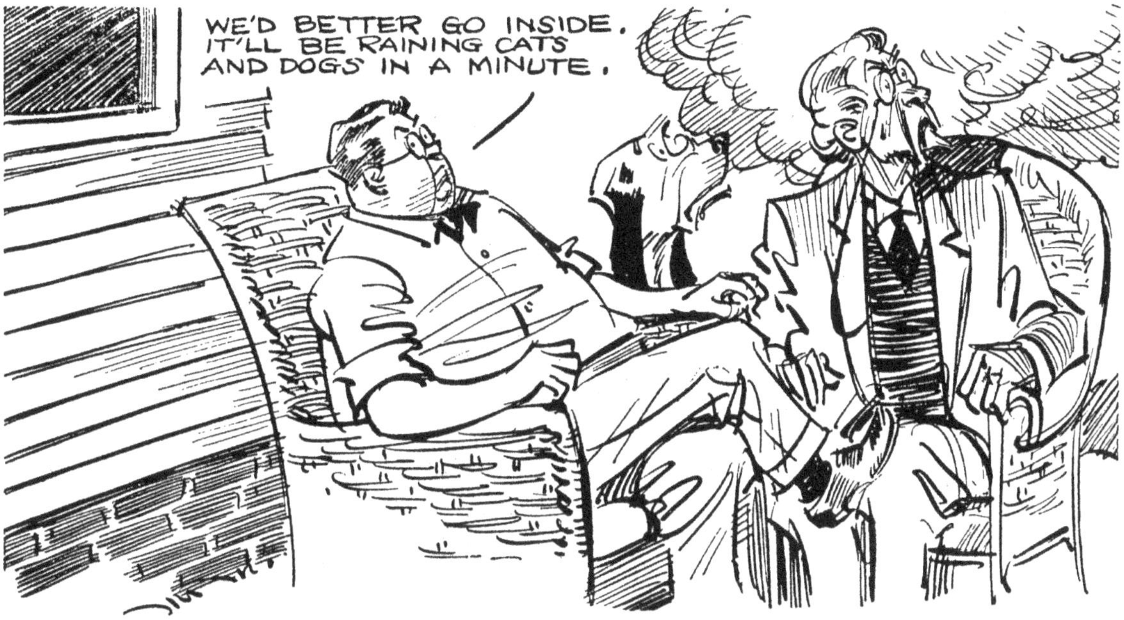
WE'D BETTER GO INSIDE. IT'LL BE RAINING CATS AND DOGS IN A MINUTE.

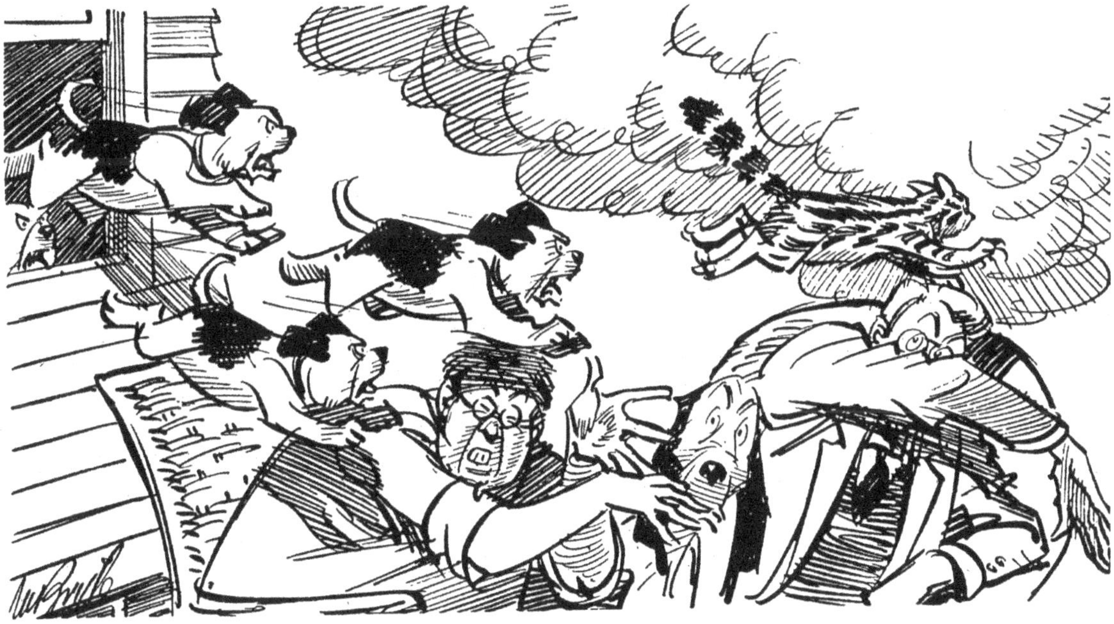

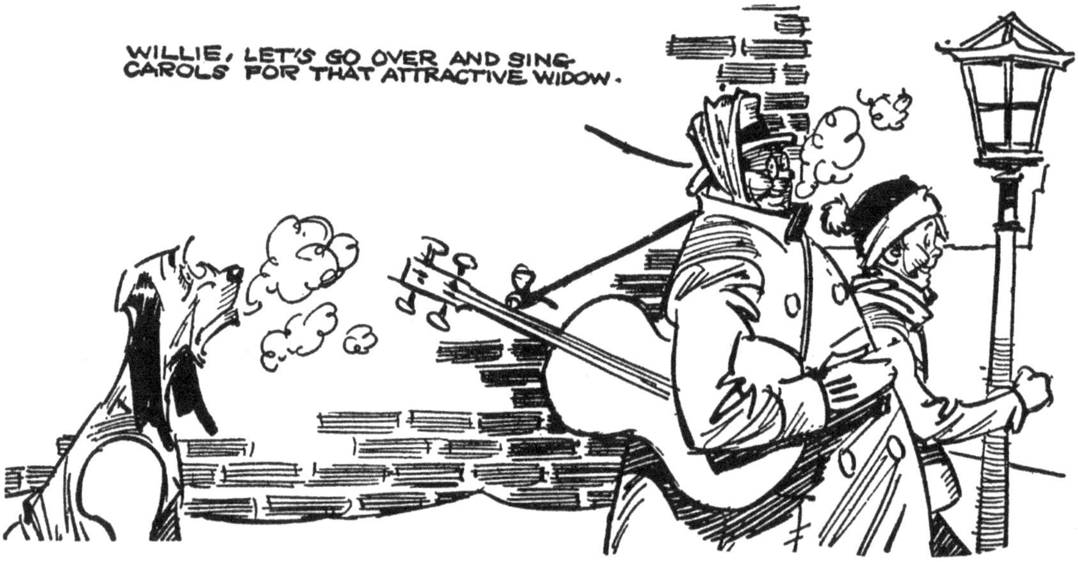
WILLIE, LET'S GO OVER AND SING CAROLS FOR THAT ATTRACTIVE WIDOW.

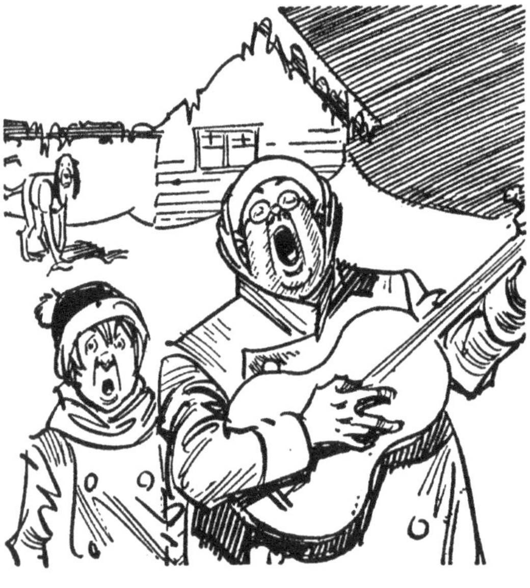

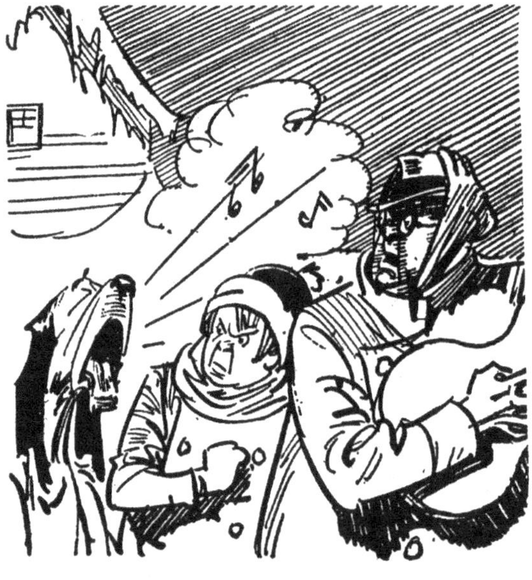

NAPOLEON AMONG THE KIDS

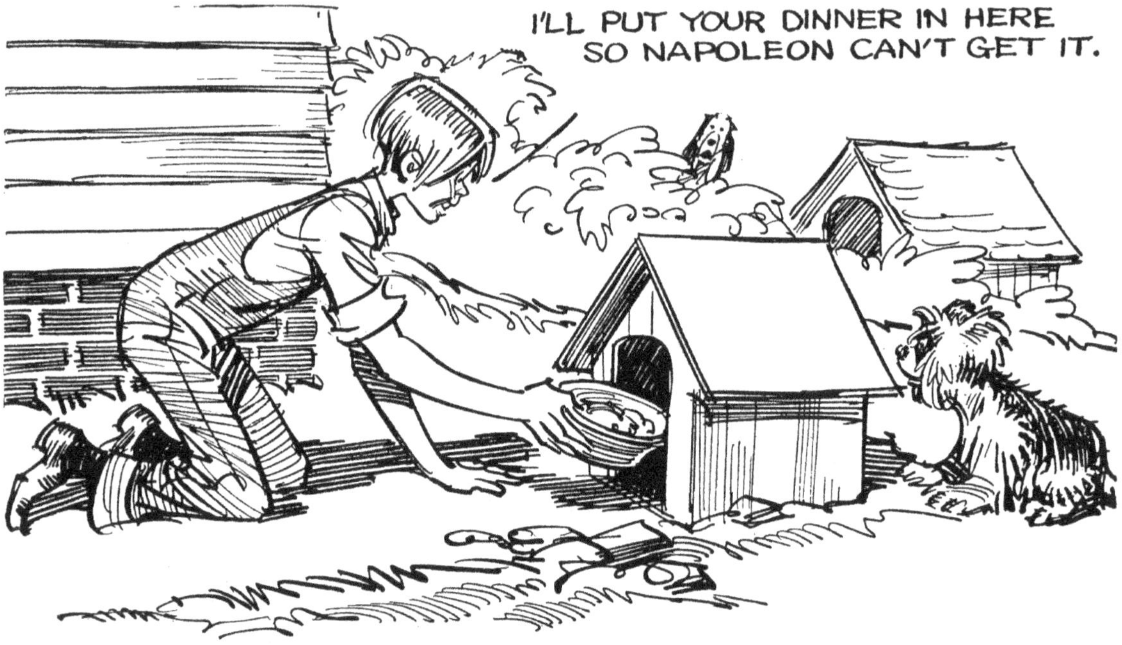
I'LL PUT YOUR DINNER IN HERE
SO NAPOLEON CAN'T GET IT.

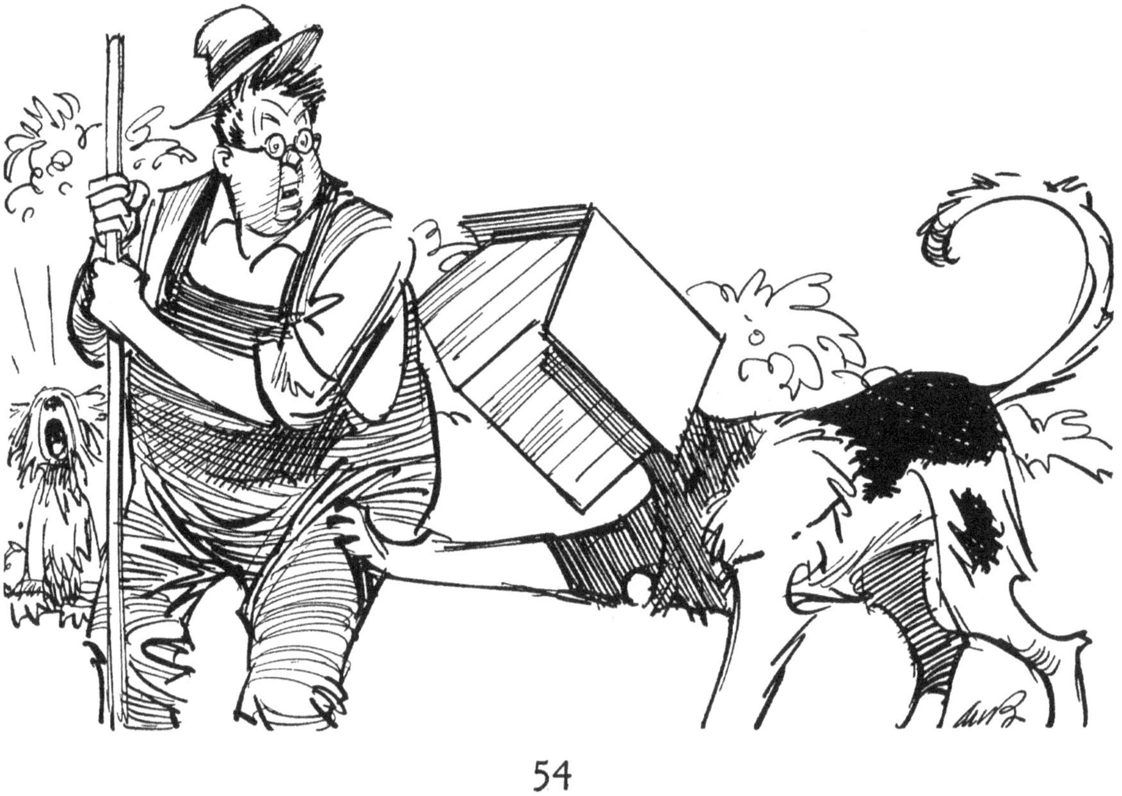

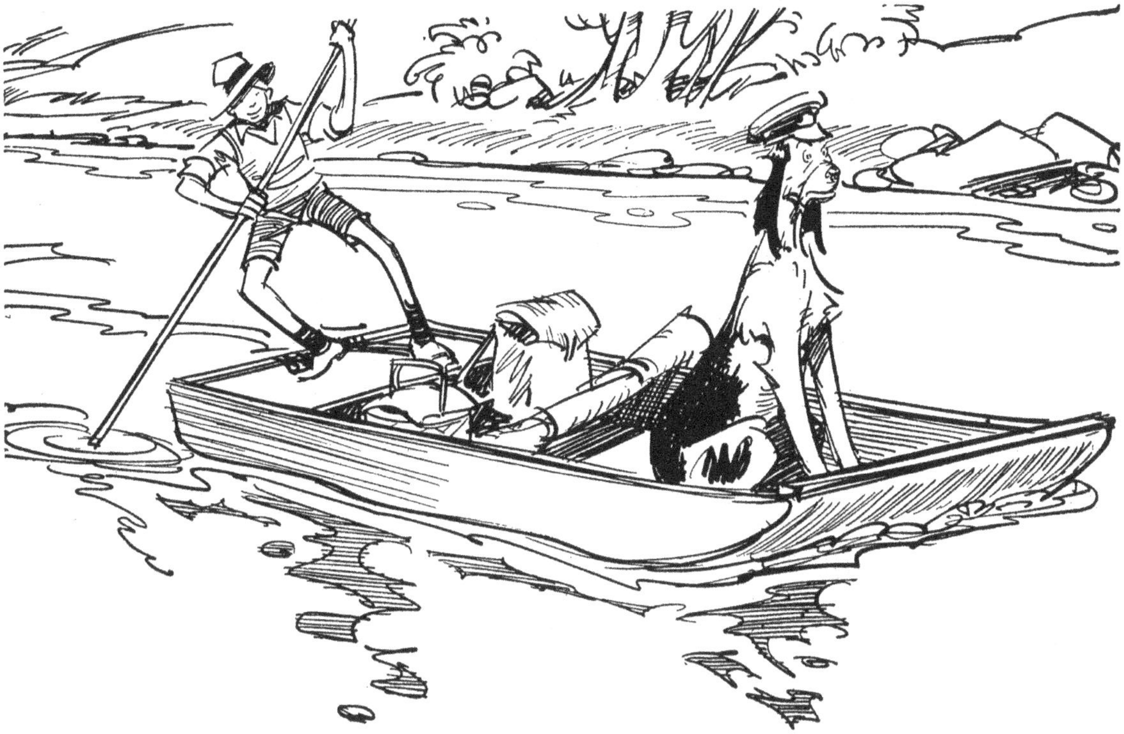

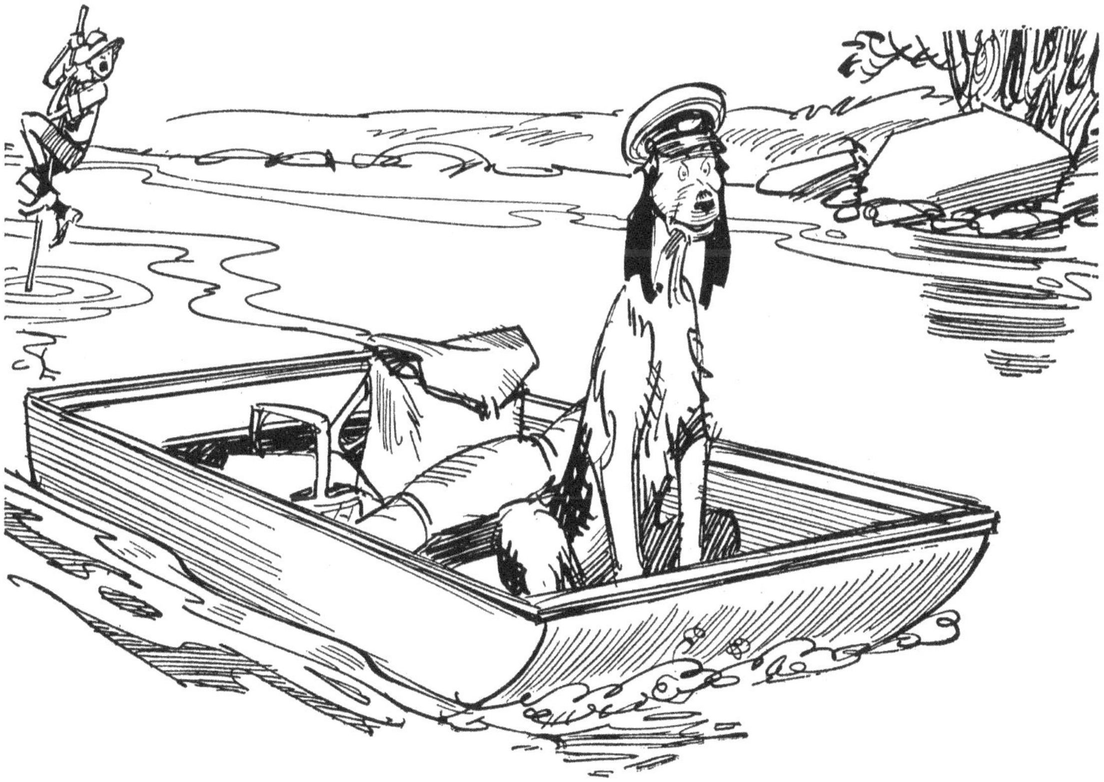

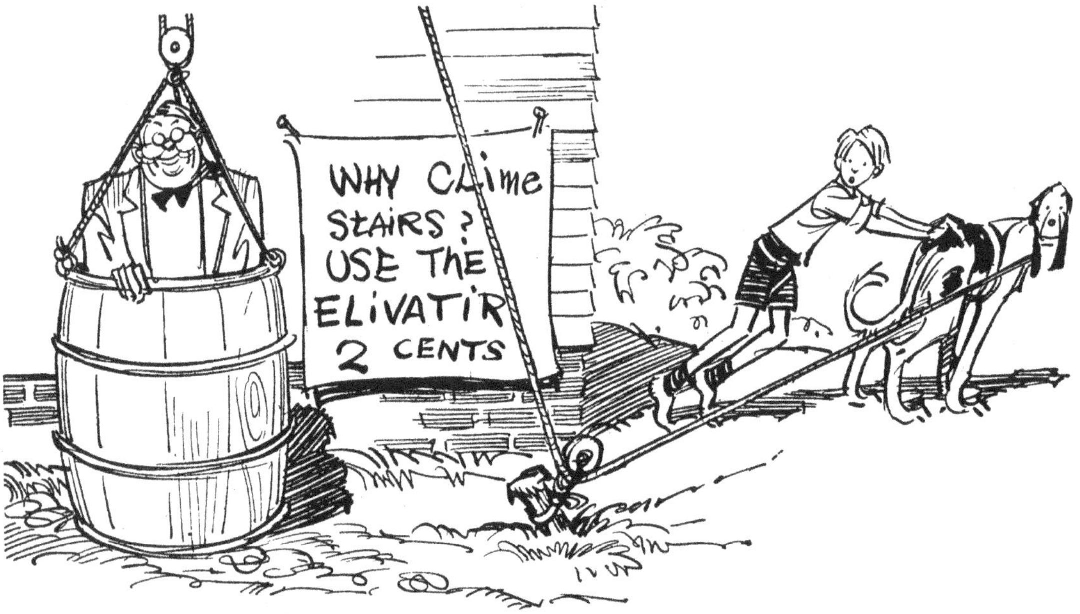
WHY CLime
STAIRS ?
USE THE
ELiVATIR
2 CENTS

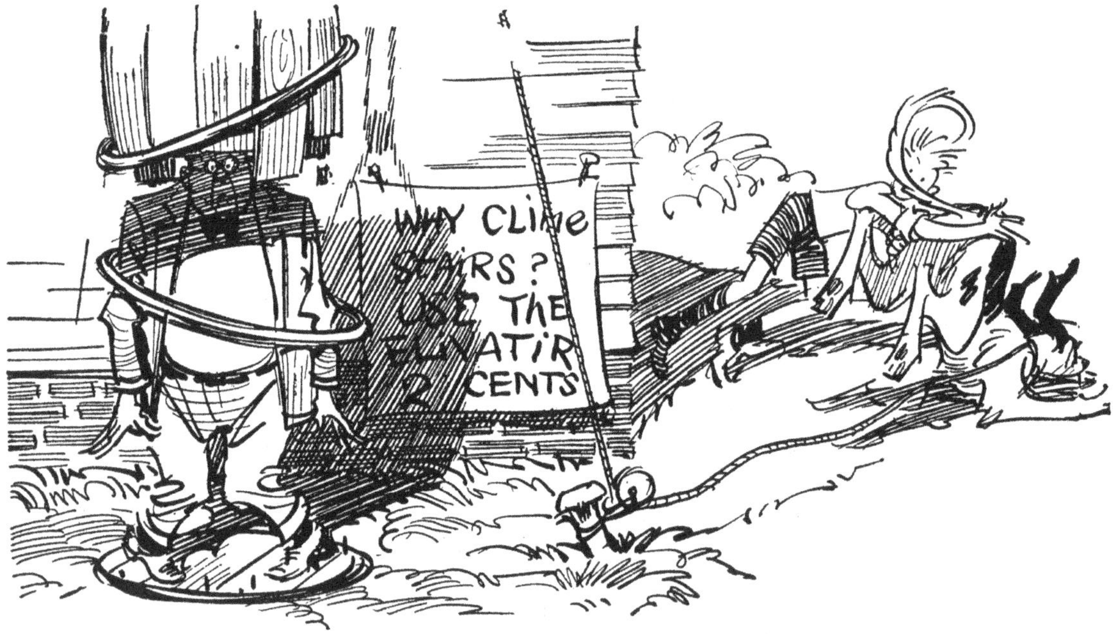
WHY CLime
STAIRS ?
USE THE
ELiVATIR
2 CENTS

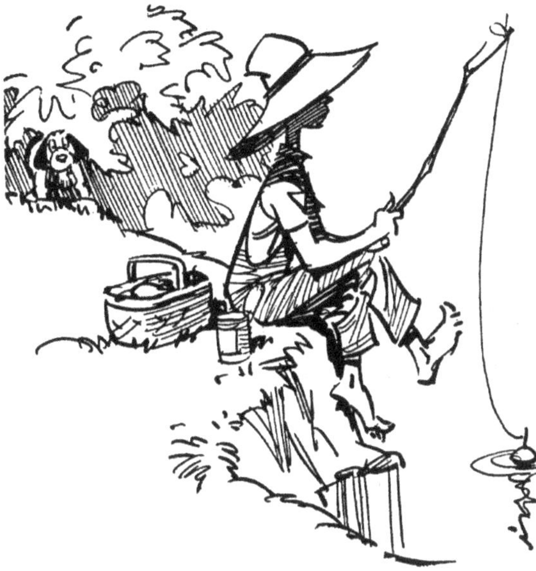

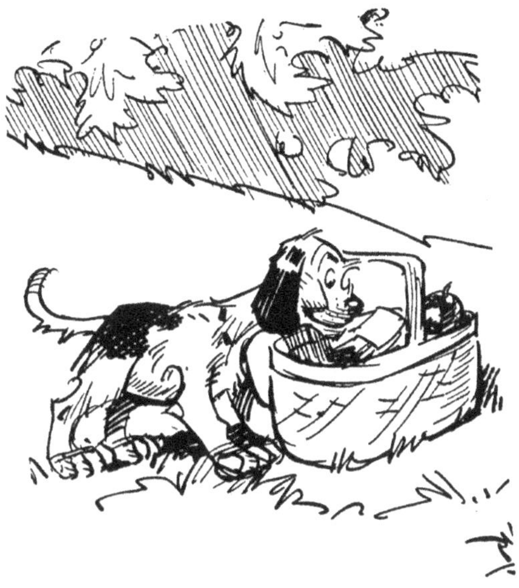

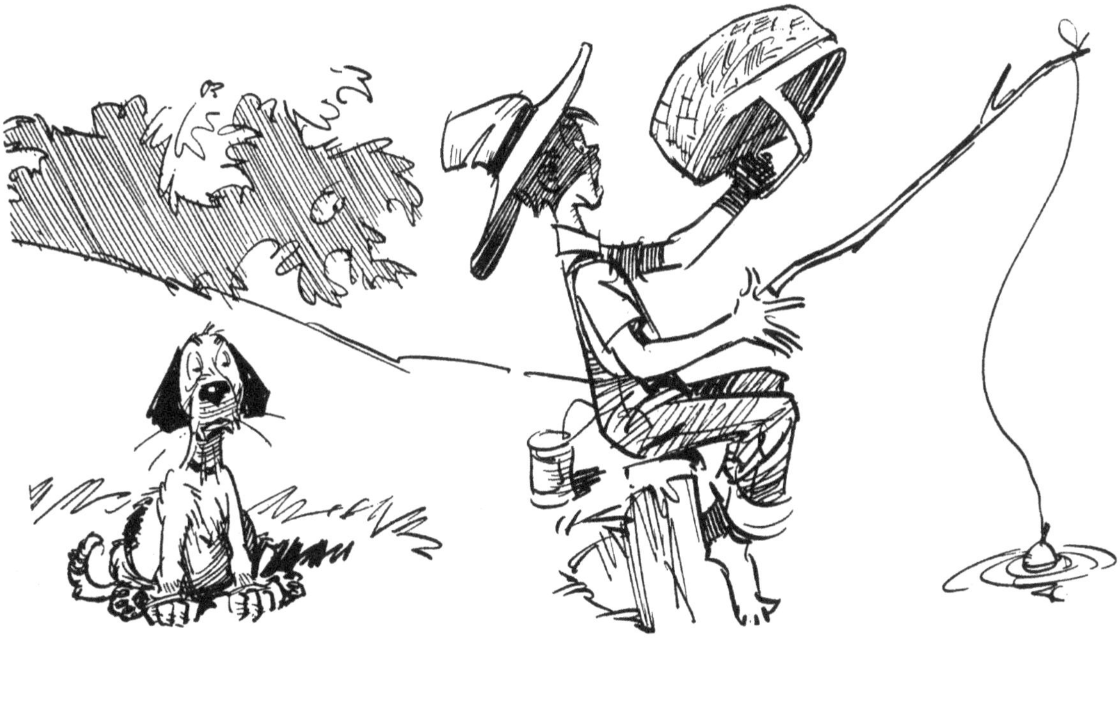

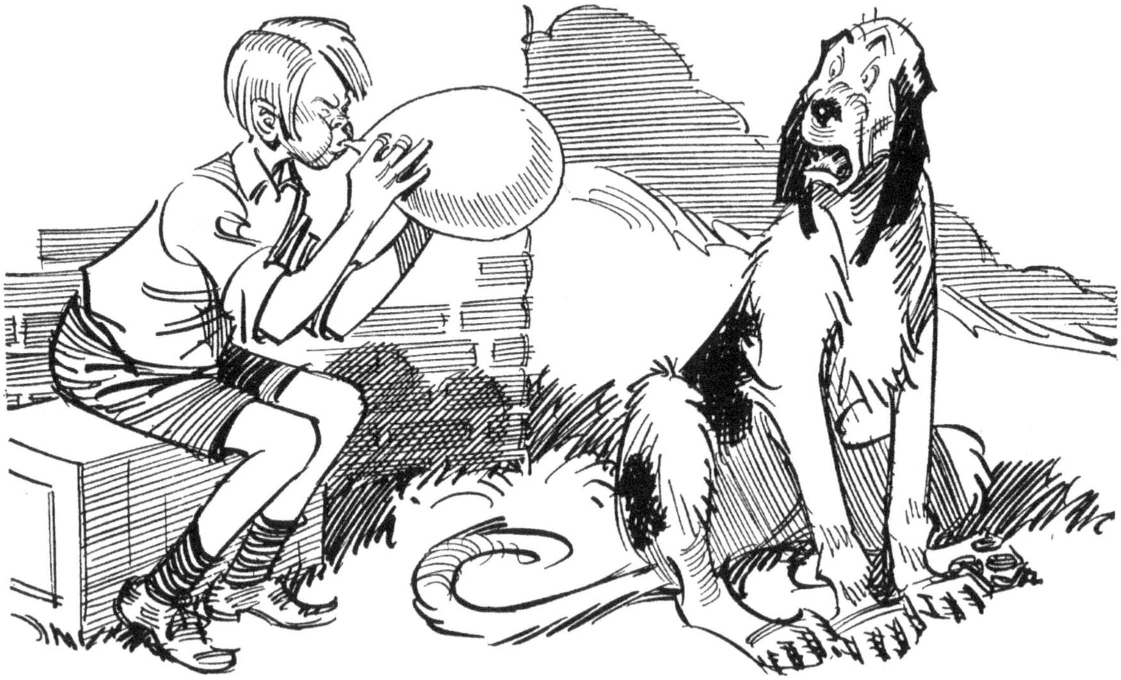

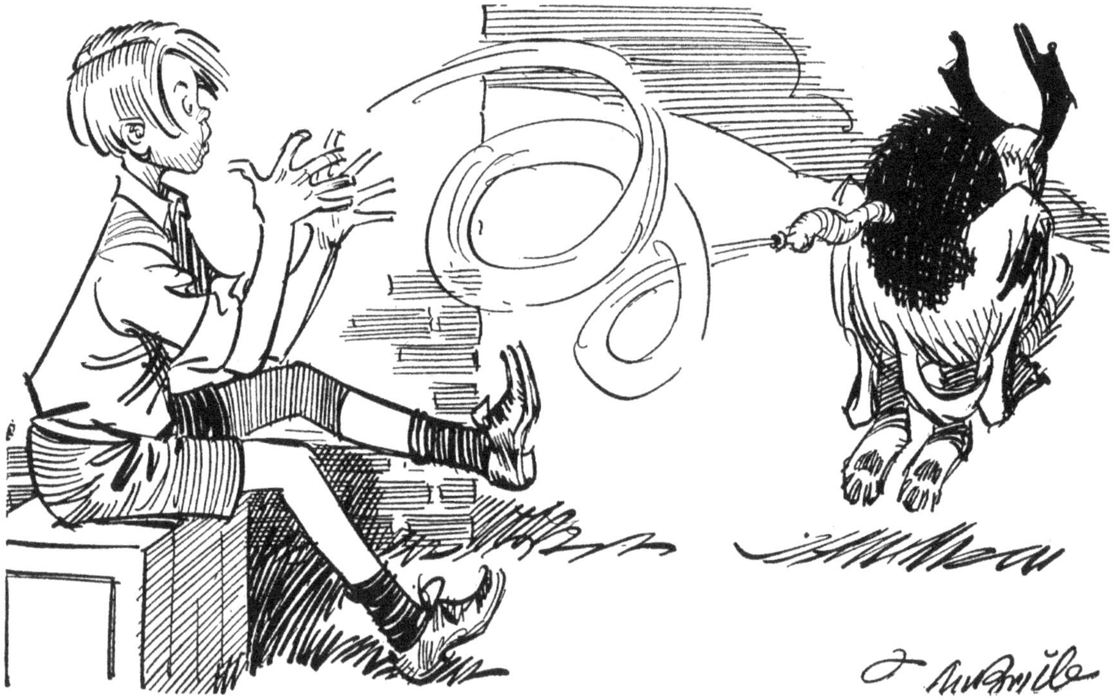

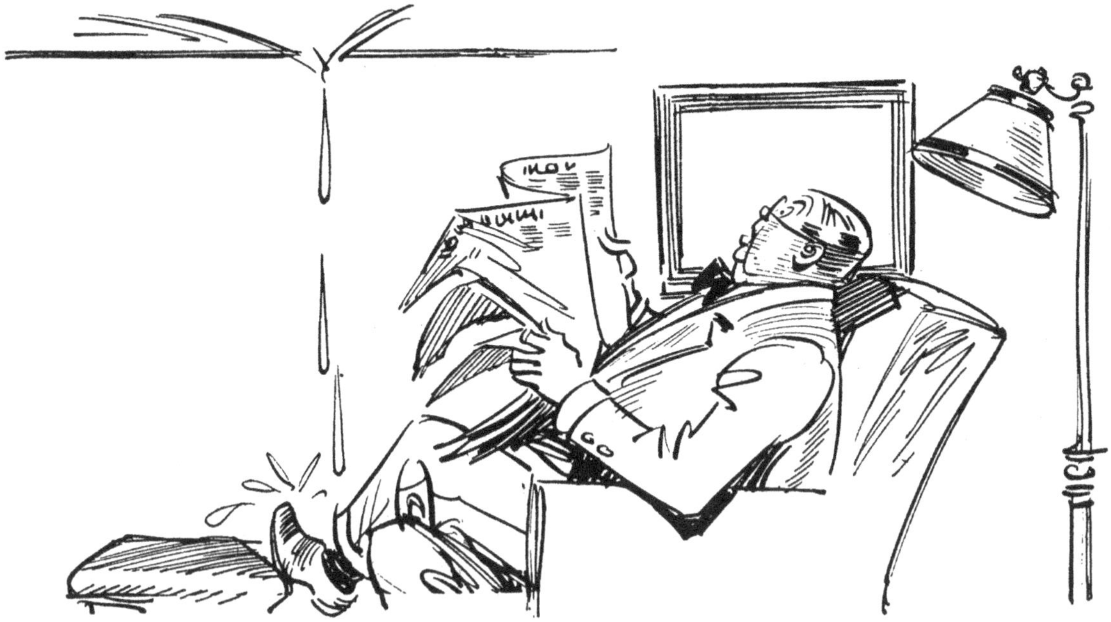

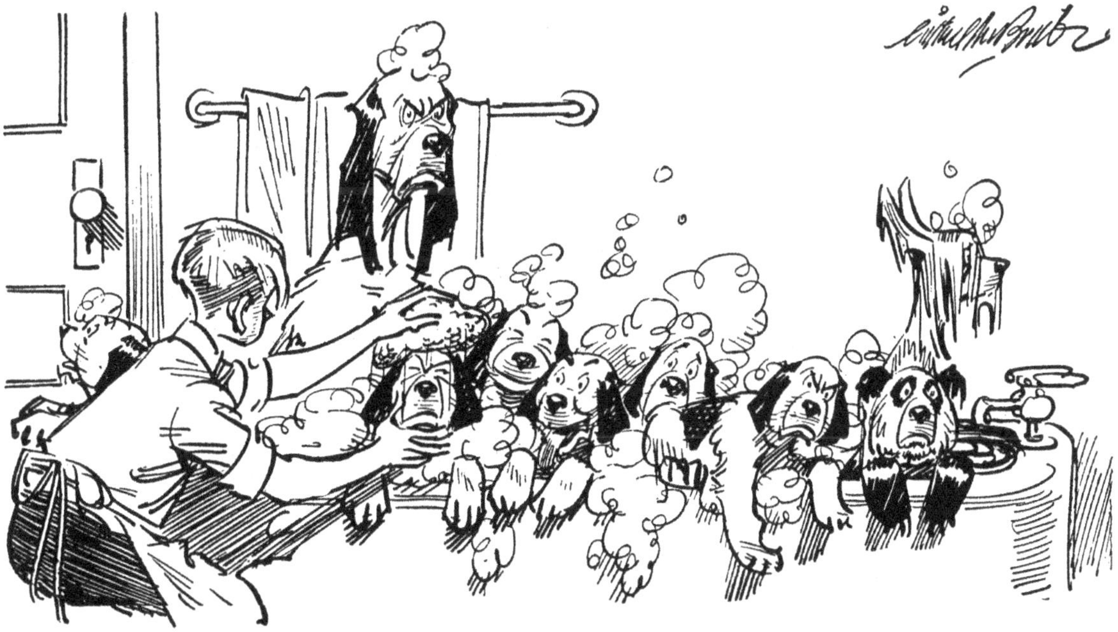

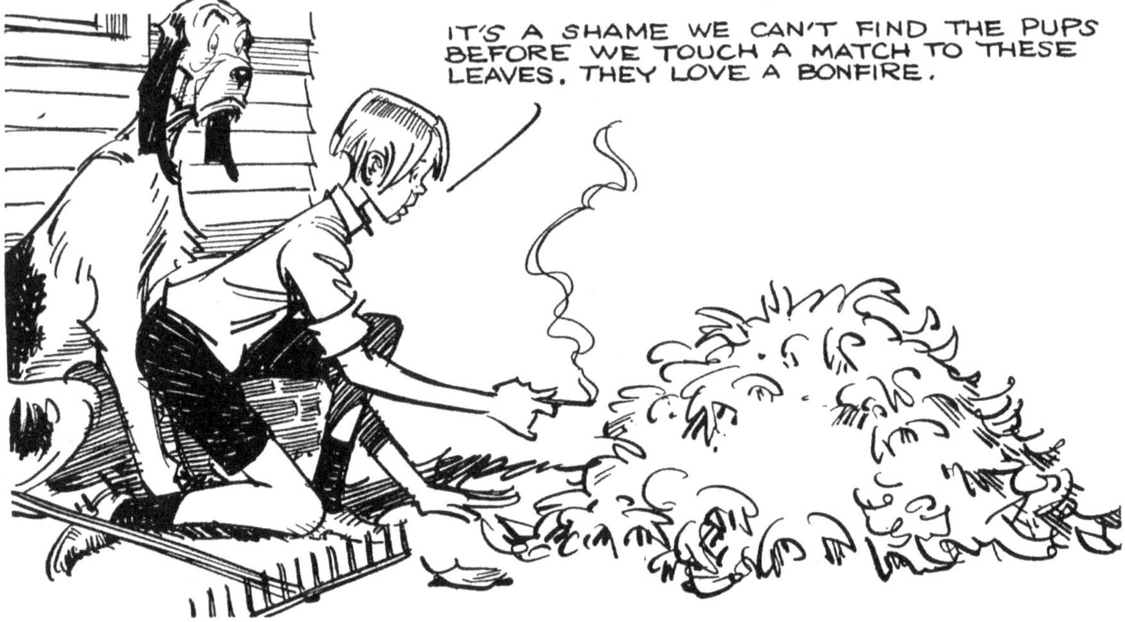
IT'S A SHAME WE CAN'T FIND THE PUPS BEFORE WE TOUCH A MATCH TO THESE LEAVES. THEY LOVE A BONFIRE.

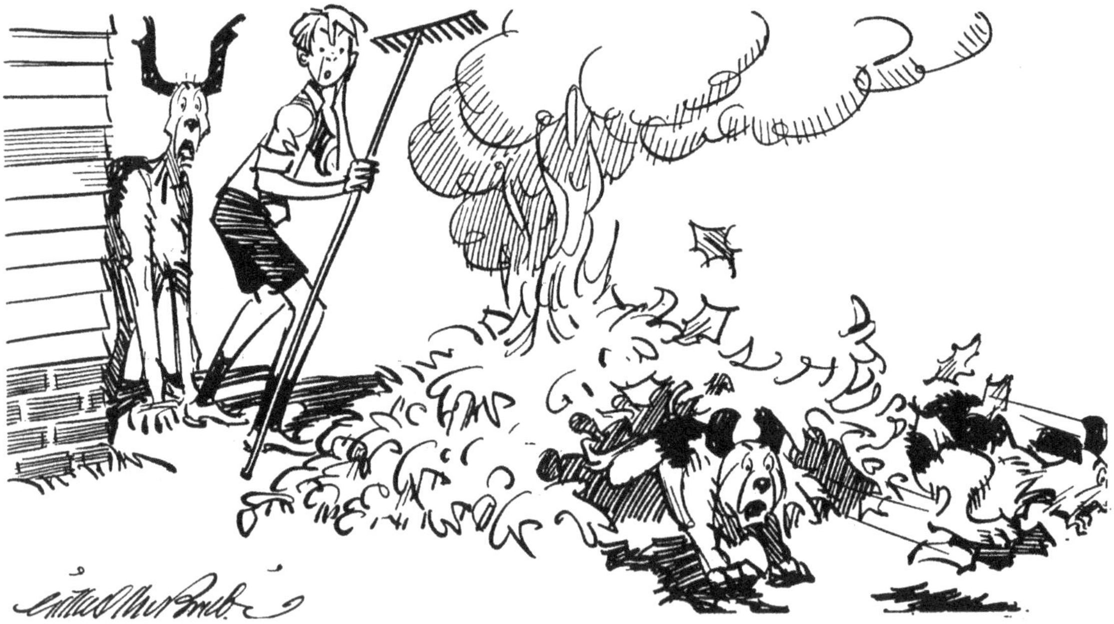

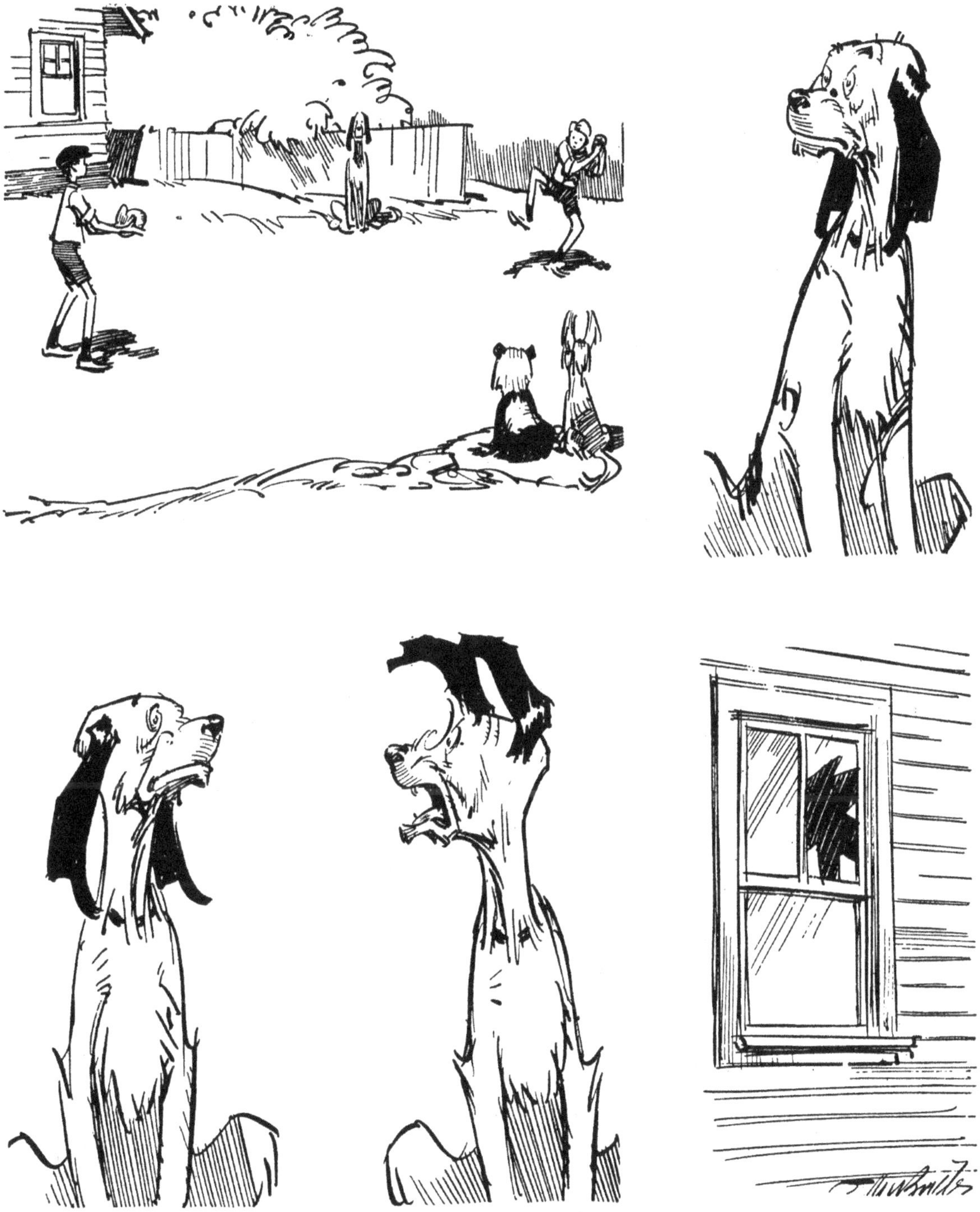

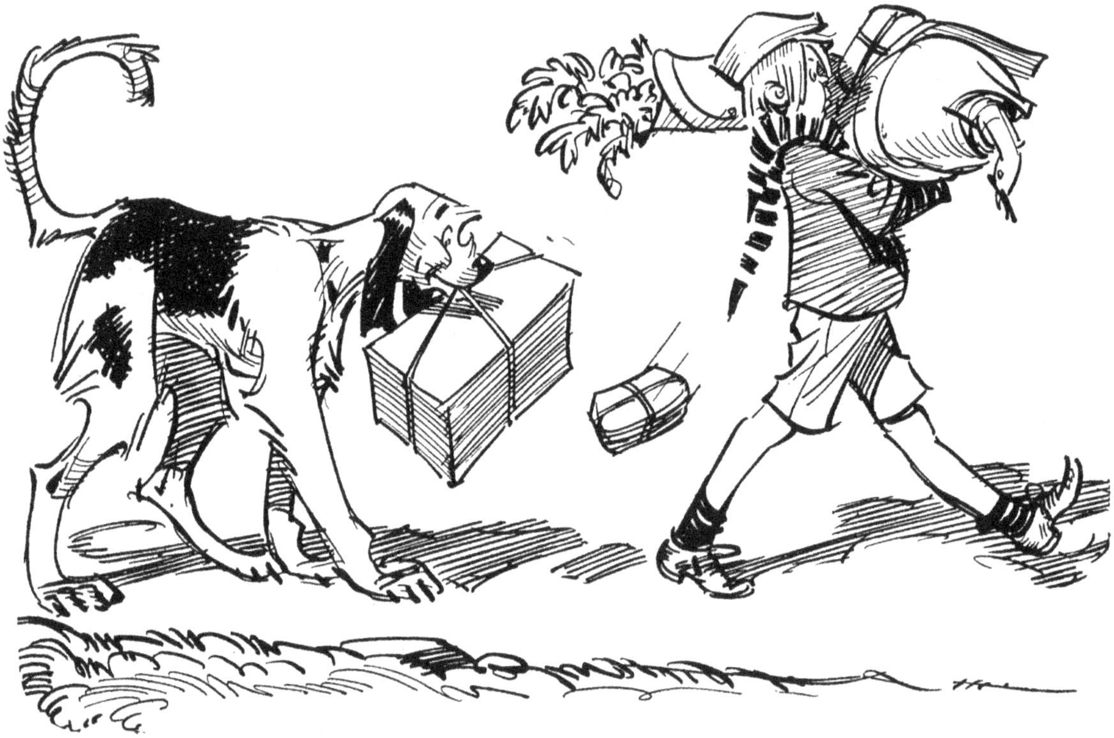

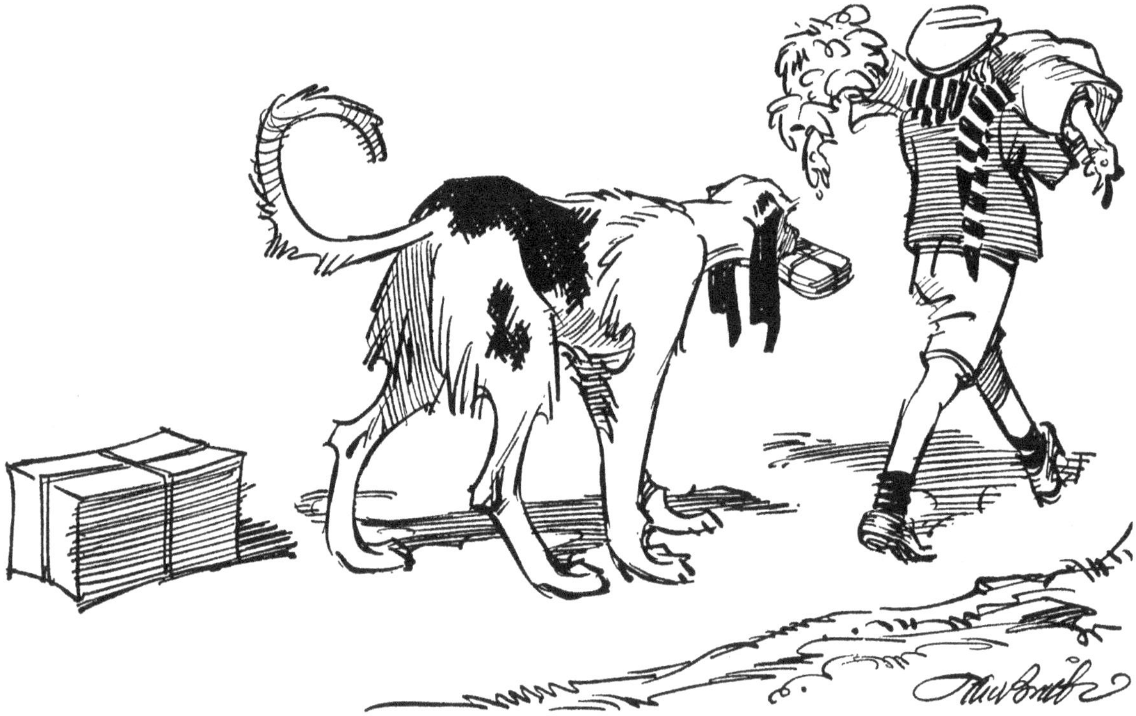

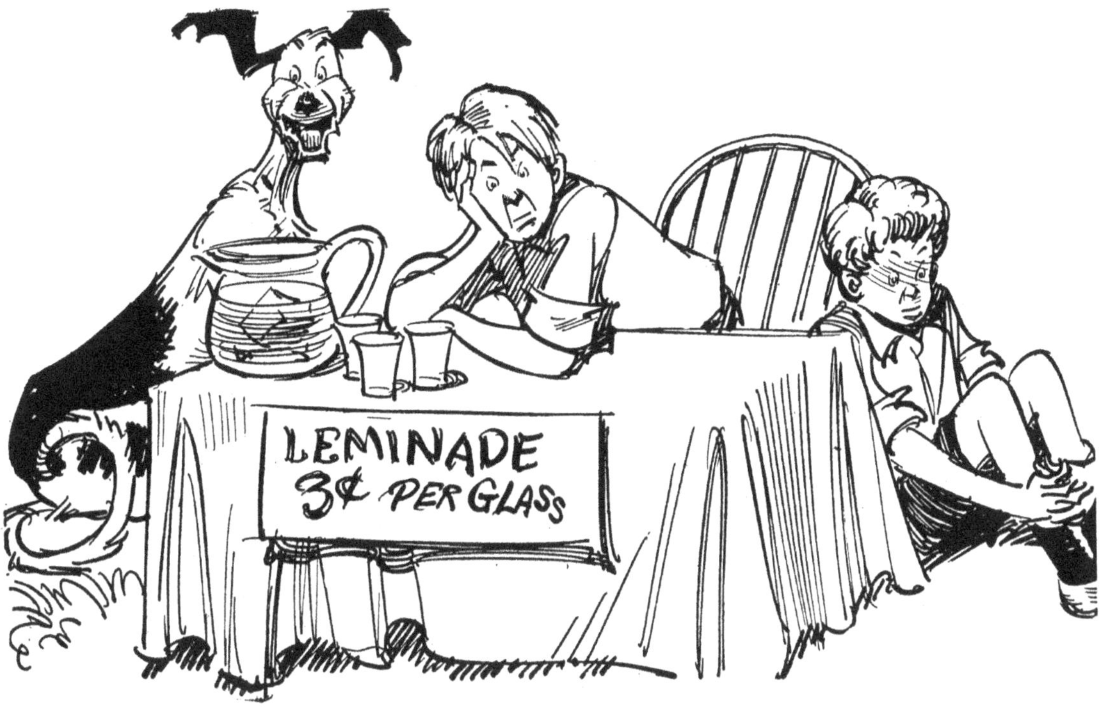
LEMINADE
3¢ PER GLASS

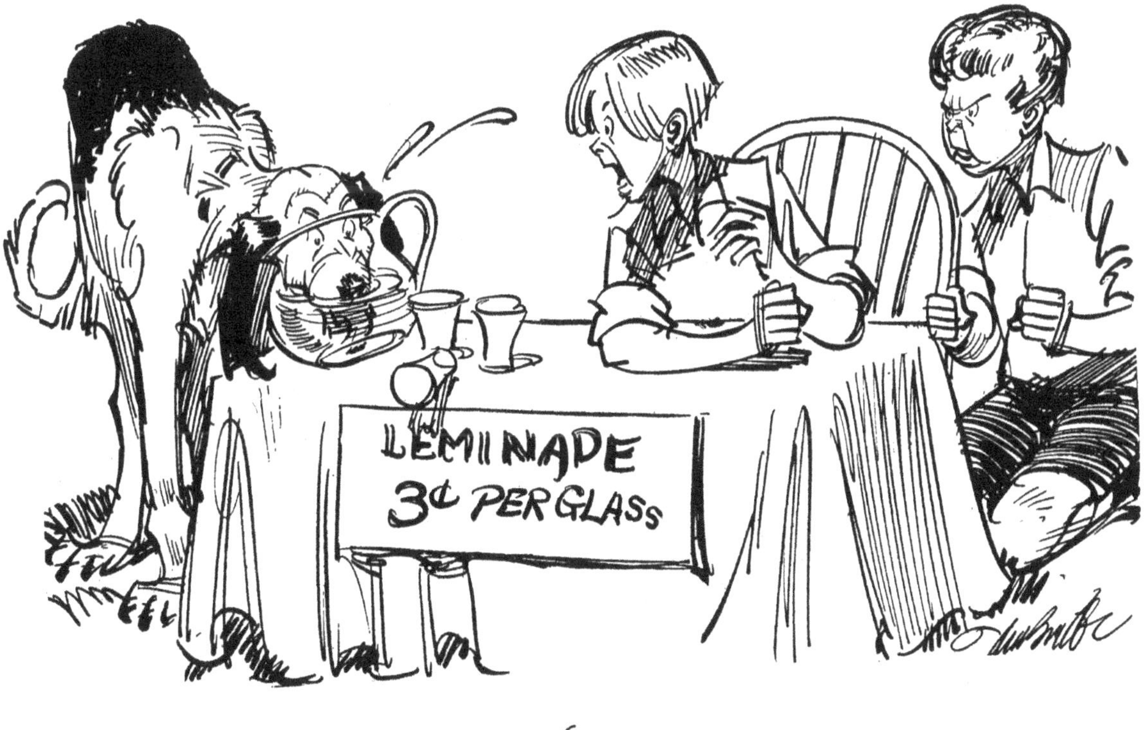
LEMINADE
3¢ PER GLASS

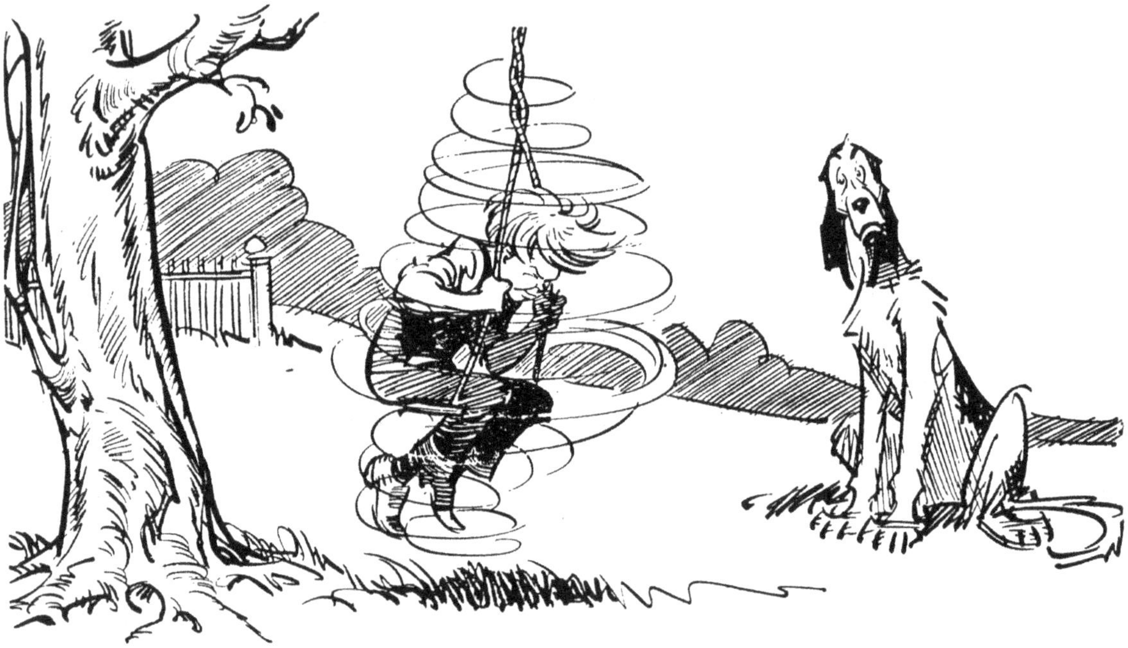

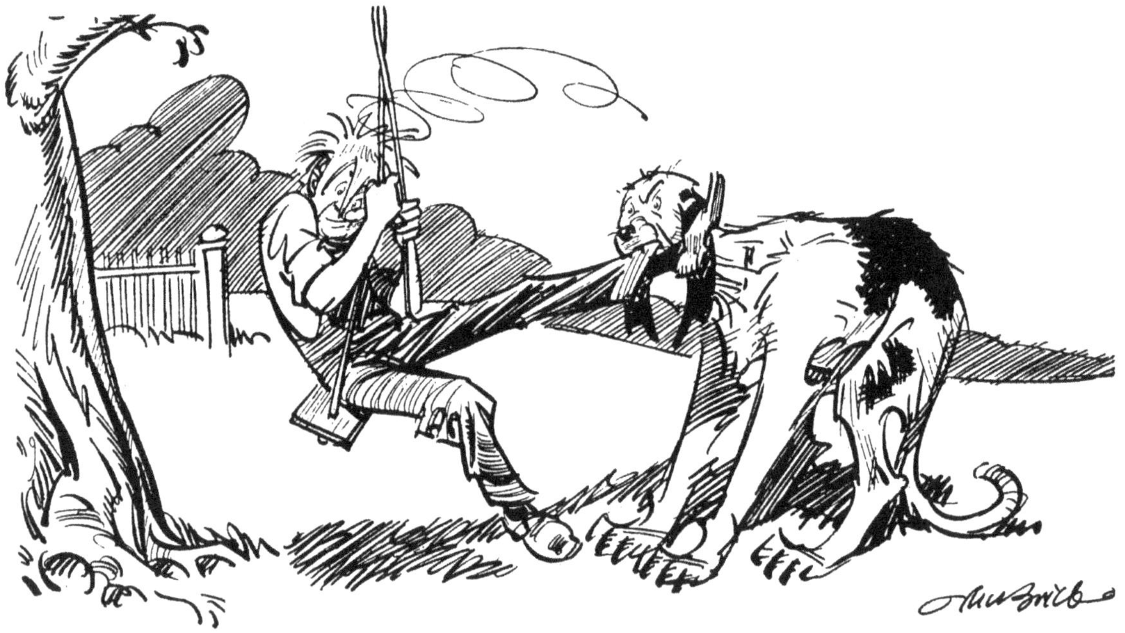

NAPOLEON HAS IDEAS

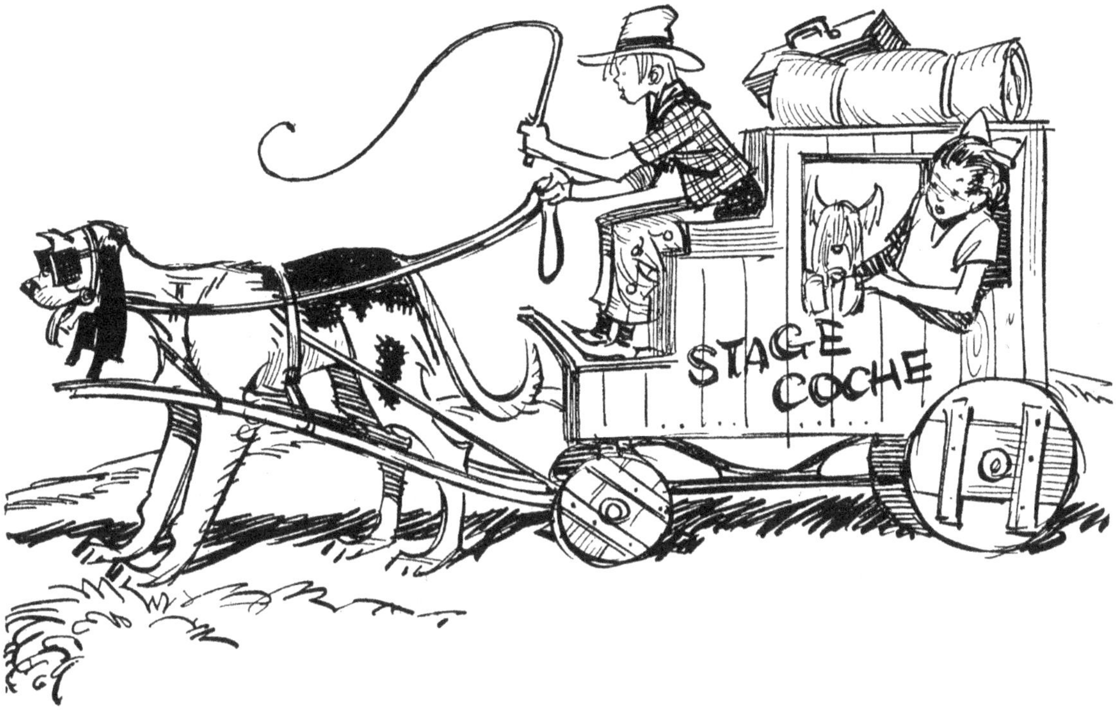
STAGE
COCHE

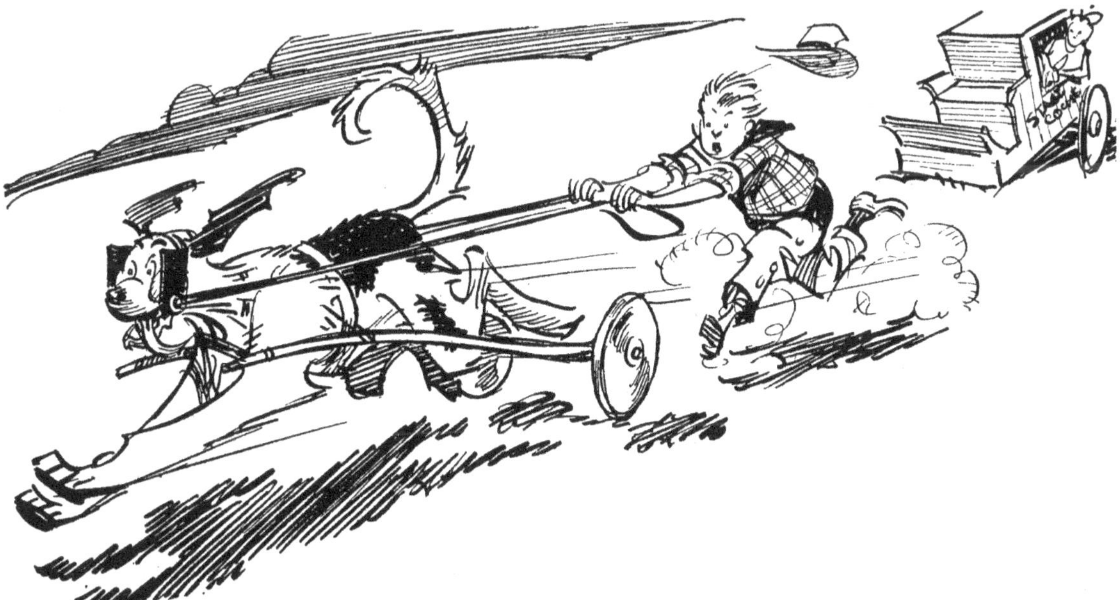

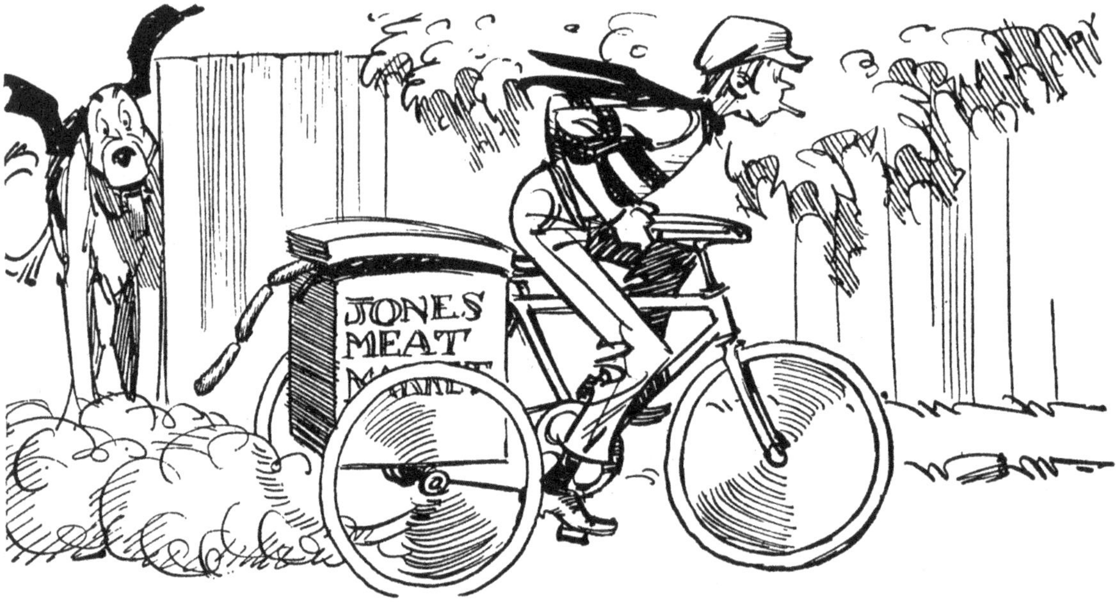
JONES
MEAT

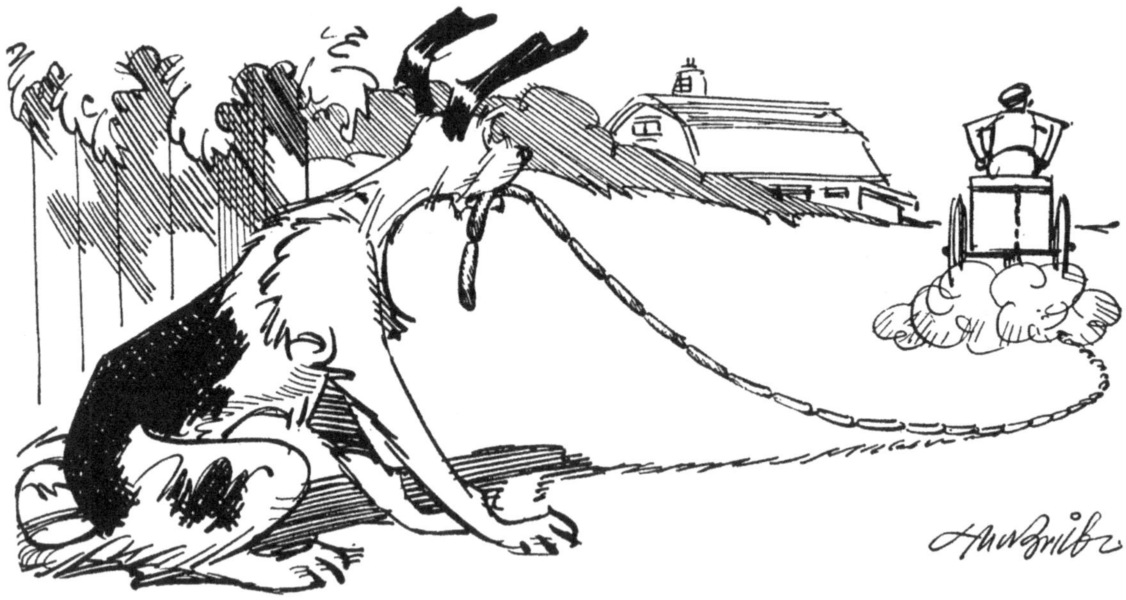

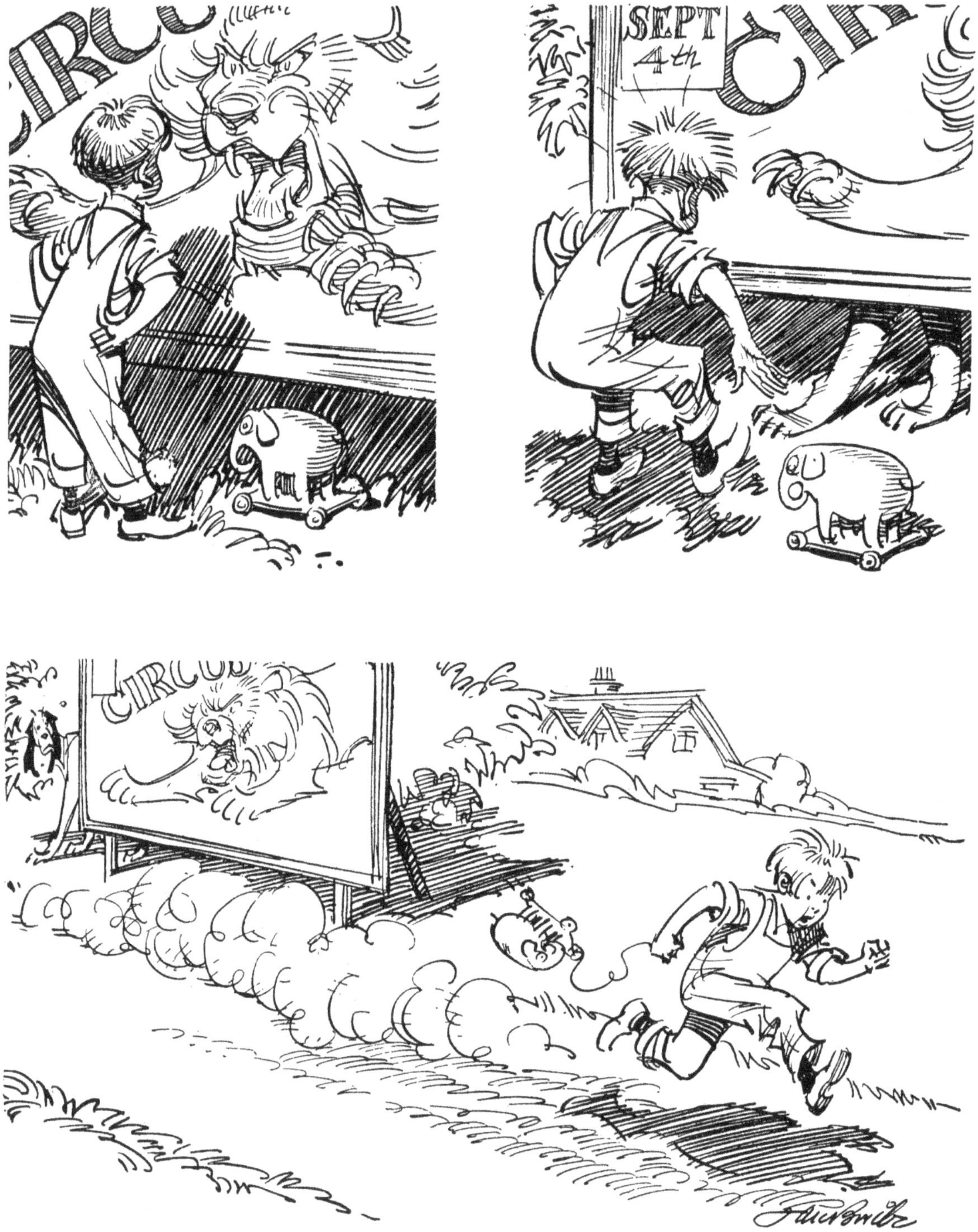
SEPT
4th

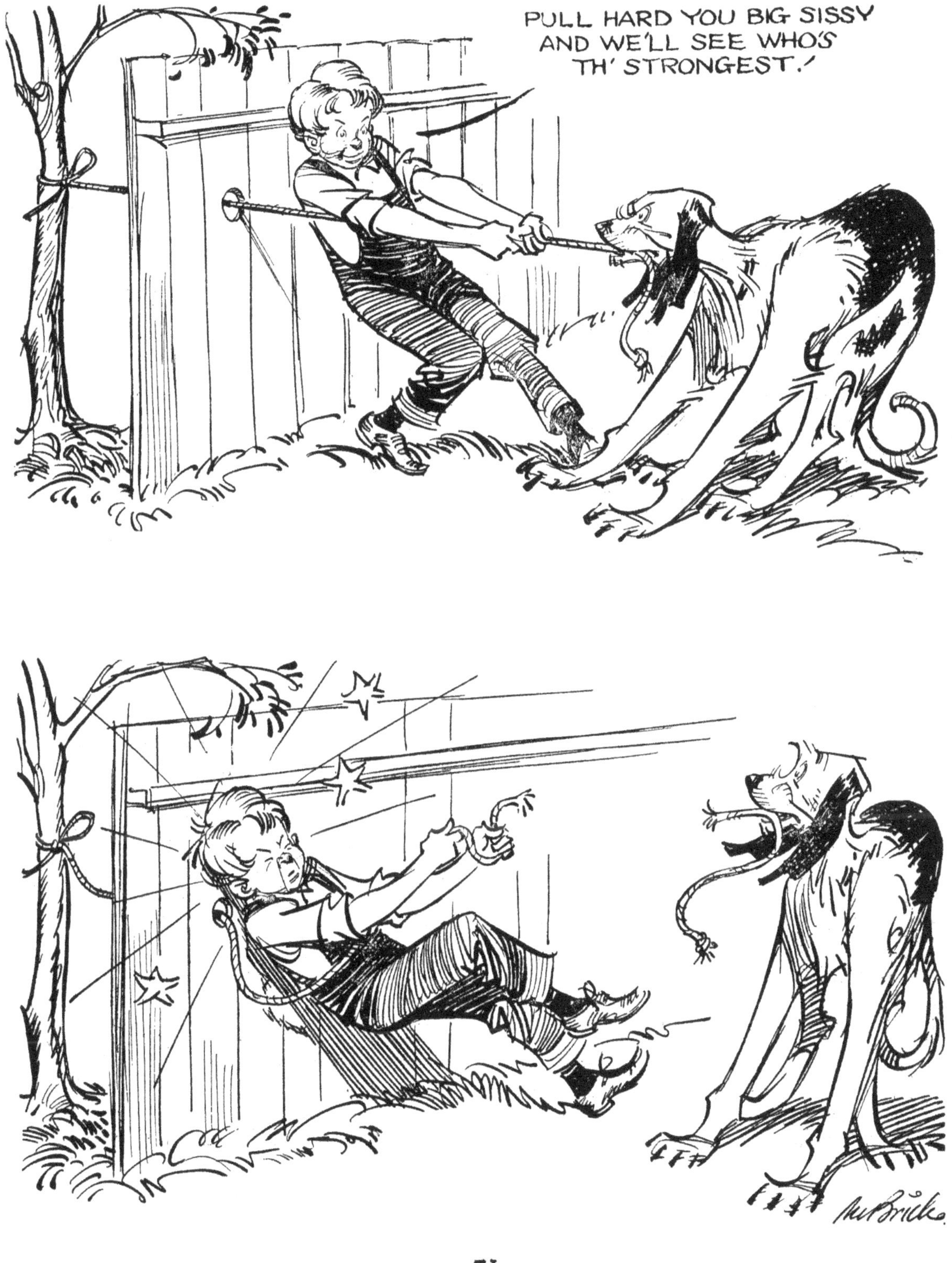
PULL HARD YOU BIG SISSY AND WE'LL SEE WHO'S TH' STRONGEST.!

TRAINS
LETTUC
LETTUC
TRAIN

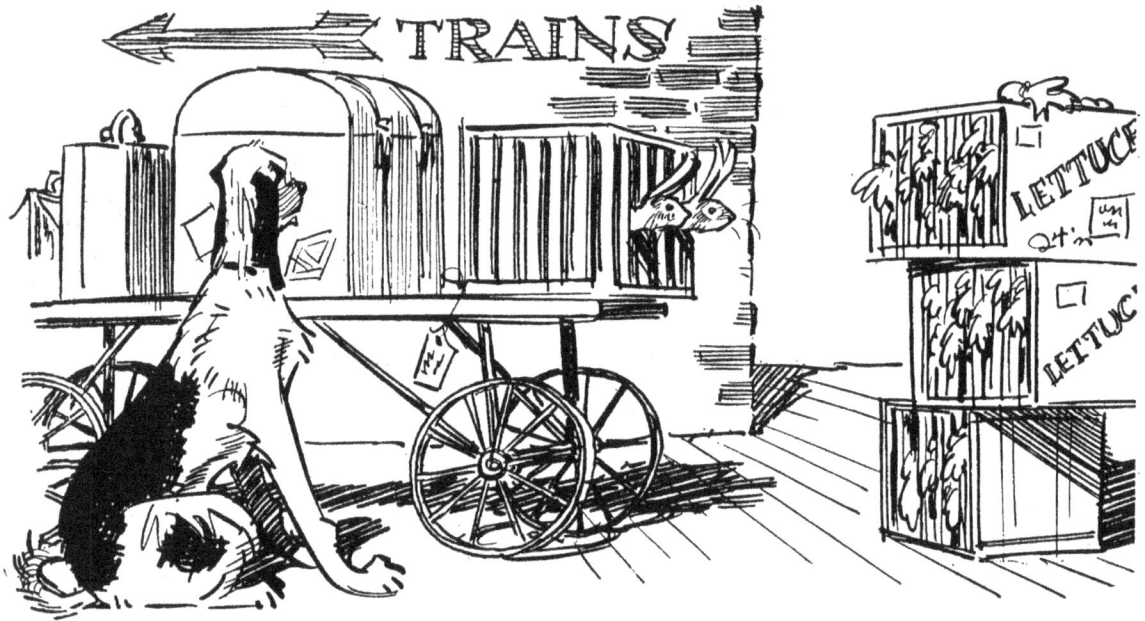

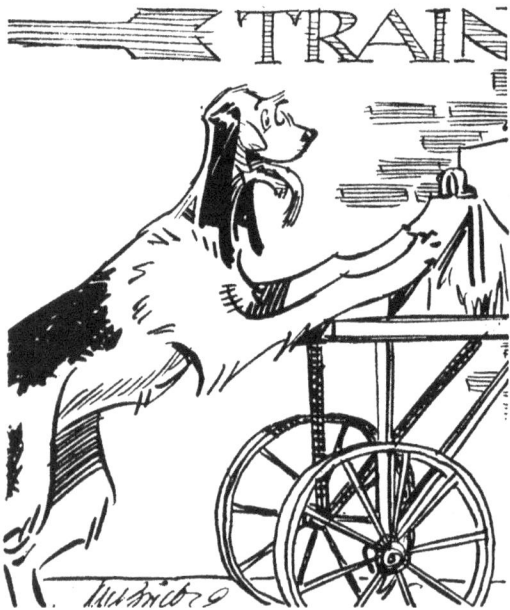

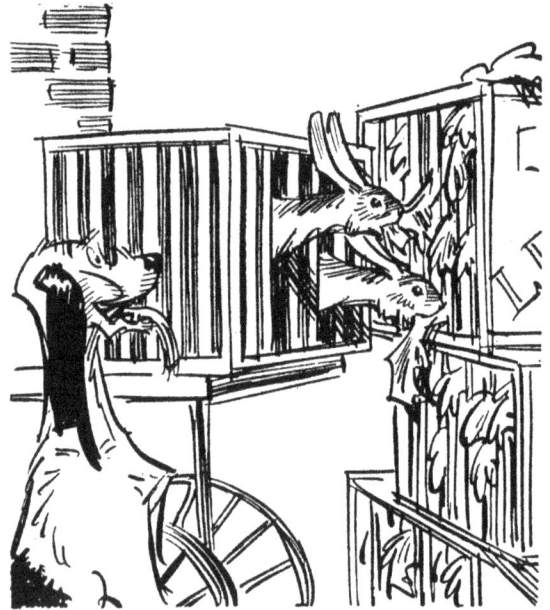

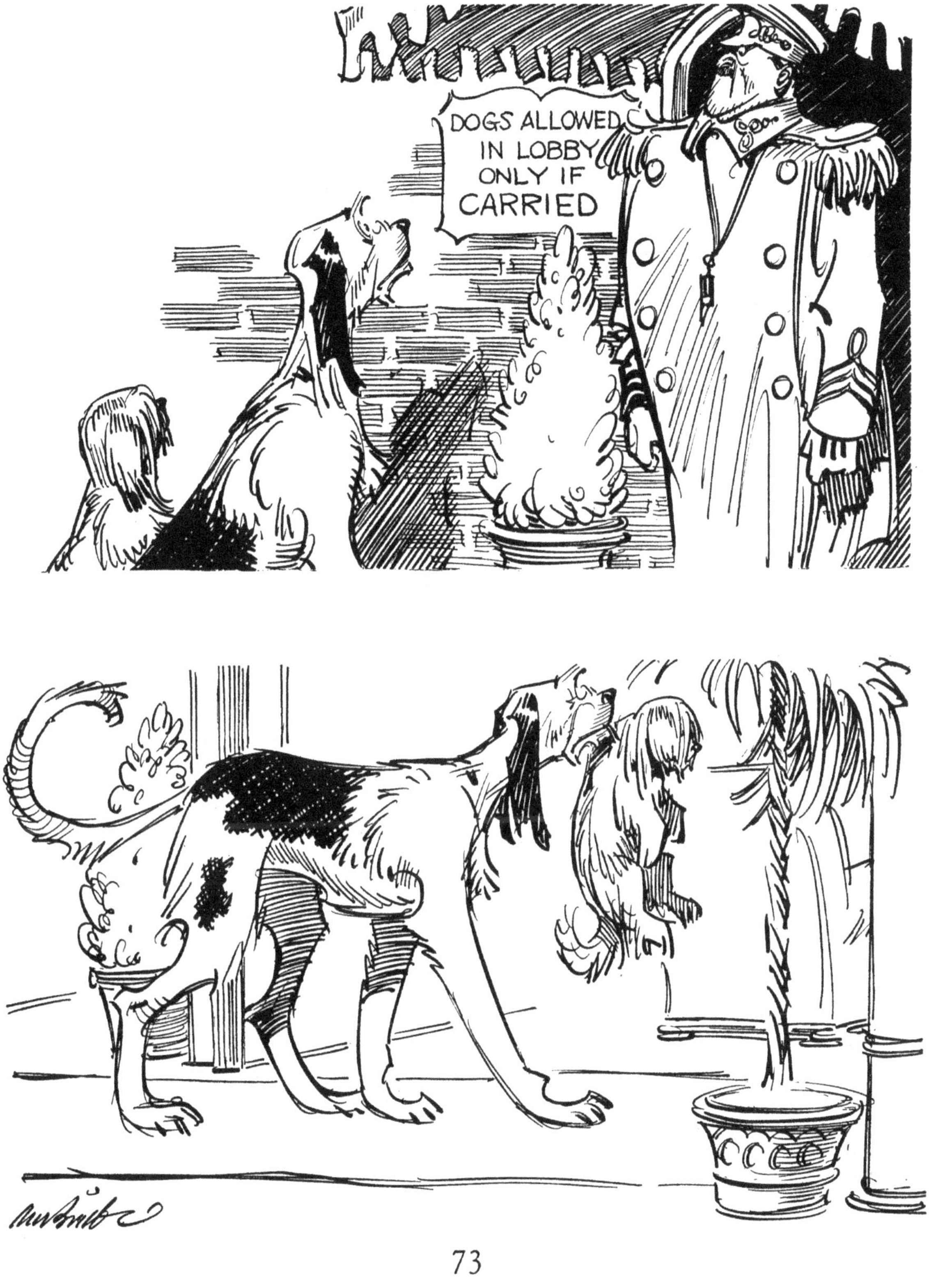
DOGS ALLOWED IN LOBBY ONLY IF CARRIED

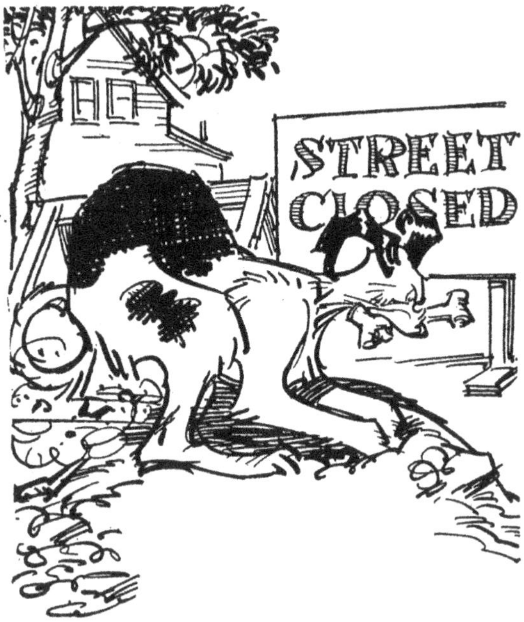
STREET
CLOSED

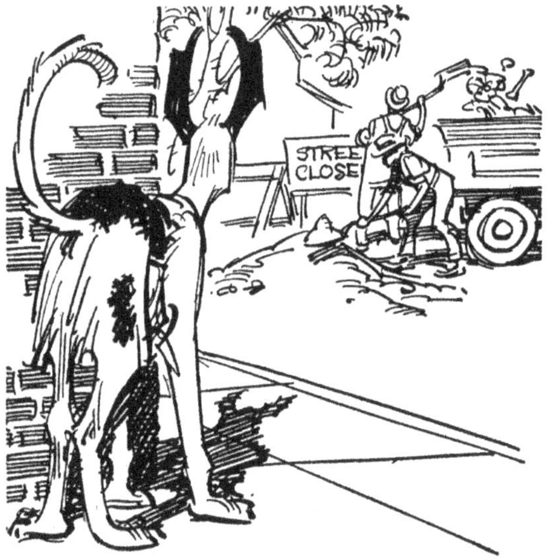
STREE
CLOSE

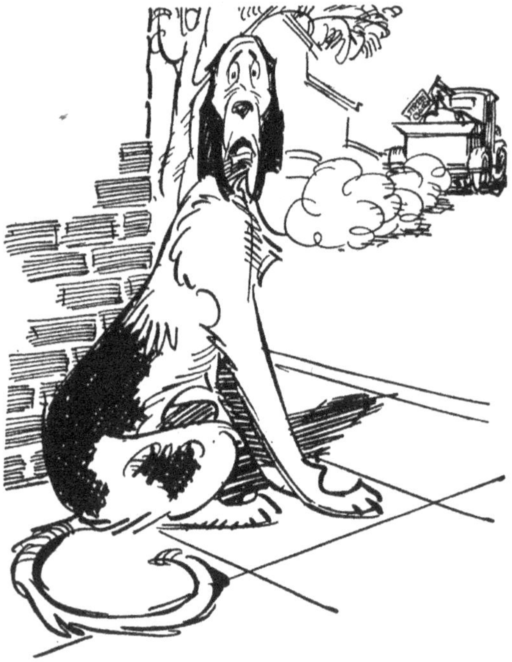

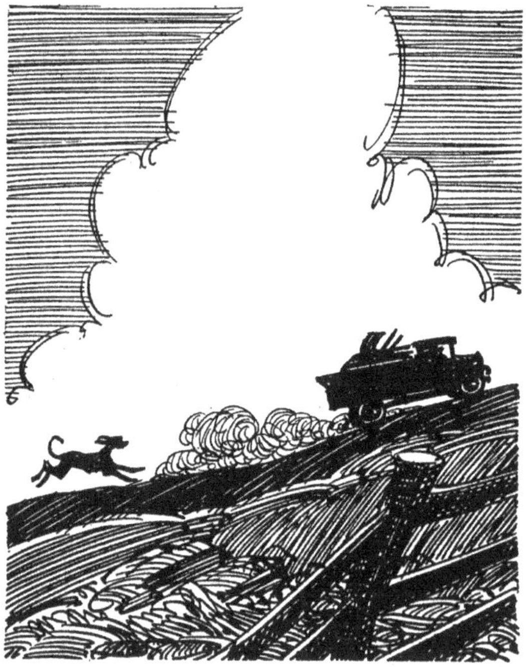

NAPOLEON GOES CAMPING

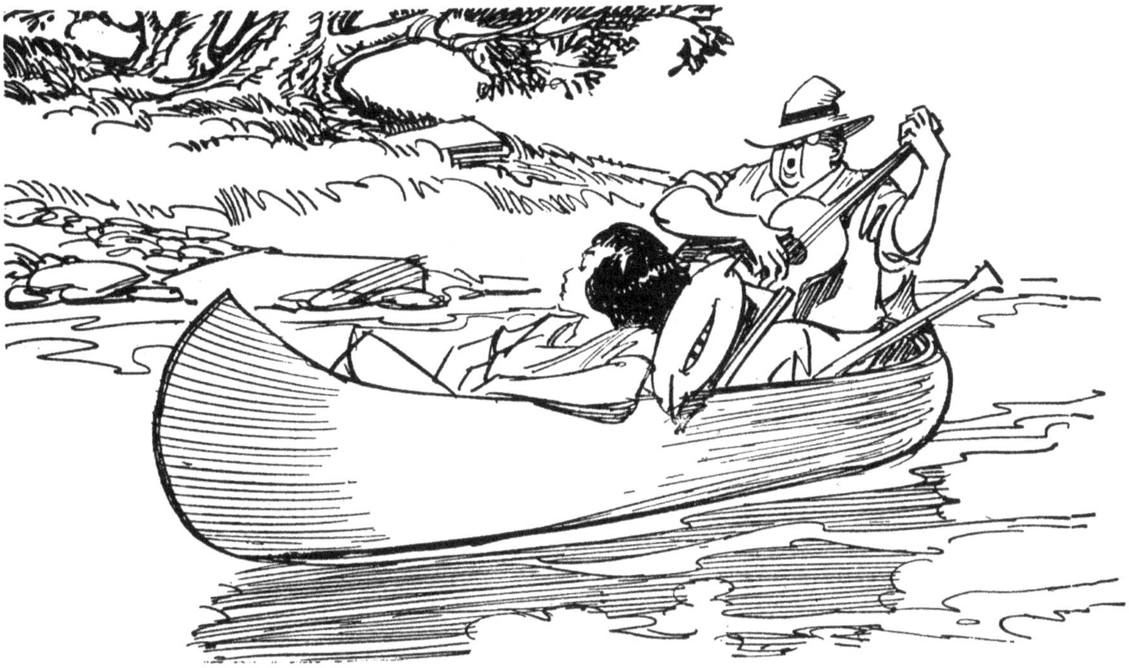

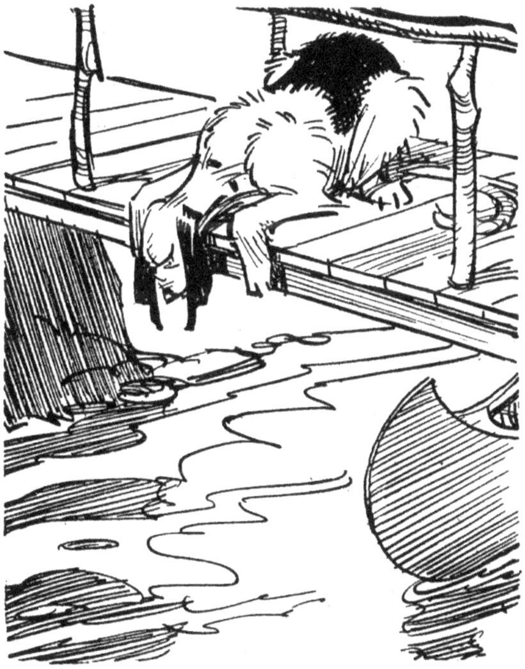

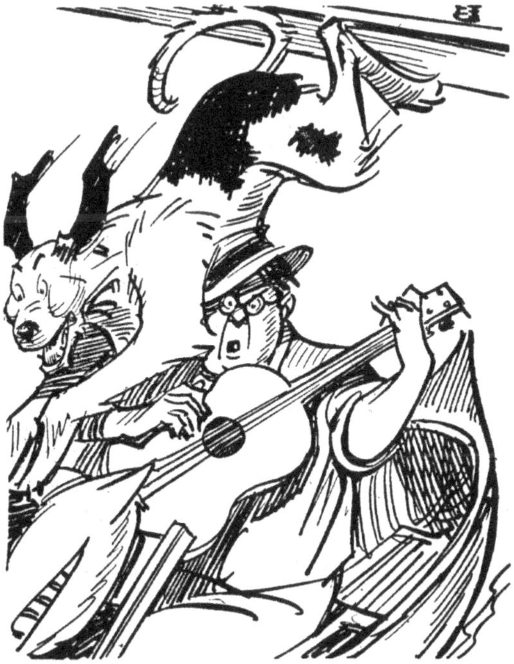

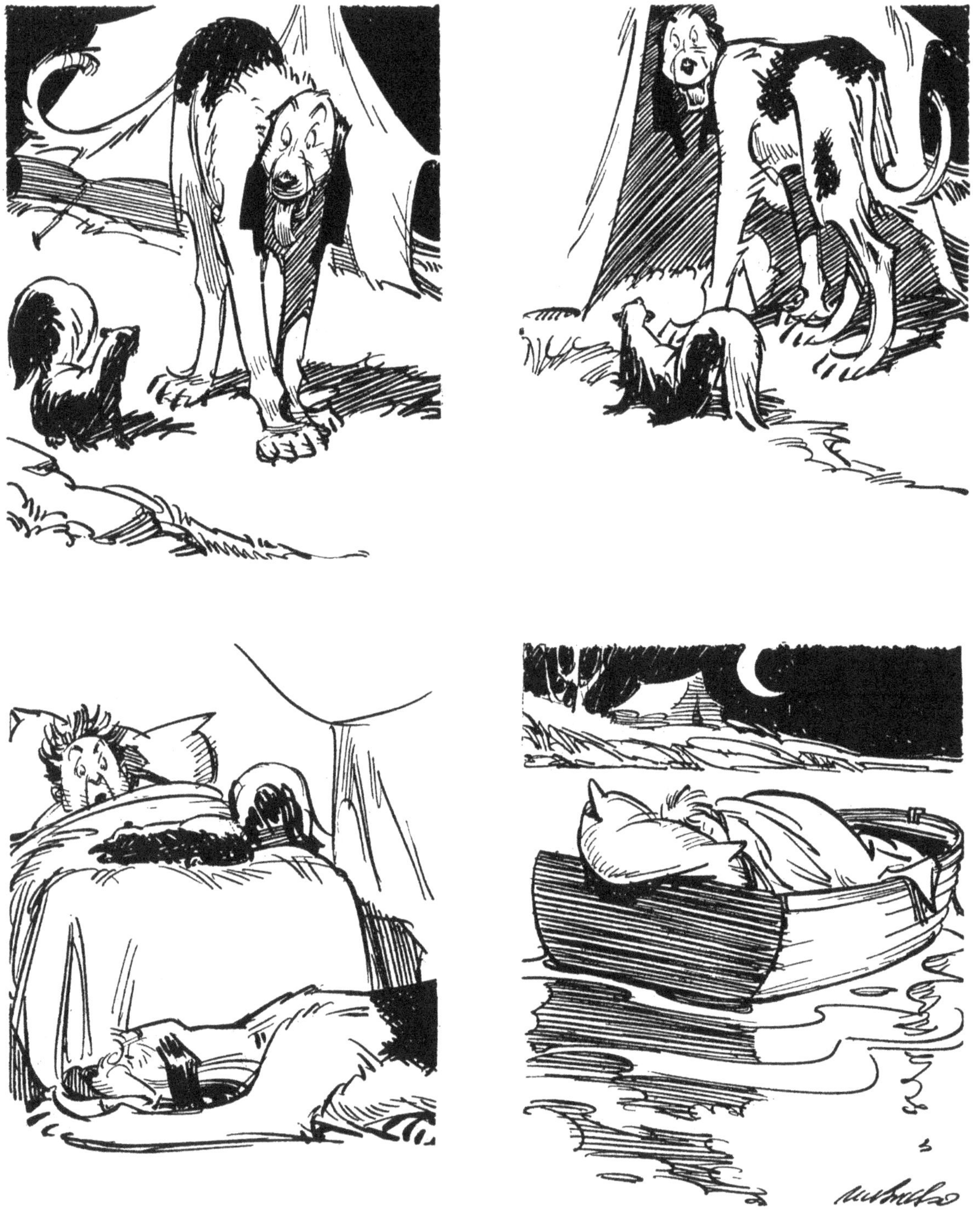

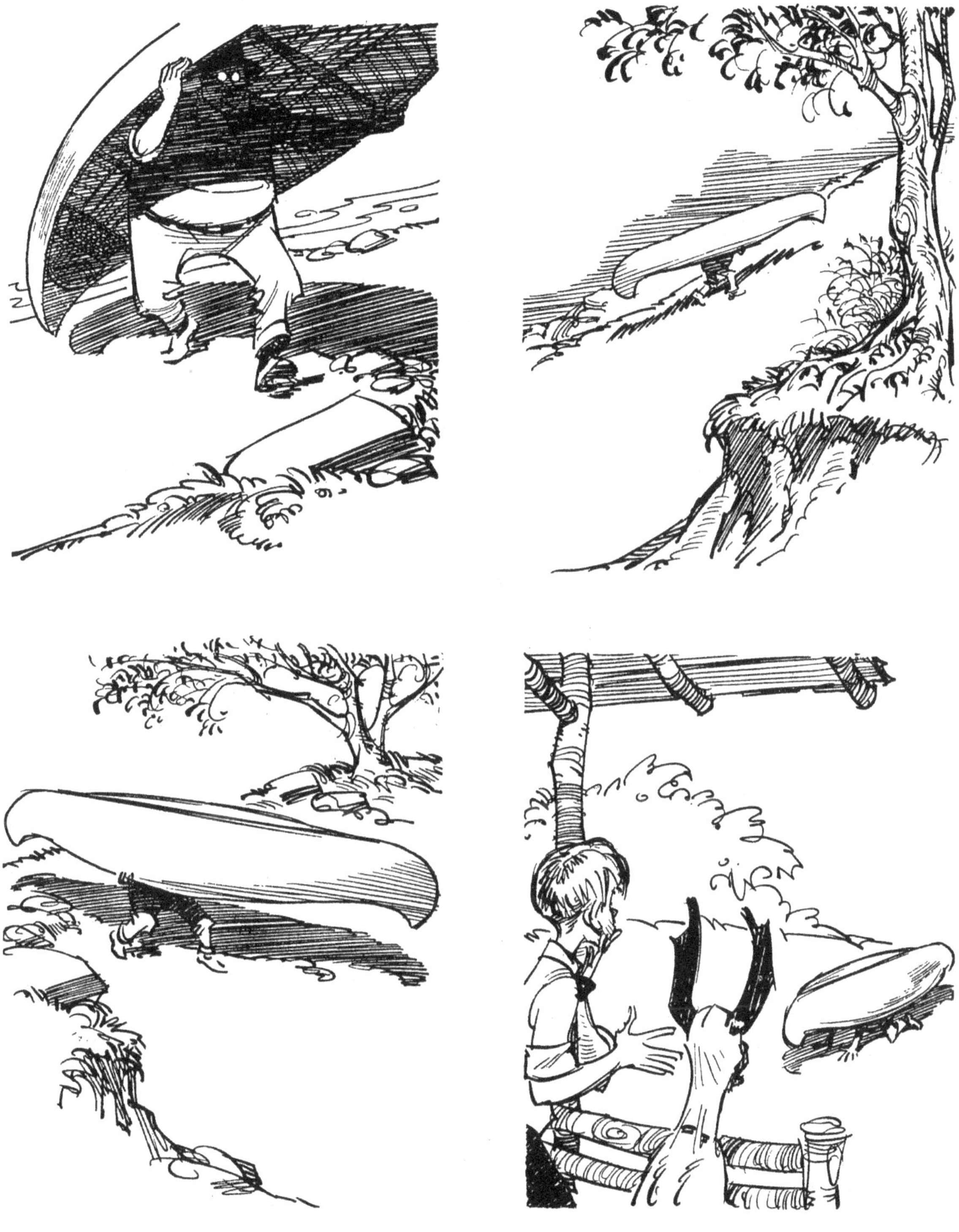

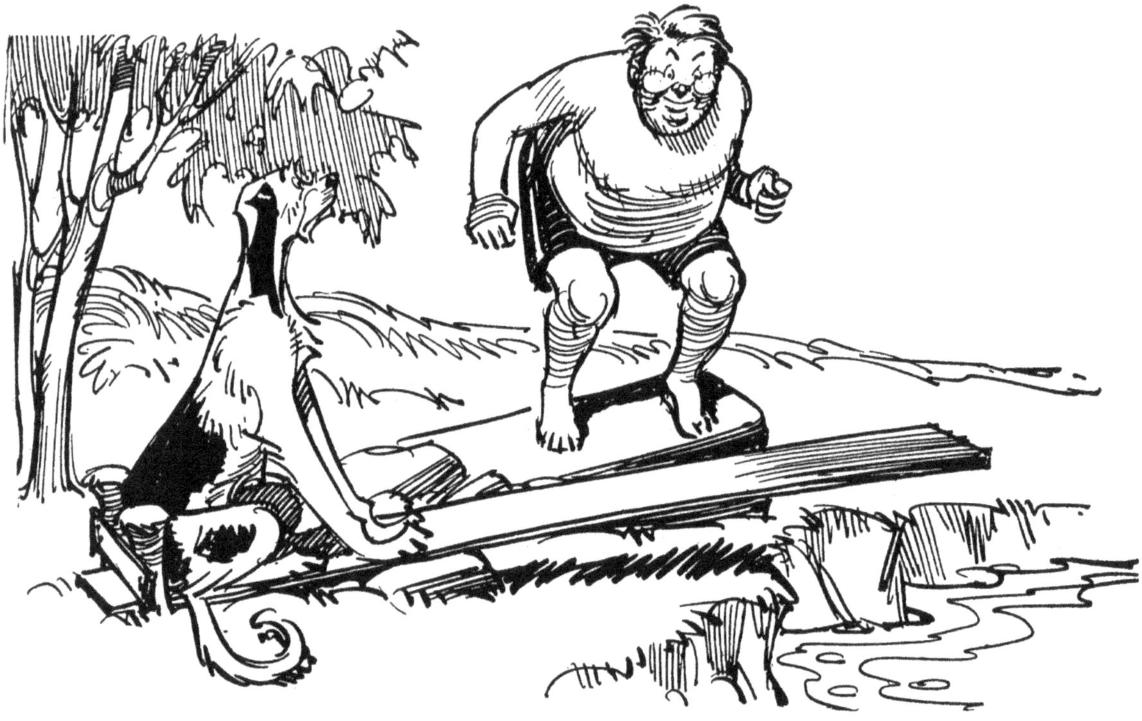

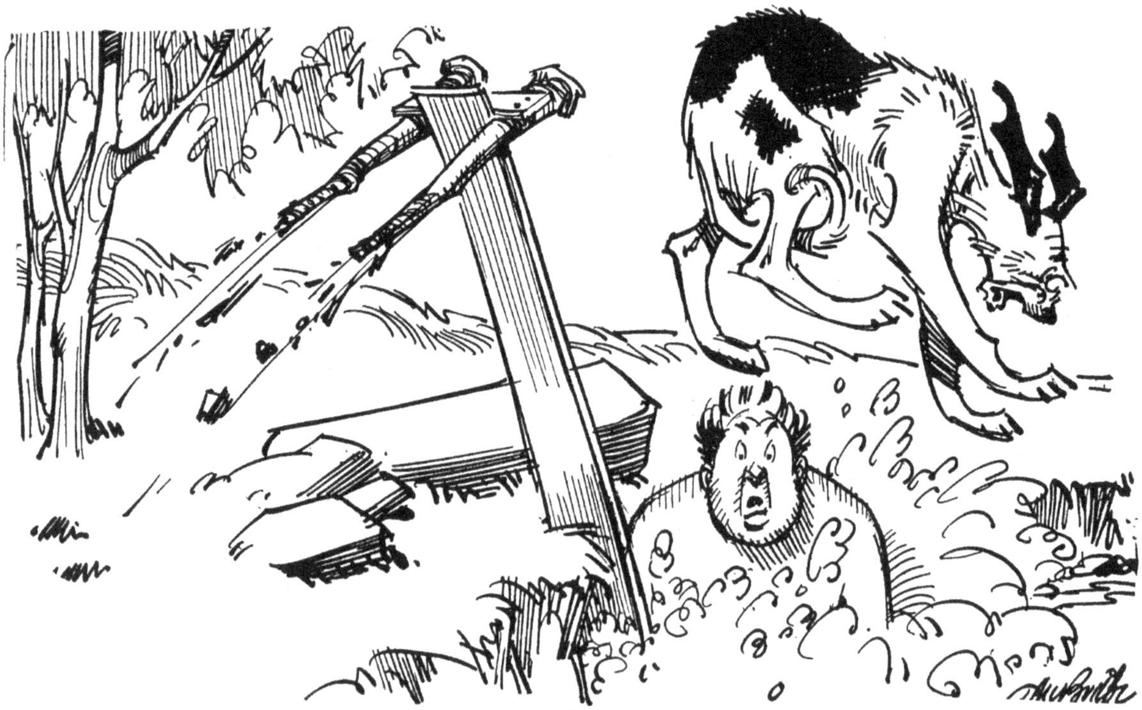

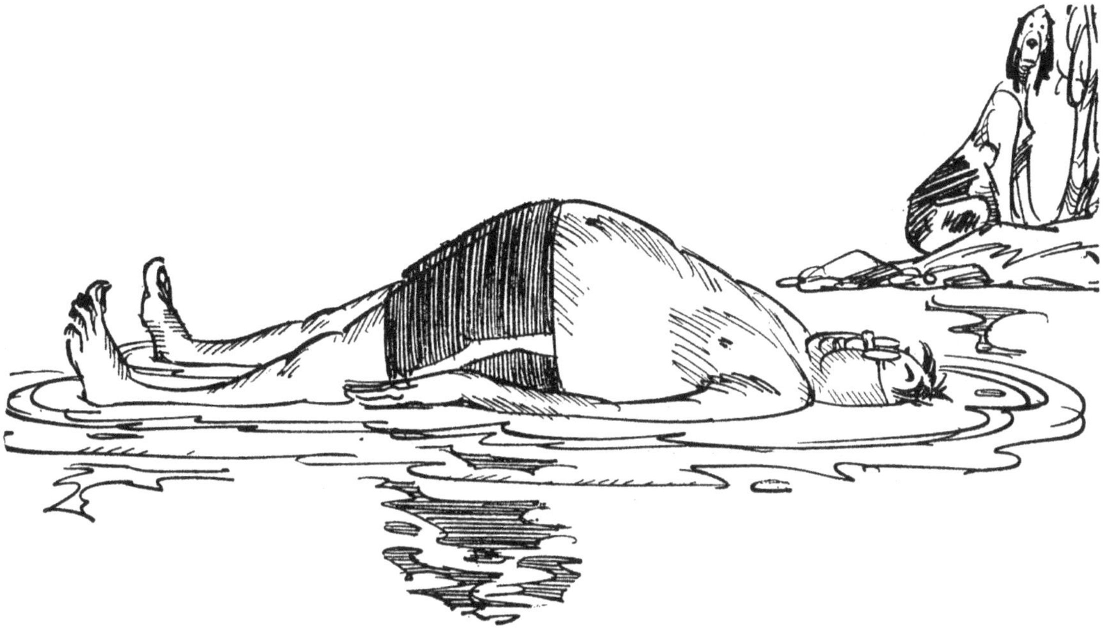

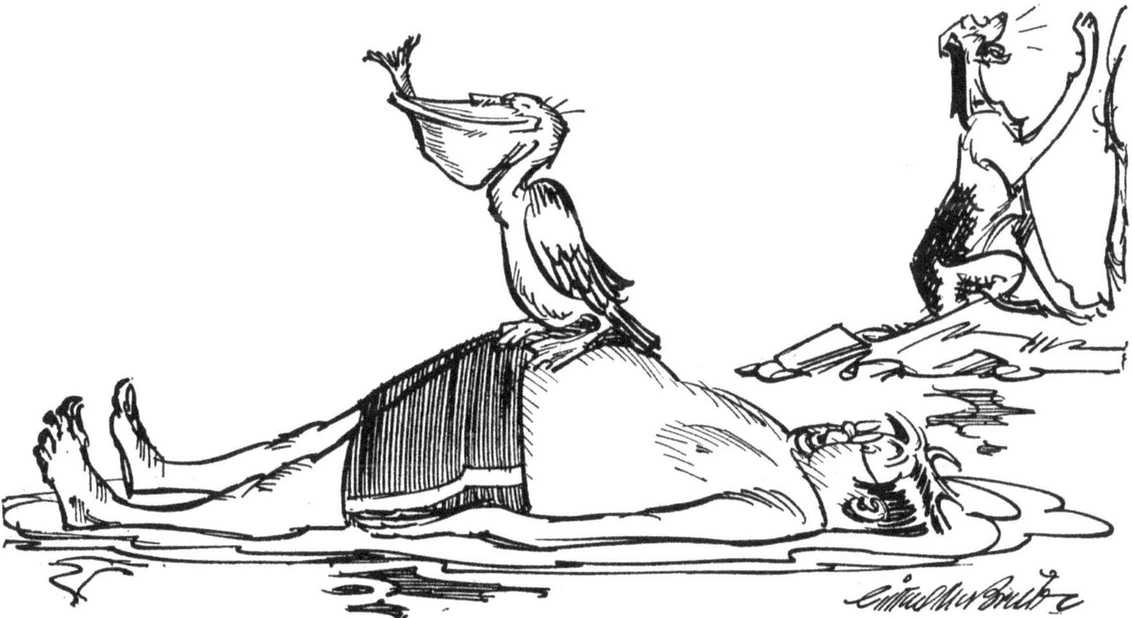

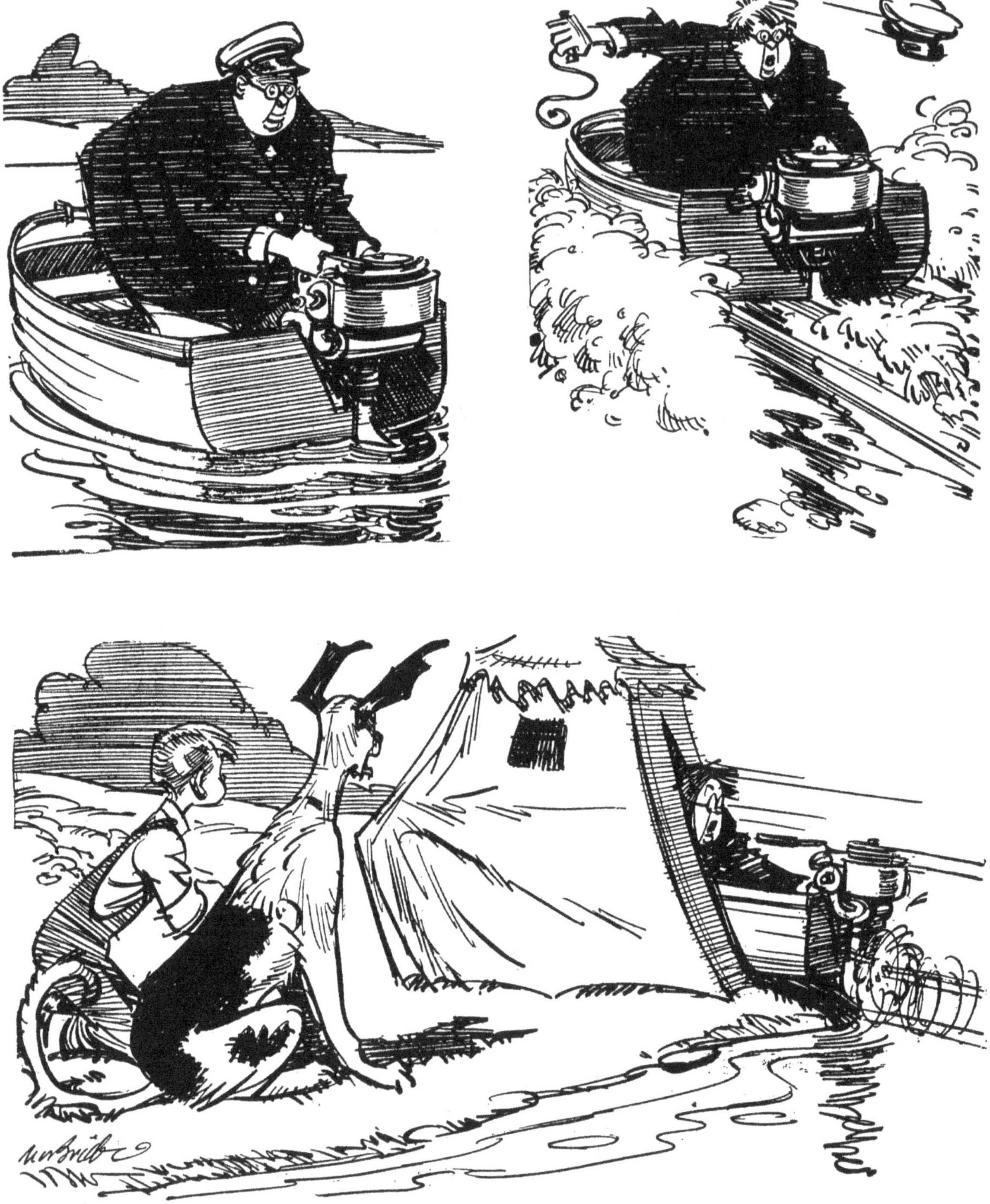

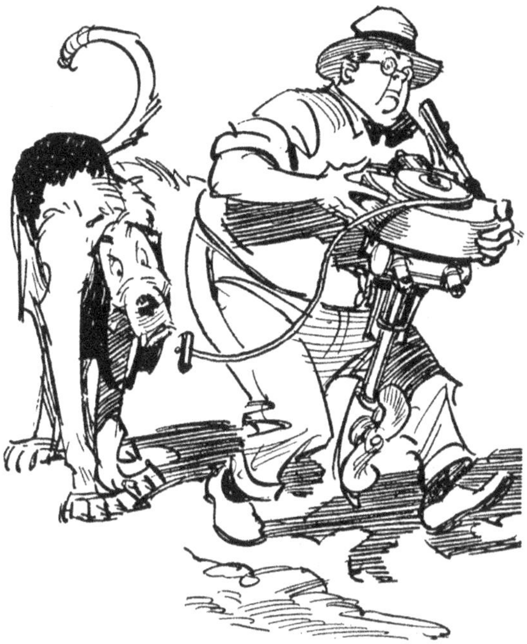

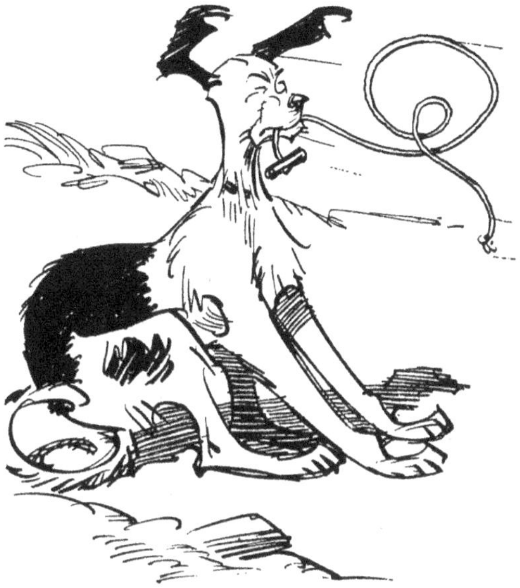

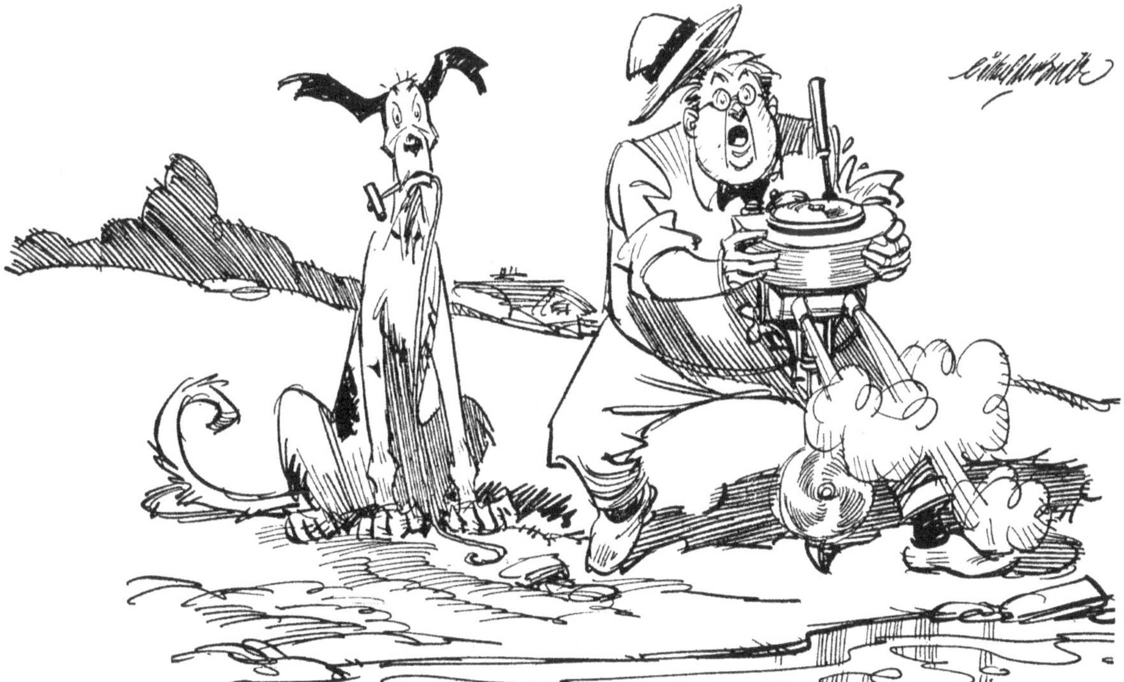

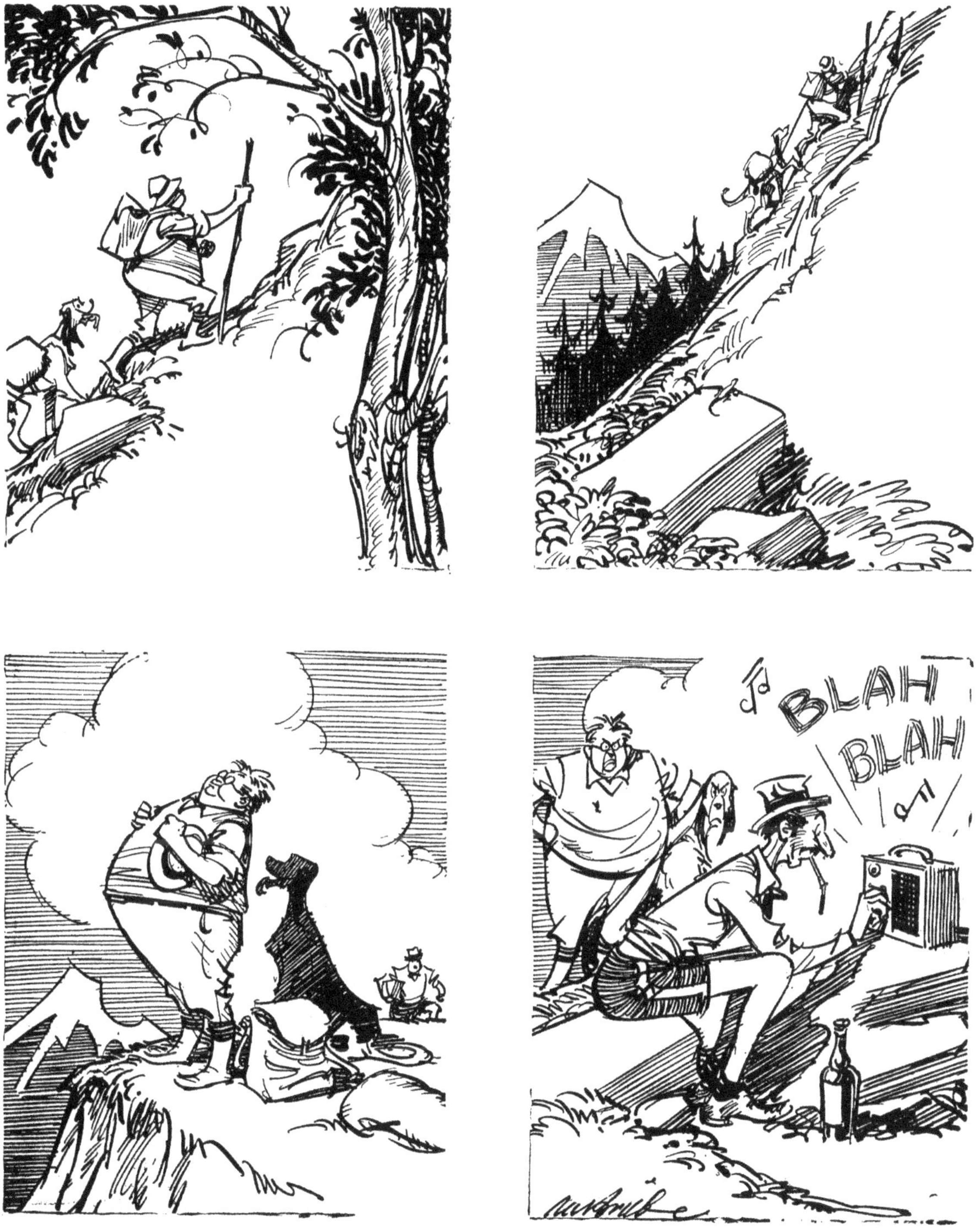
BLAH
BLAH

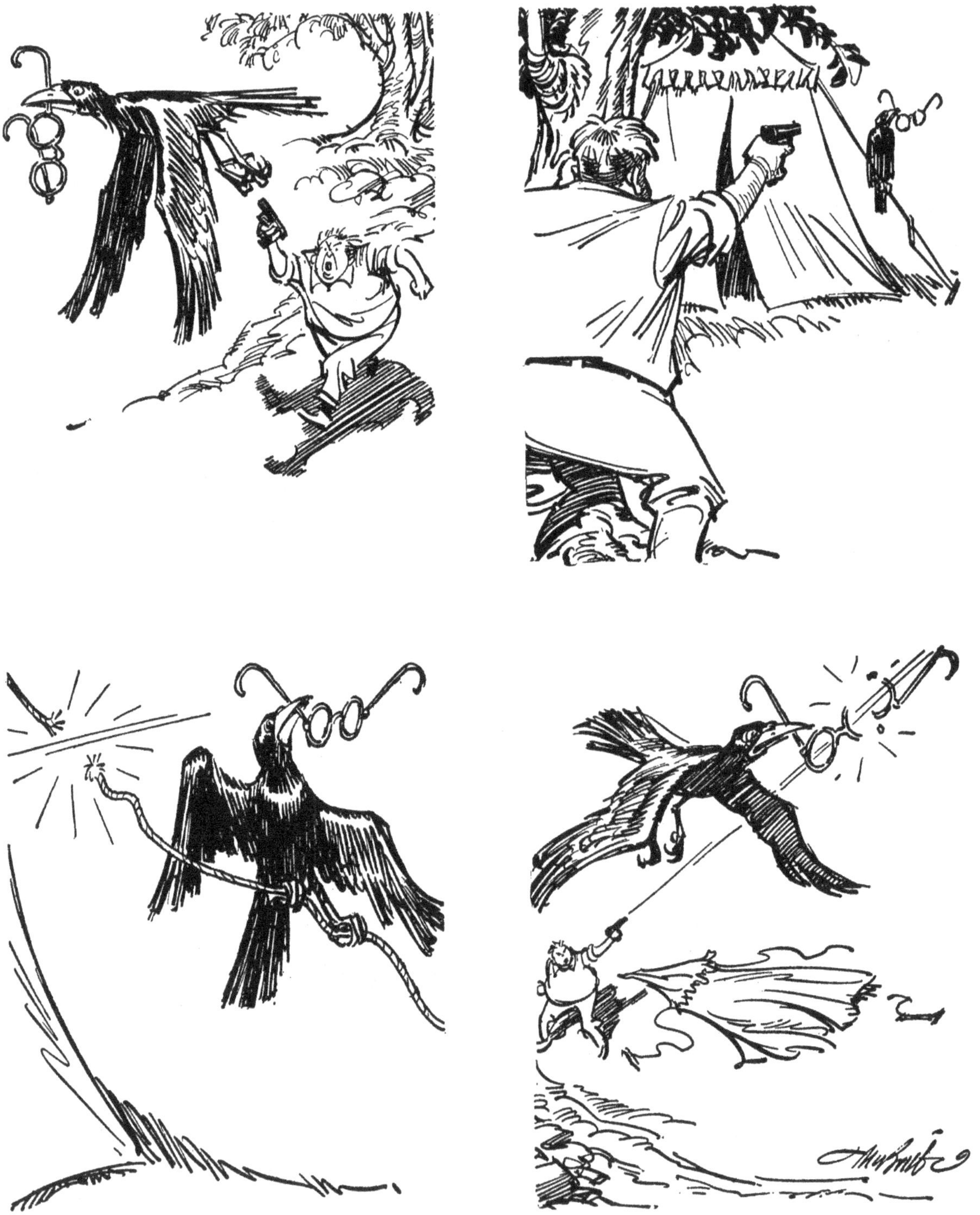

OBSERVE, WILLIE, HOW MOTHER NATURE HAS ENDOWED HER FURRY CHILDREN WITH NATIVE INTELLIGENCE. THE RABBIT SEEKS THE COOL OF THE HOLLOW LOG INSTINCTIVELY, AND---

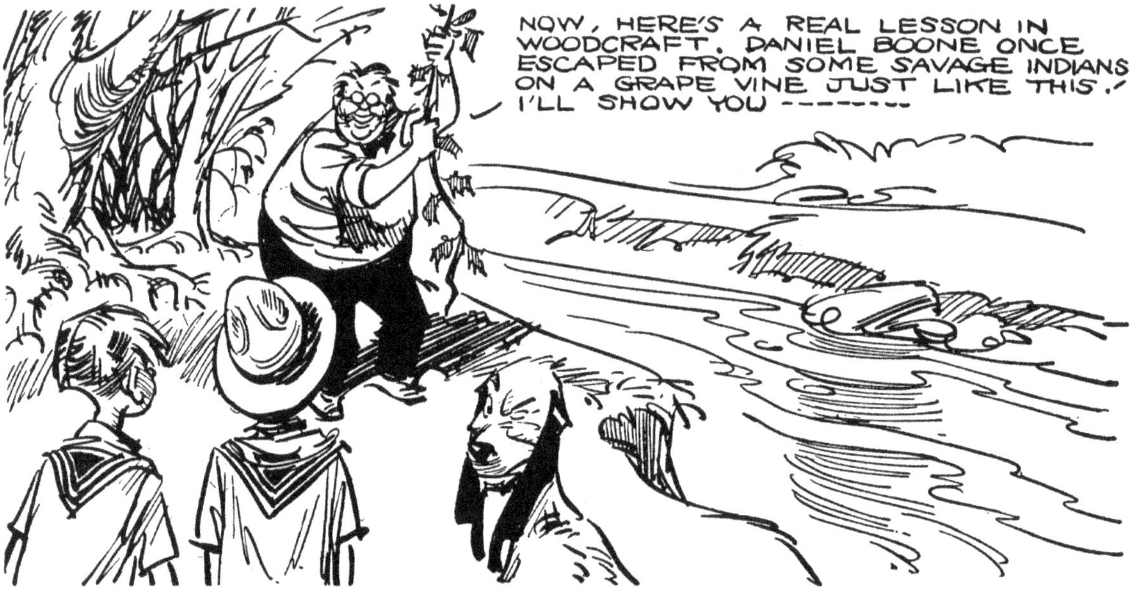
NOW, HERE'S A REAL LESSON IN WOODCRAFT. DANIEL BOONE ONCE ESCAPED FROM SOME SAVAGE INDIANS ON A GRAPE VINE JUST LIKE THIS! I'LL SHOW YOU --------

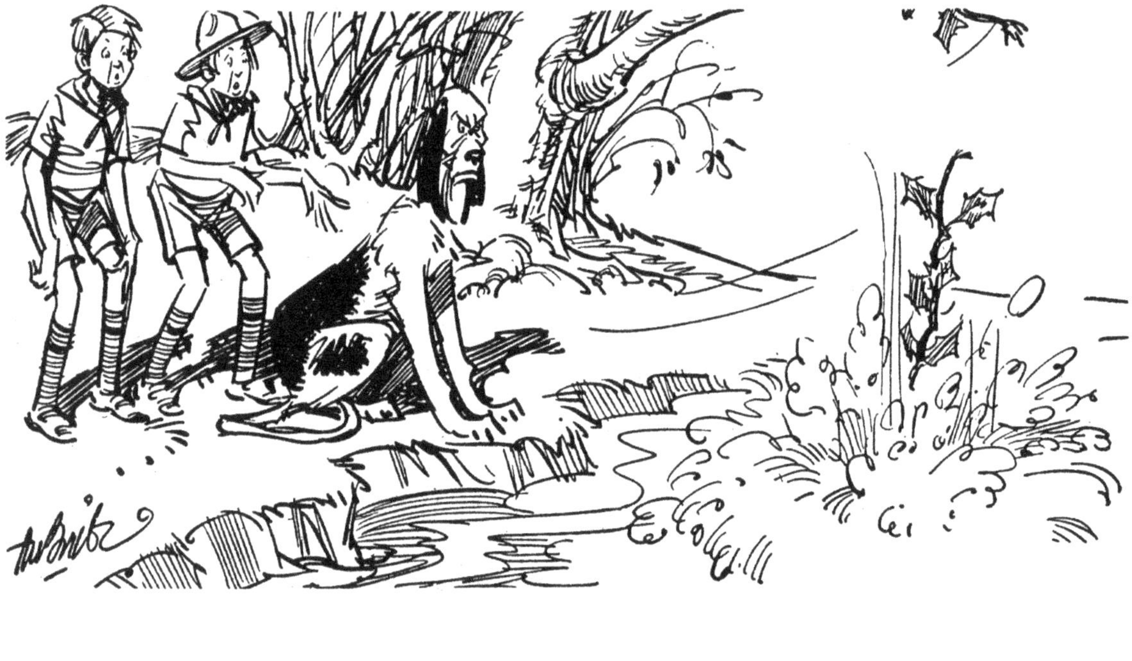

ALL RIGHT, THERE YOU GO ON TH' CANOE RIDE YOU'VE BEEN BEGGIN' FOR, I'LL RUN ACROSS AND TOW YOU ASHORE WHEN YOU GET AROUND TH' NEXT BEND.

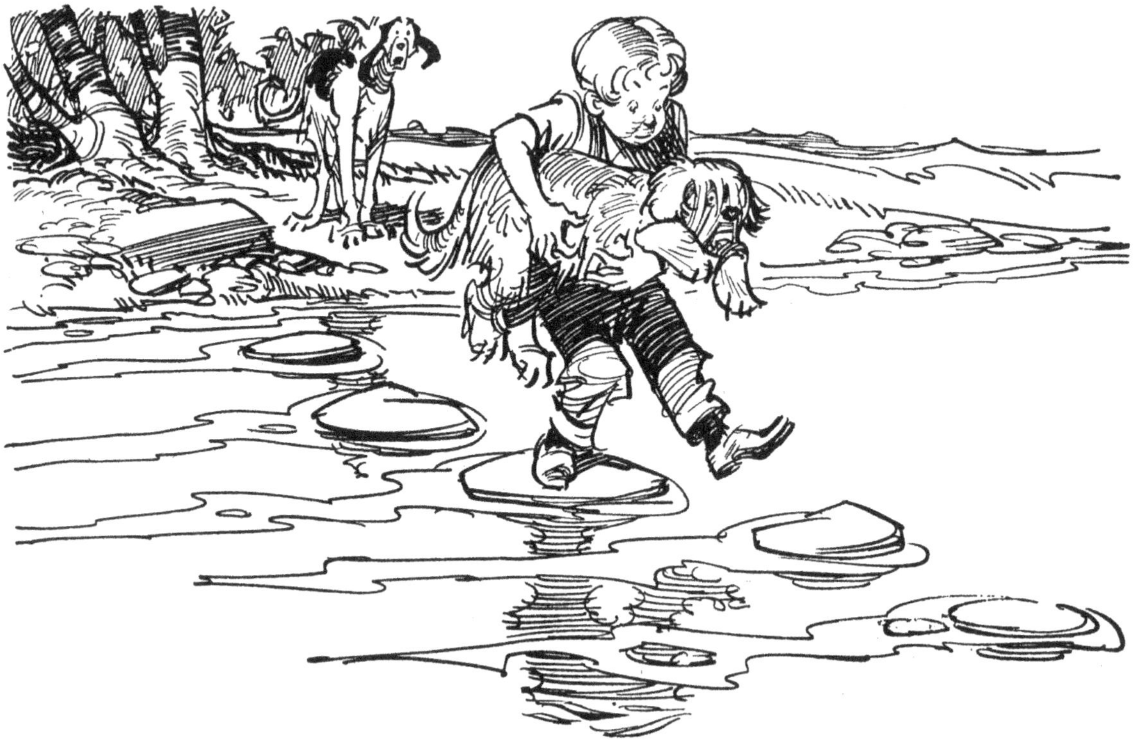

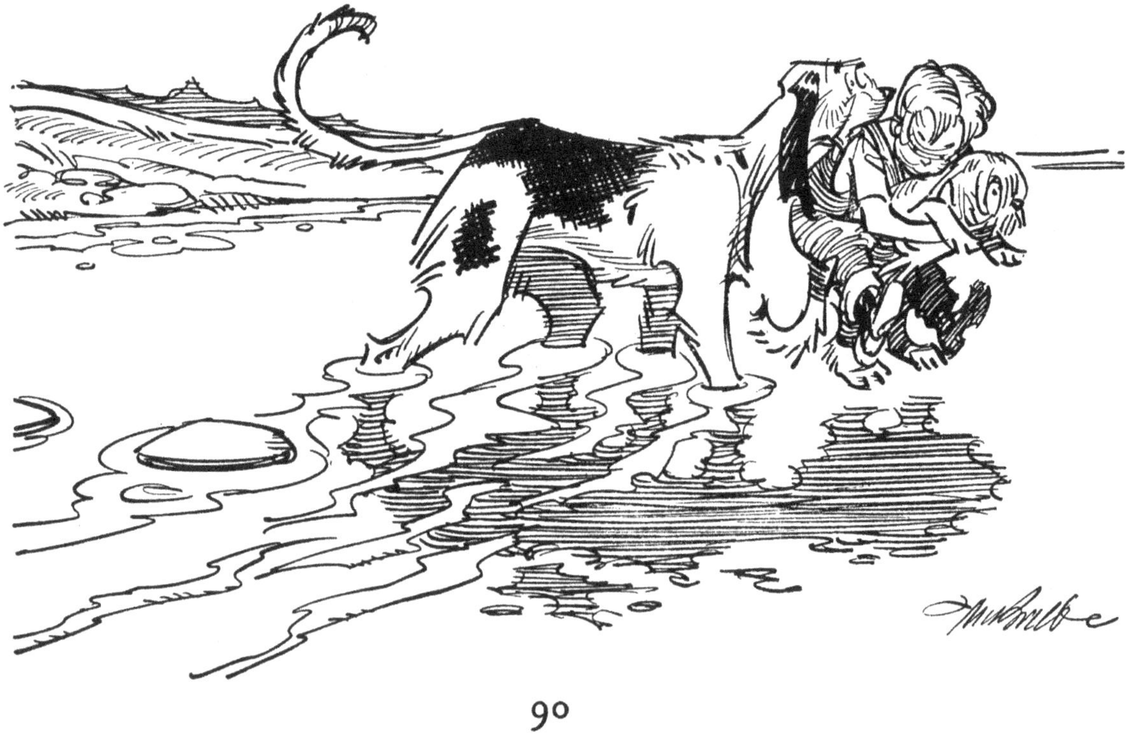

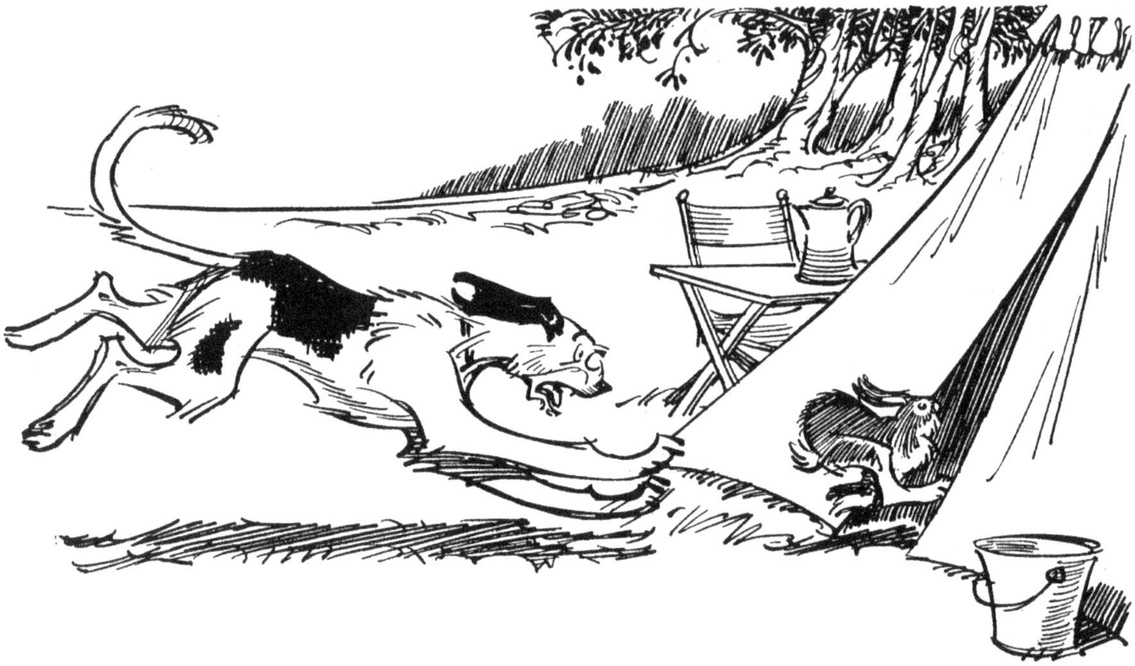

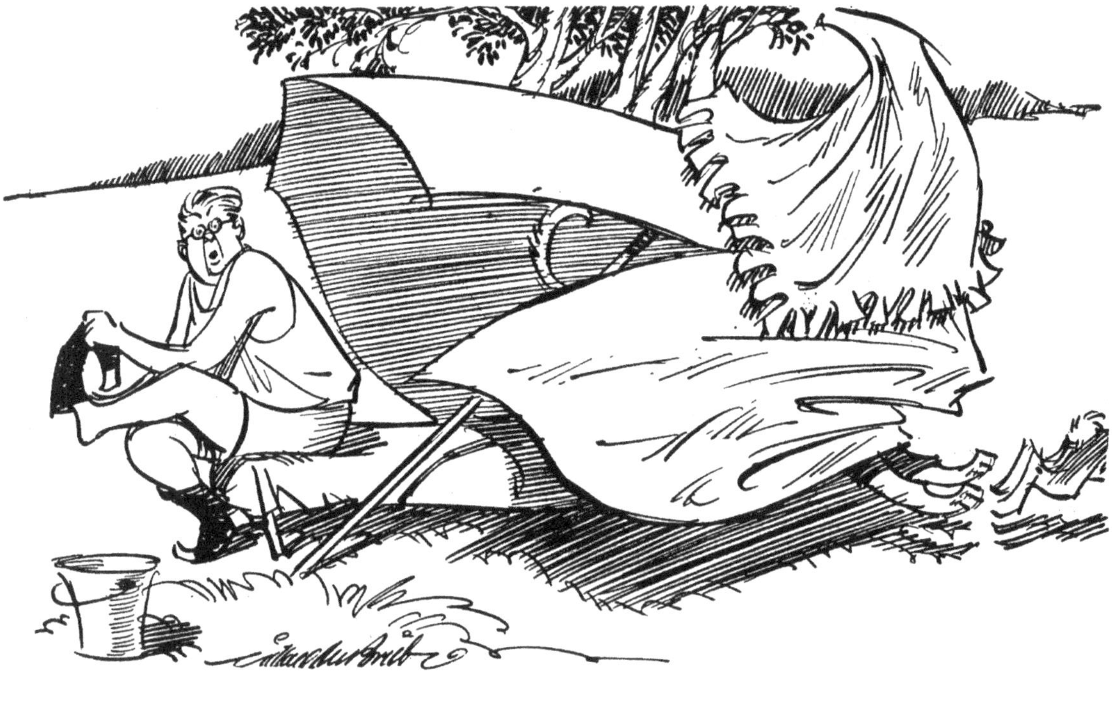

NAPOLEON LIKES FISHING

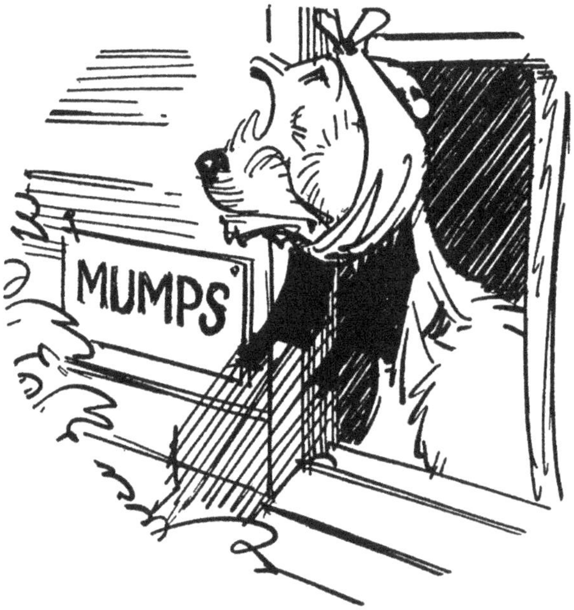
MUMPS

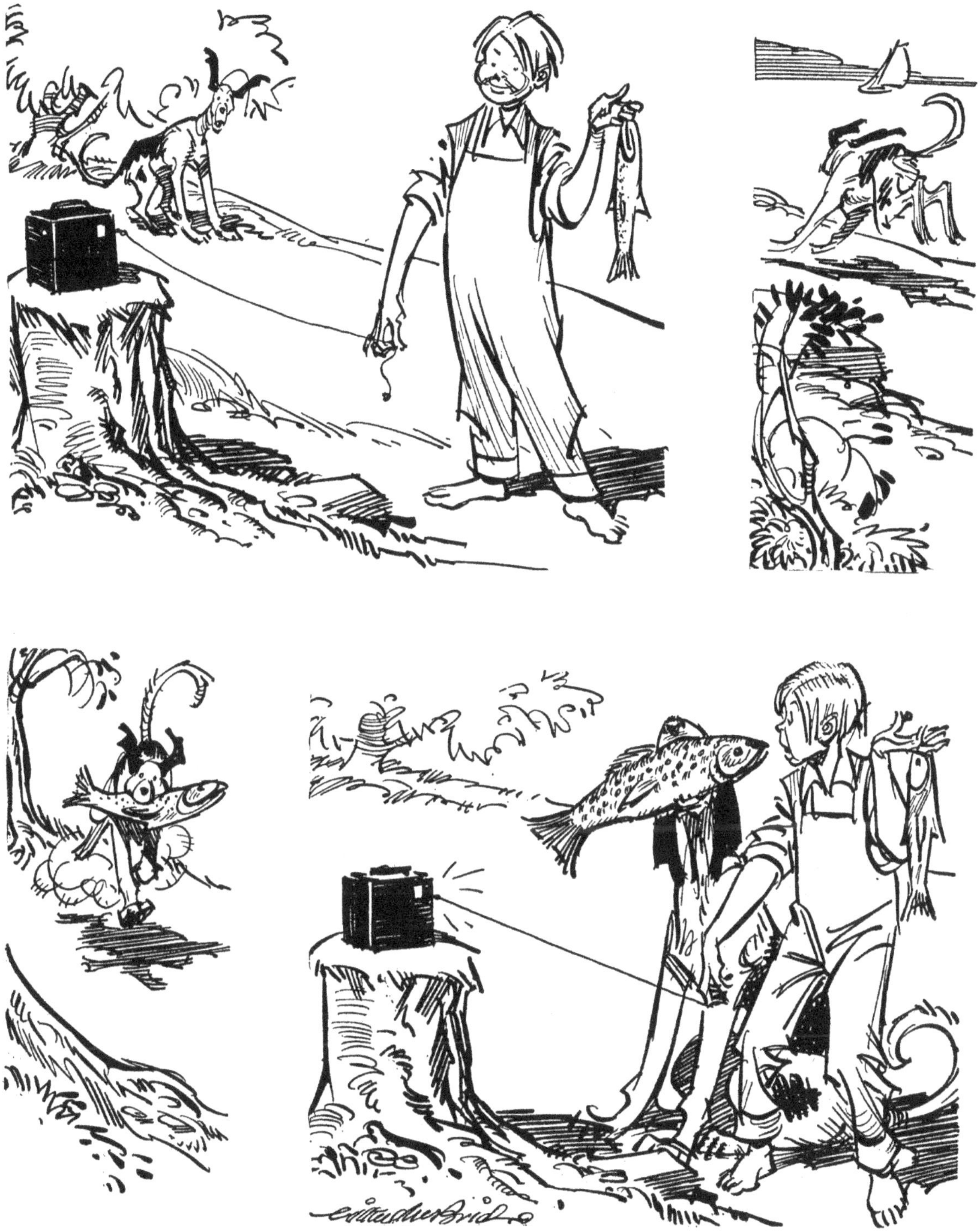

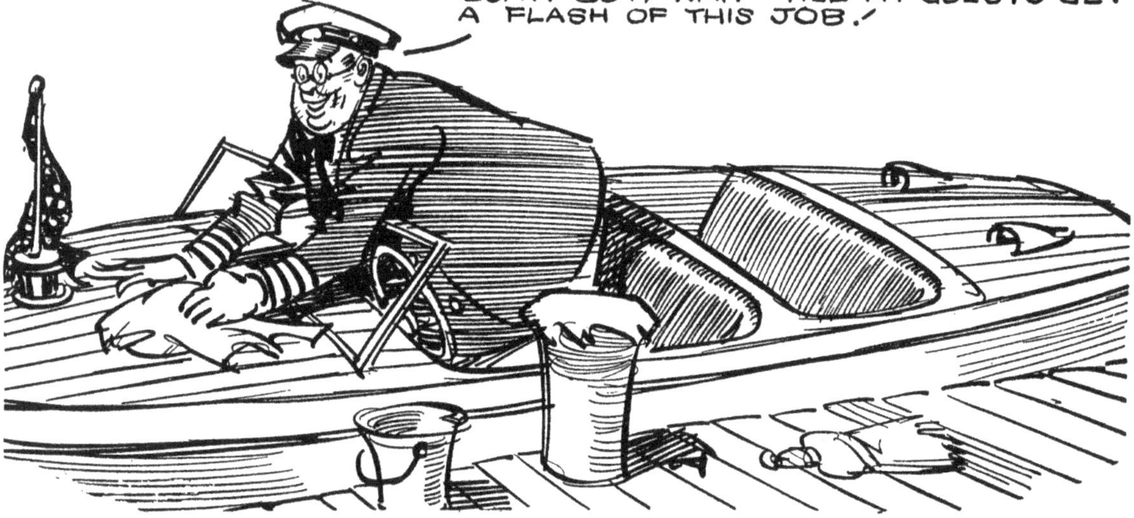
I BELIEVE IN KEEPING A BOAT UP SHIP SHAPE AND BRISTOL FASHION. NOTHING LOOKS WORSE THAN A DIRTY UNTIDY BOAT. BOY, WAIT 'TILL MY GUESTS GET A FLASH OF THIS JOB.!

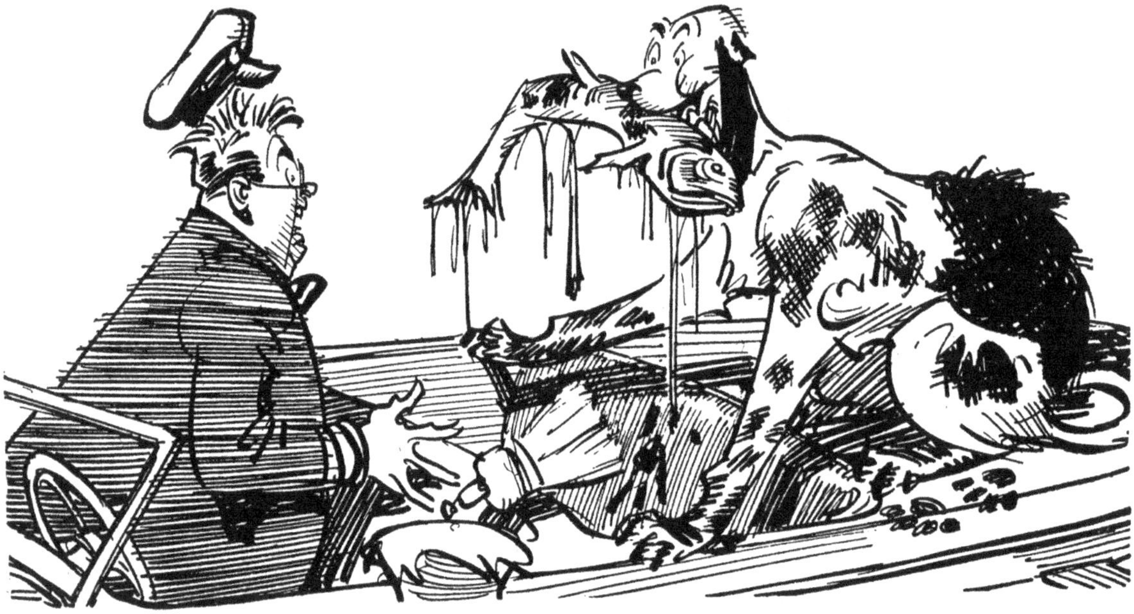

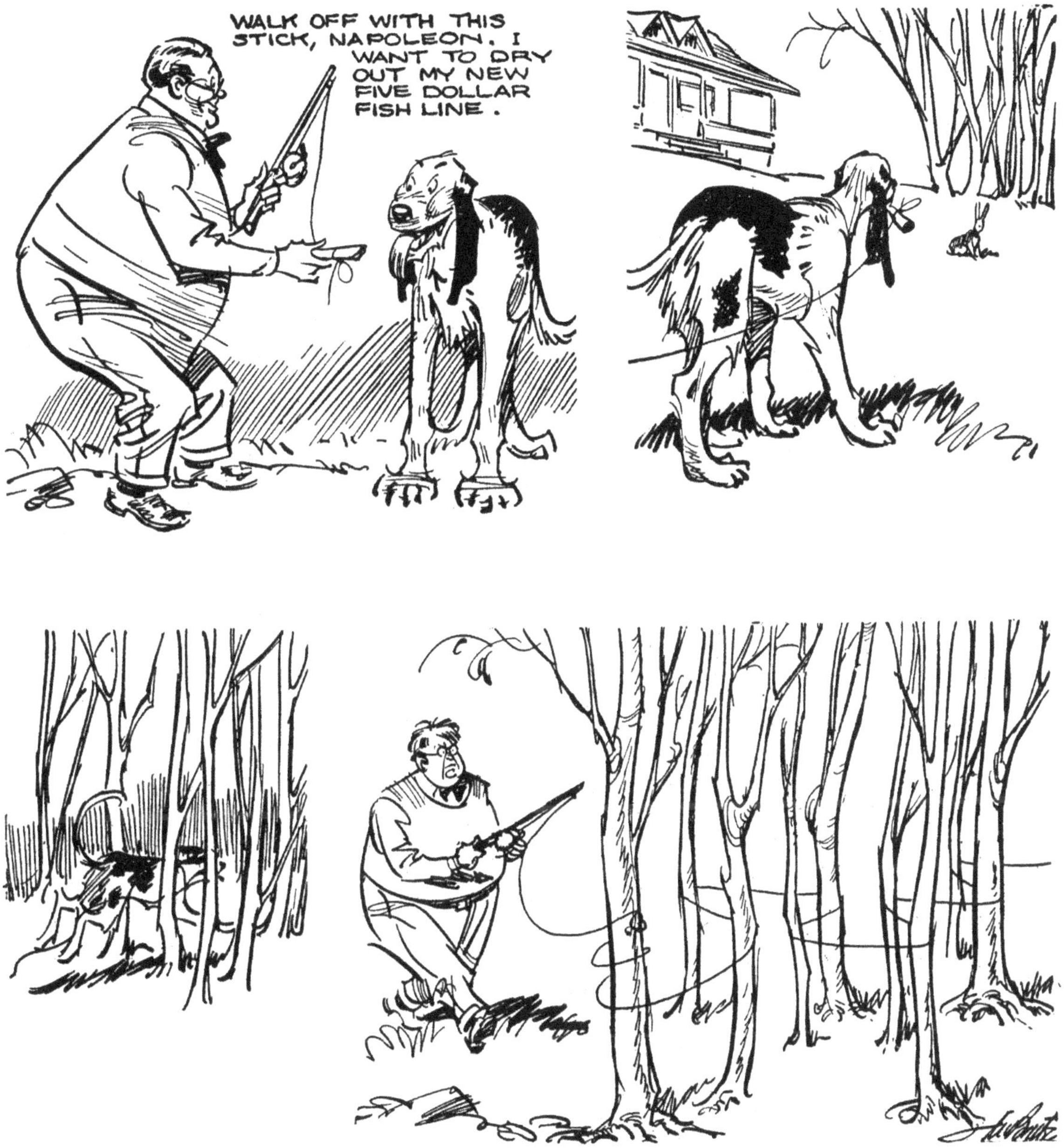
WALK OFF WITH THIS STICK, NAPOLEON. I WANT TO DRY OUT MY NEW FIVE DOLLAR FISH LINE.

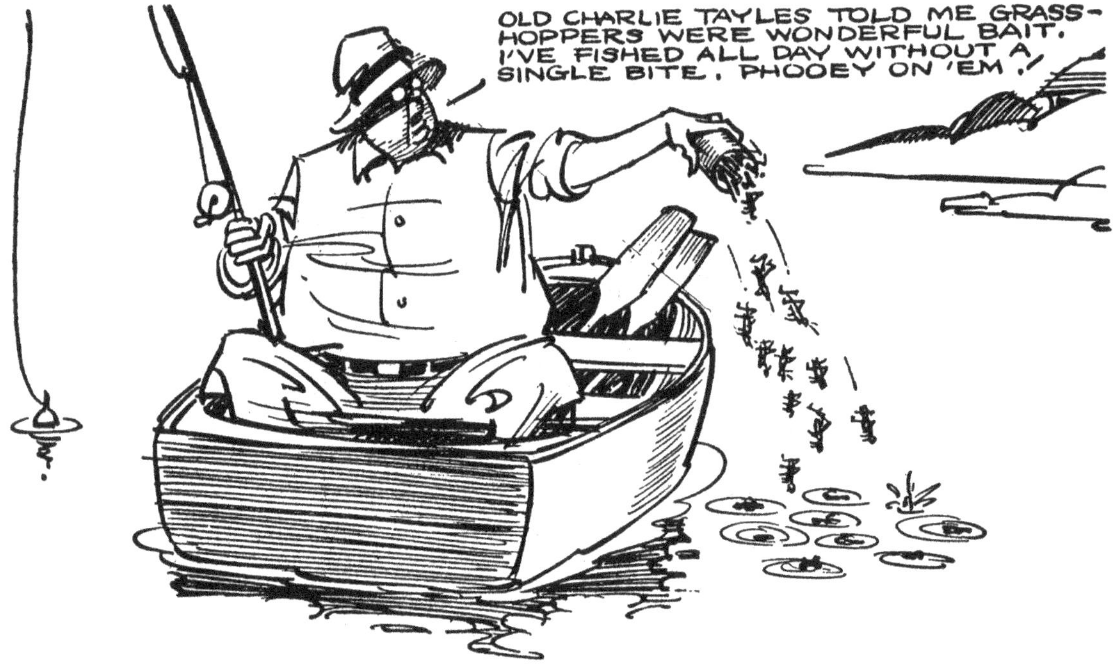
OLD CHARLIE TAYLES TOLD ME GRASS-HOPPERS WERE WONDERFUL BAIT. I'VE FISHED ALL DAY WITHOUT A SINGLE BITE. PHOOEY ON 'EM!

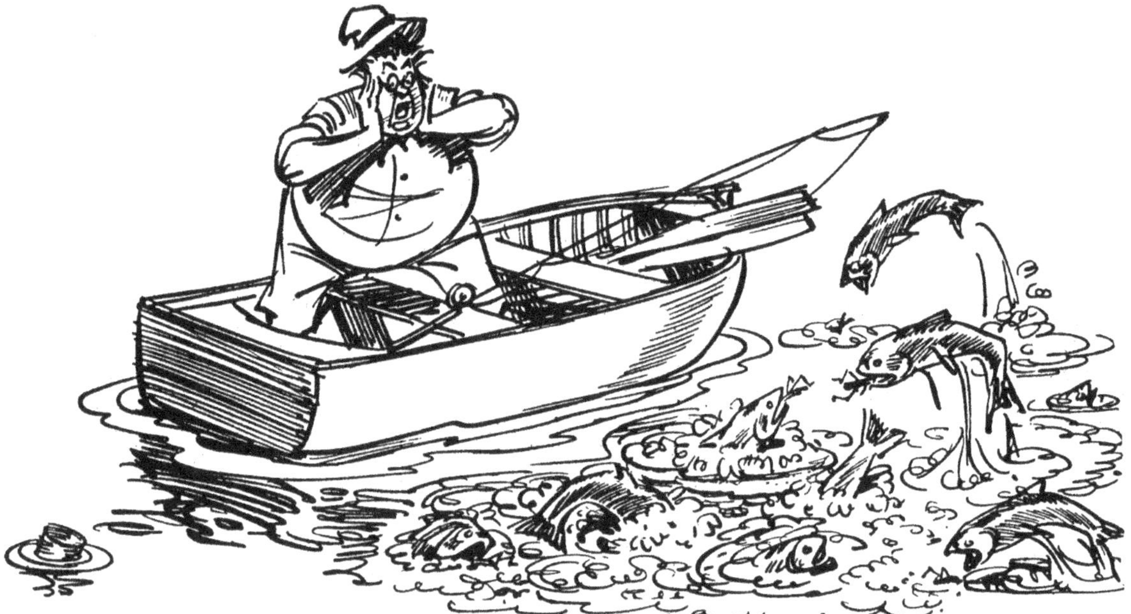

BY GOLLY! HERE'S TH' OL' FISHIN' ROD! I CAN HARDLY WAIT 'TIL SUMMER. YOU KNOW WHAT THIS IS, DON'T YOU, NAPOLEON?

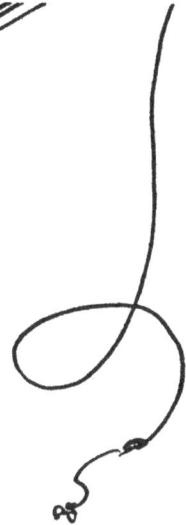

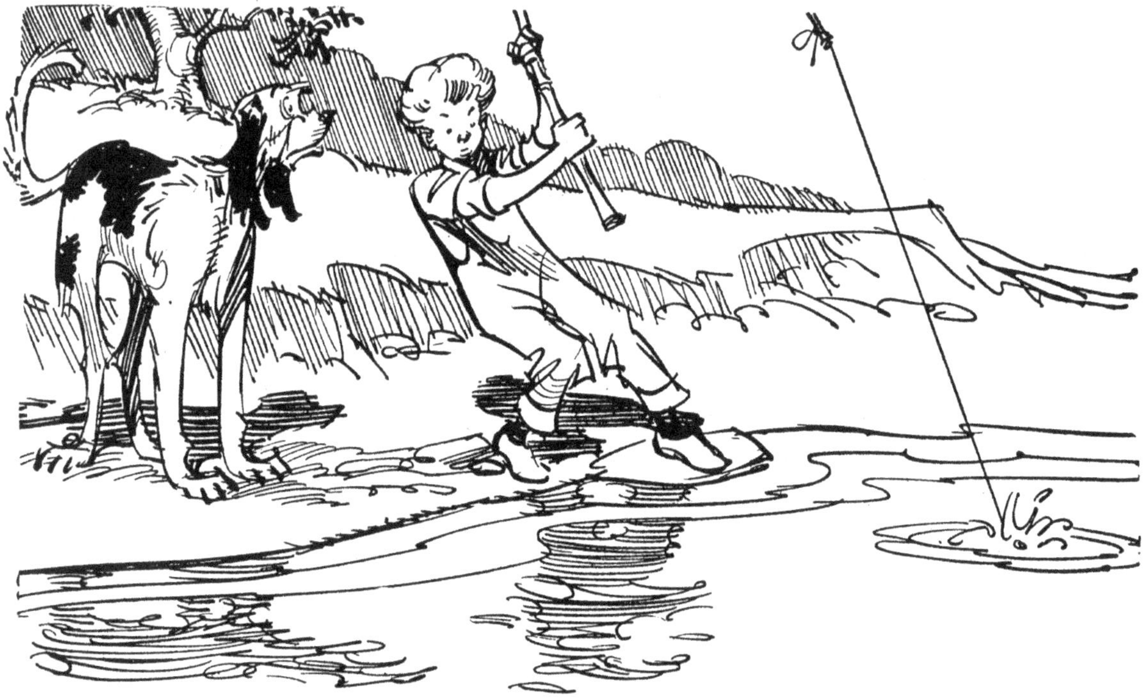

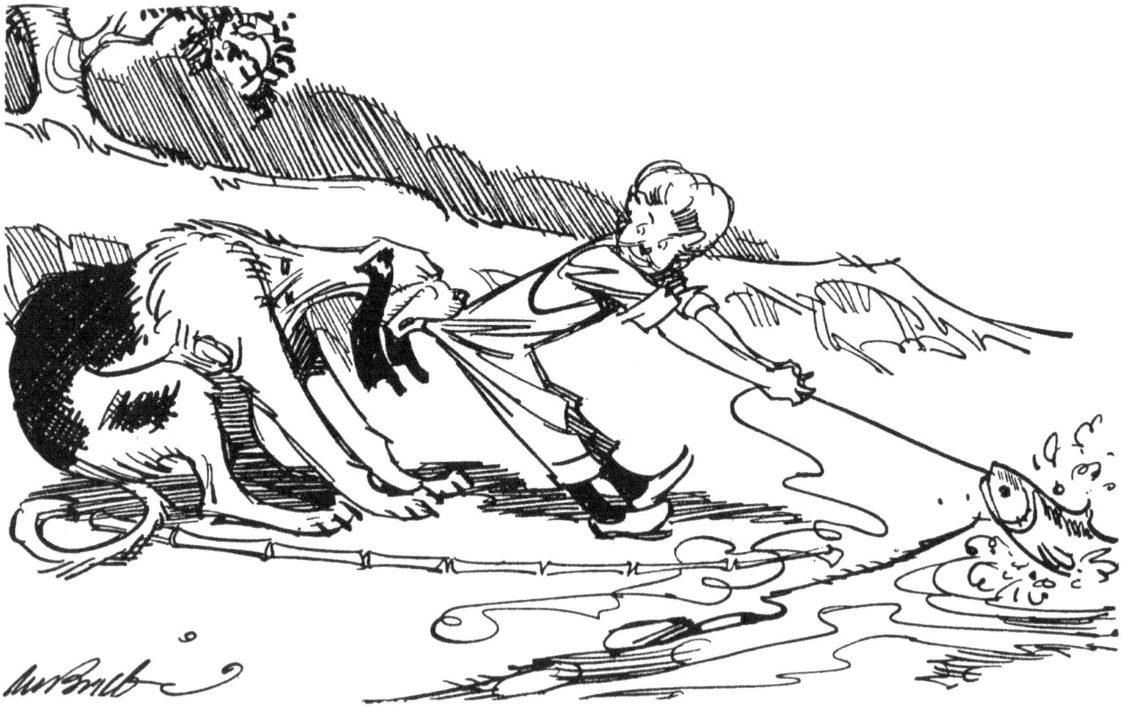

NAPOLEON WATCHES BICYCLIST
UNCLE ELBY

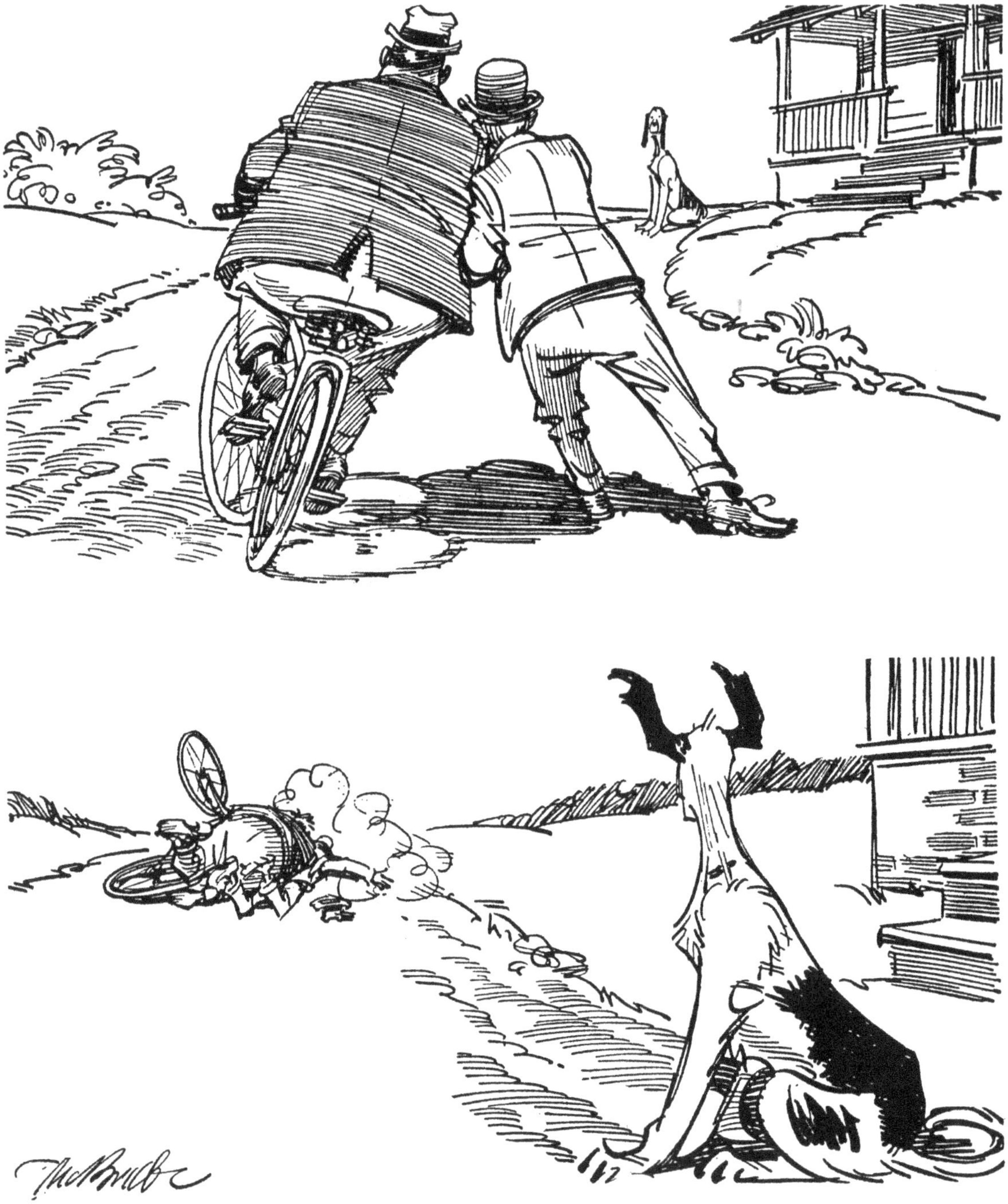

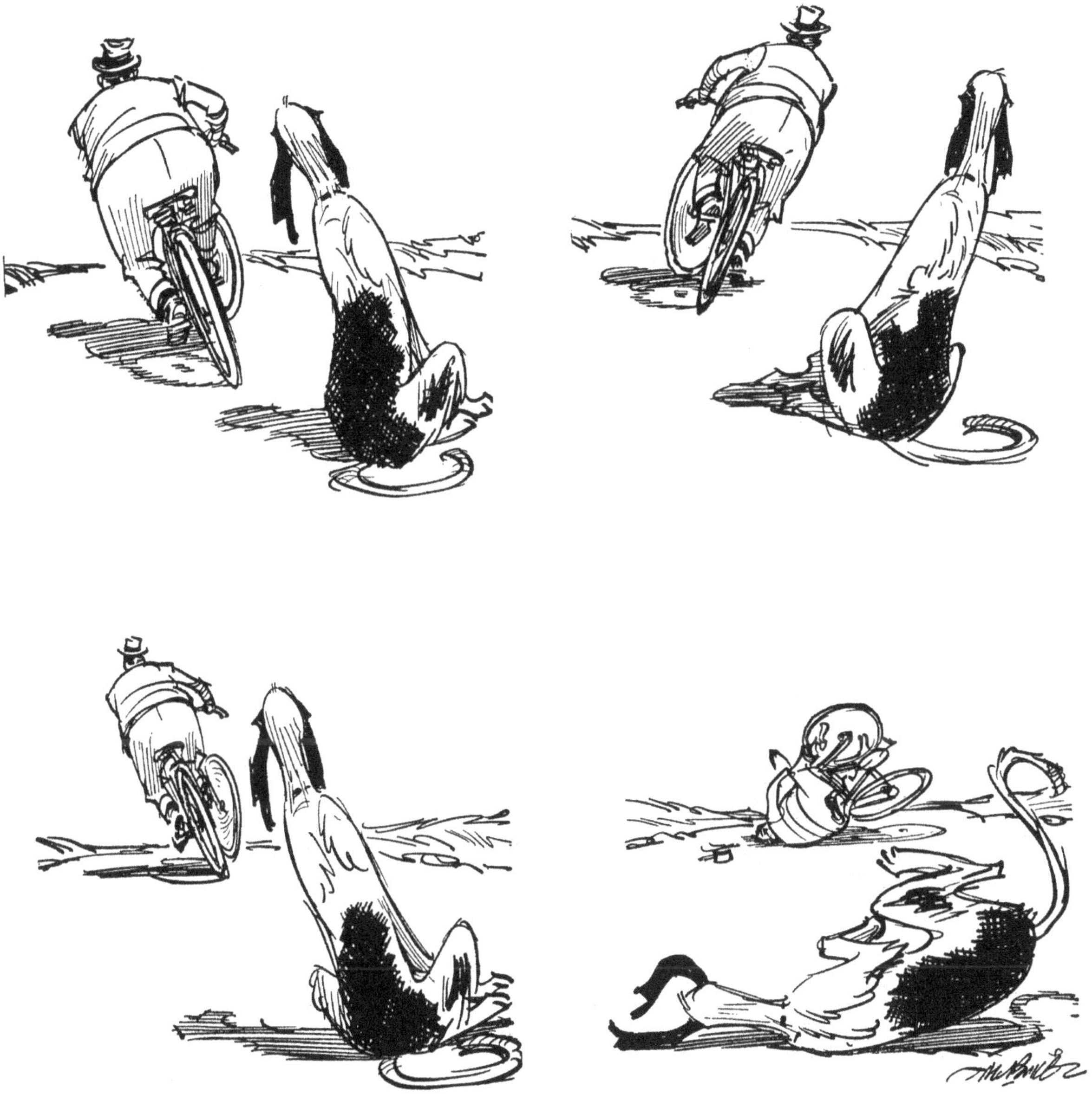

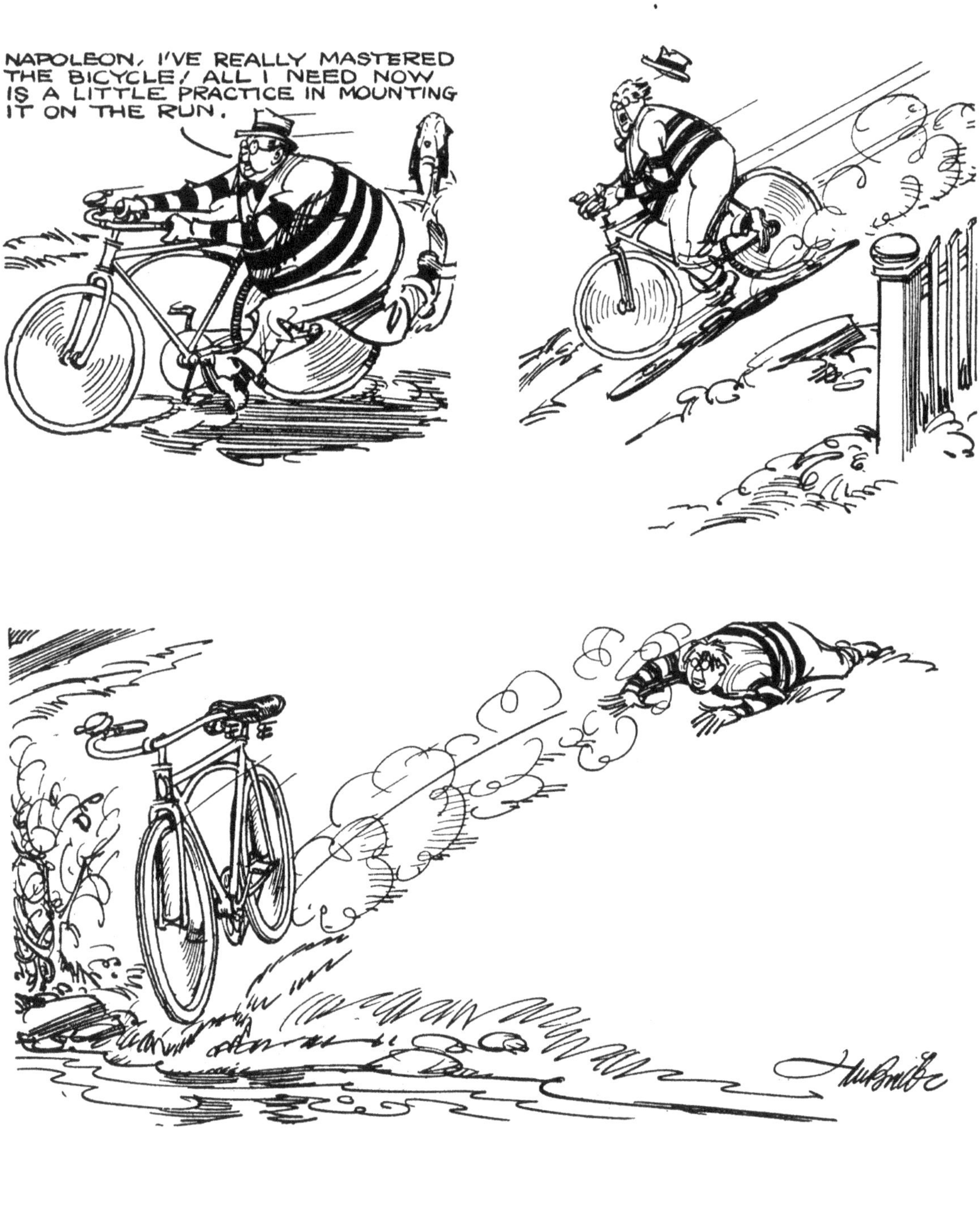
NAPOLEON, I'VE REALLY MASTERED THE BICYCLE! ALL I NEED NOW IS A LITTLE PRACTICE IN MOUNTING IT ON THE RUN.

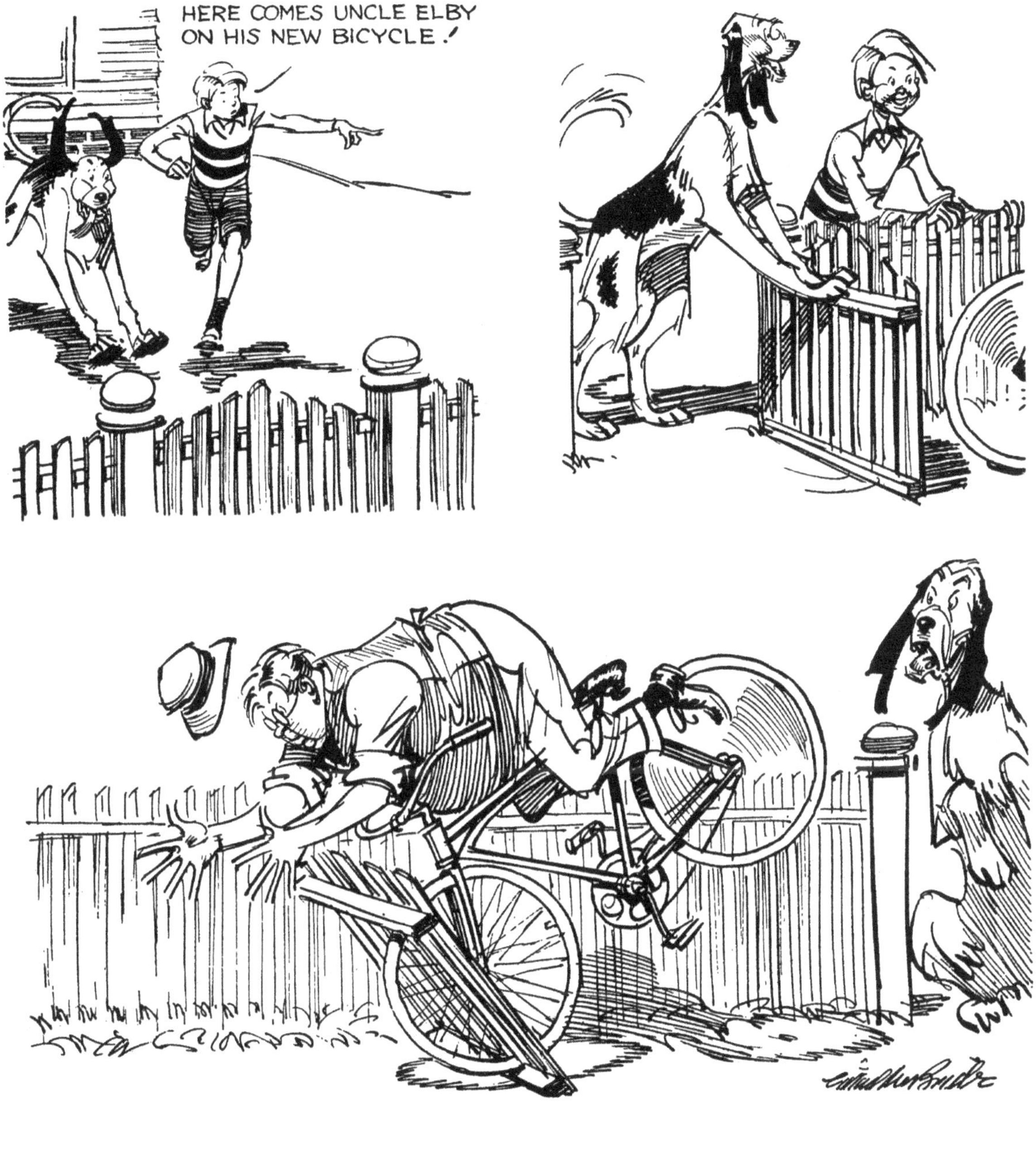
HERE COMES UNCLE ELBY ON HIS NEW BICYCLE!

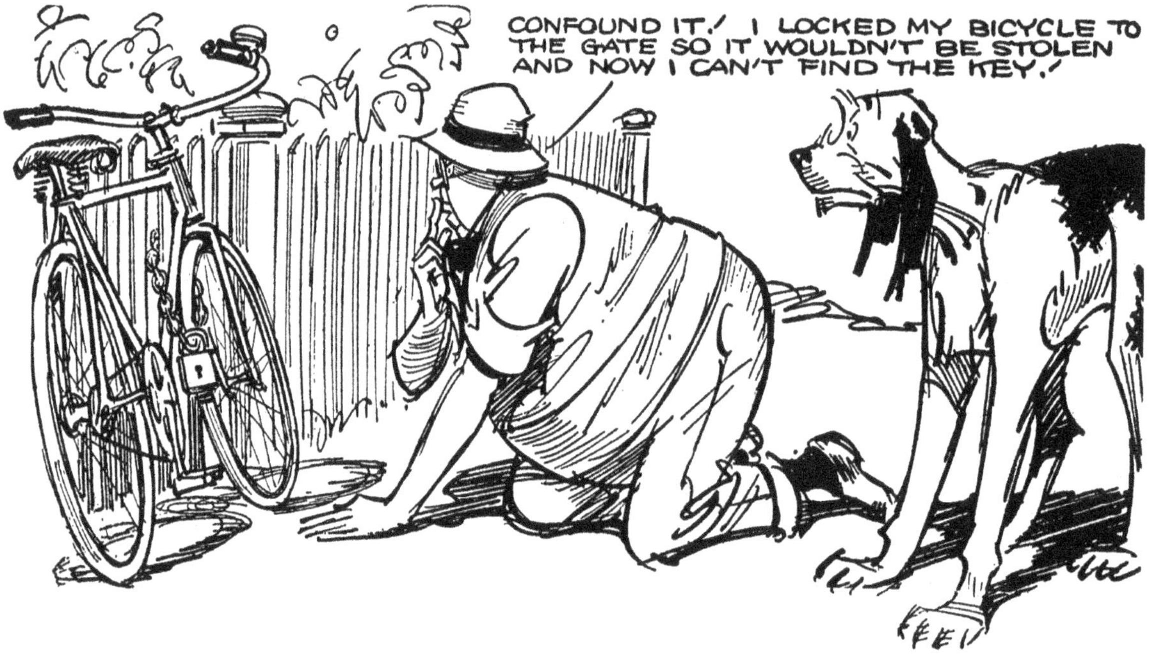
CONFOUND IT! I LOCKED MY BICYCLE TO THE GATE SO IT WOULDN'T BE STOLEN AND NOW I CAN'T FIND THE KEY!

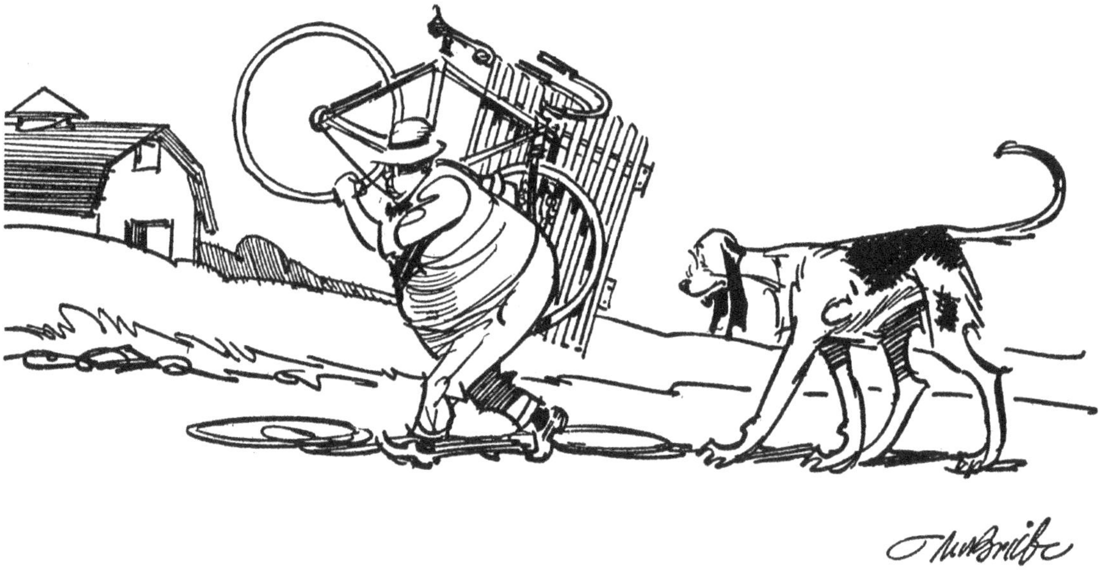

NAPOLEON AND SOME SURPRISING SPORTS

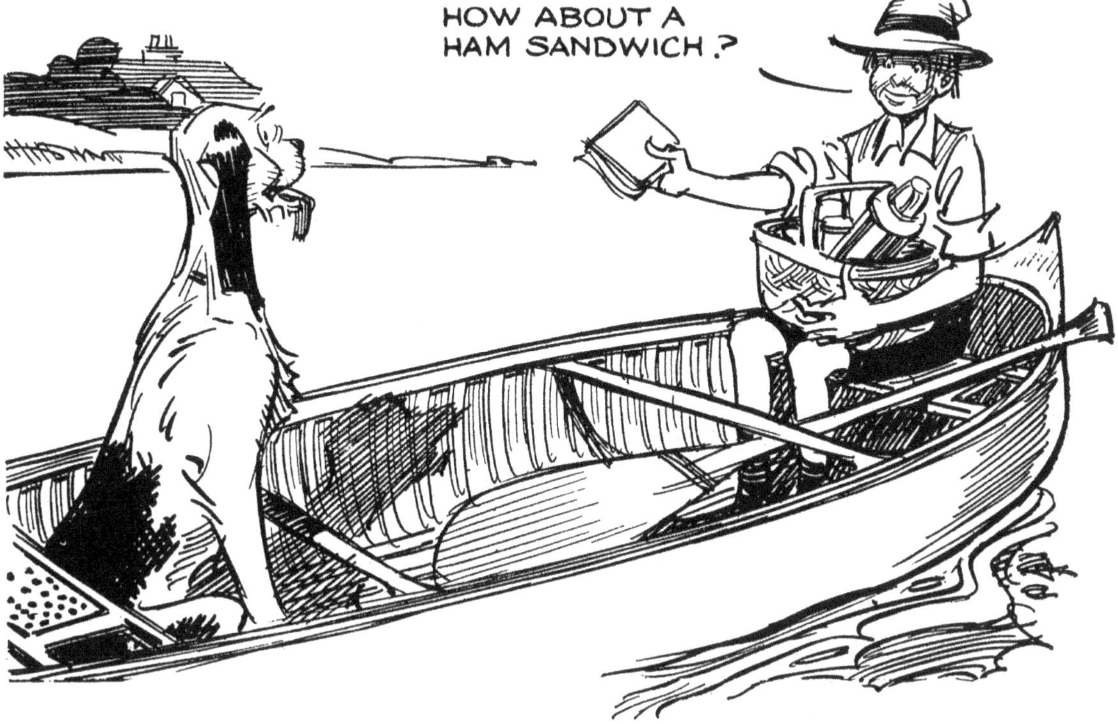
HOW ABOUT A
HAM SANDWICH ?

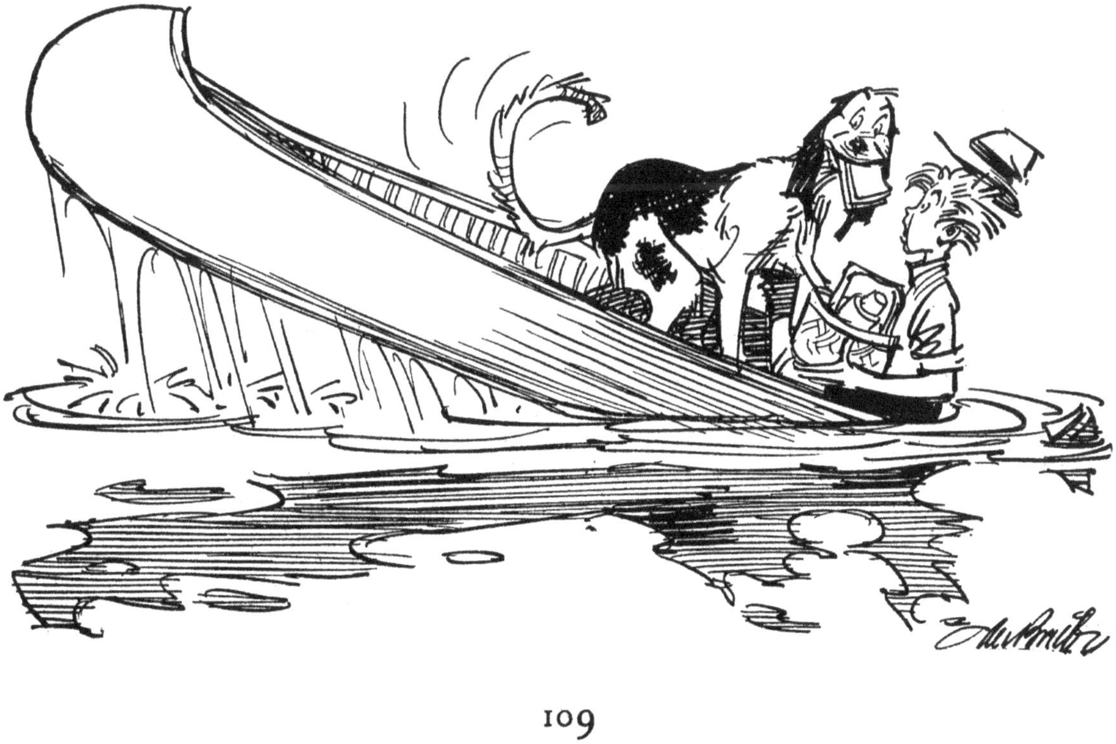

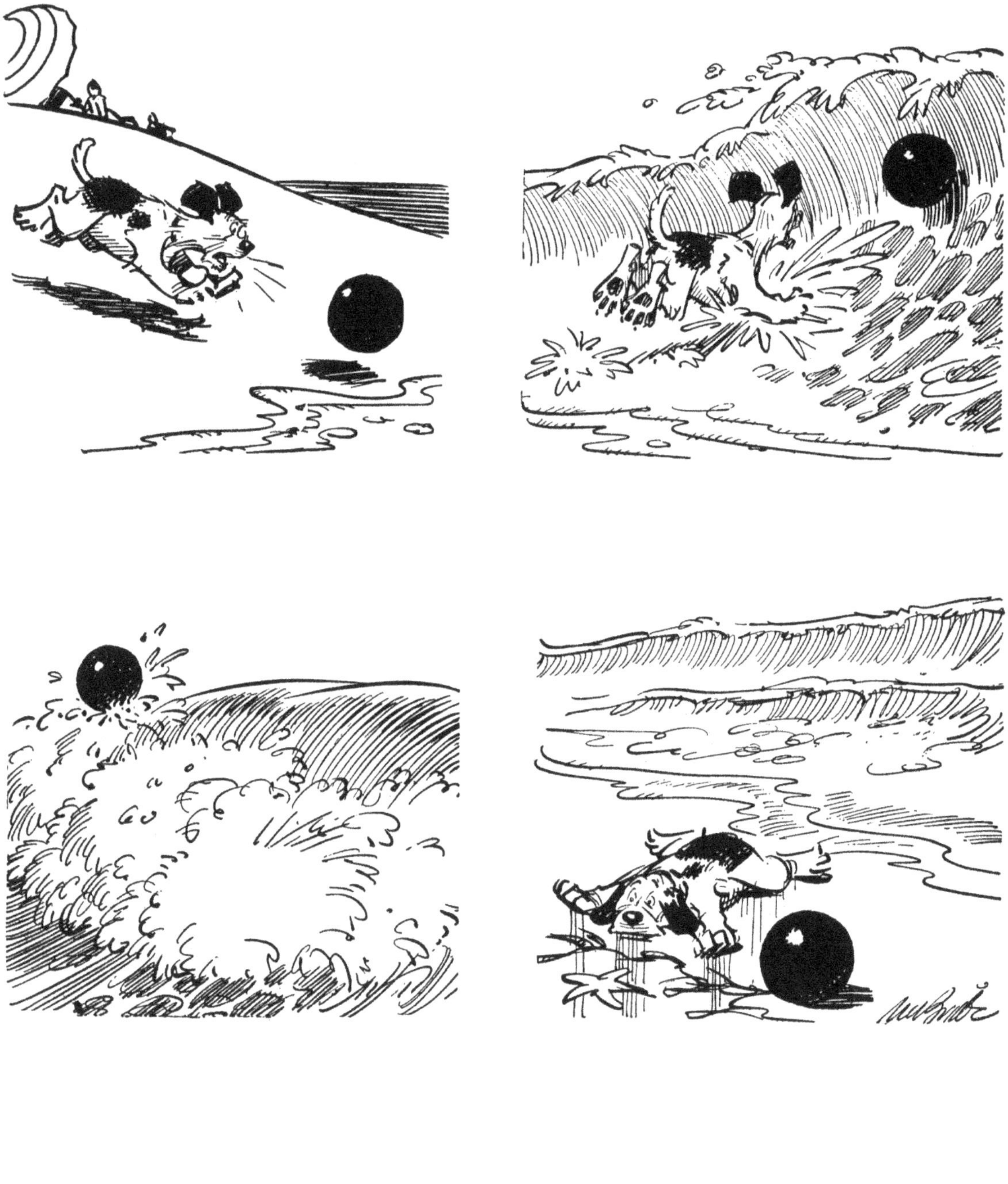

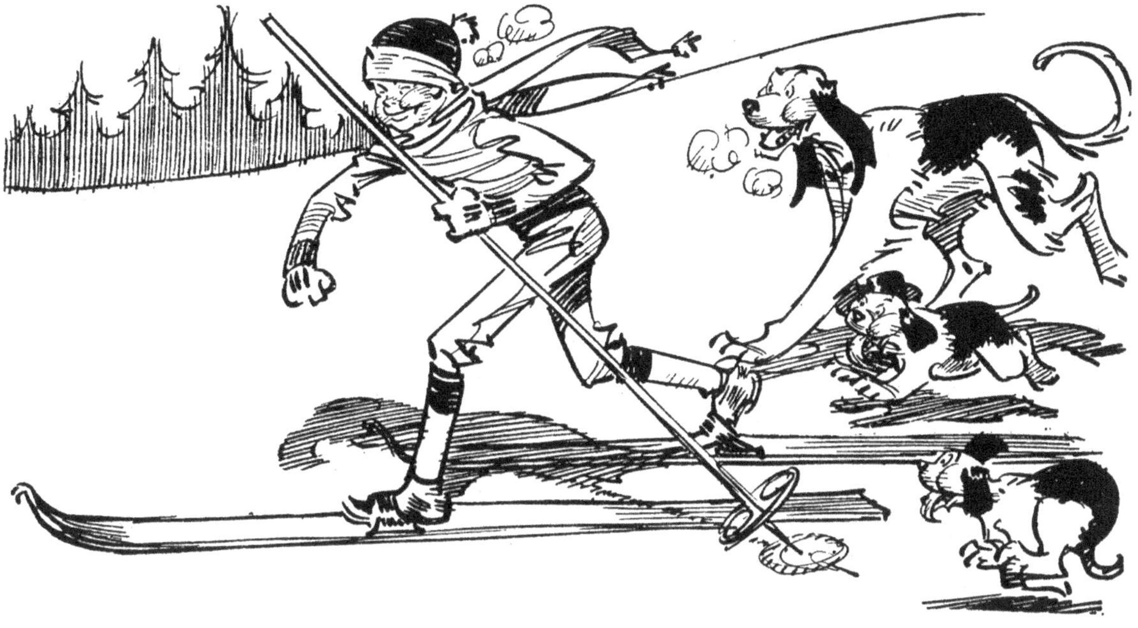

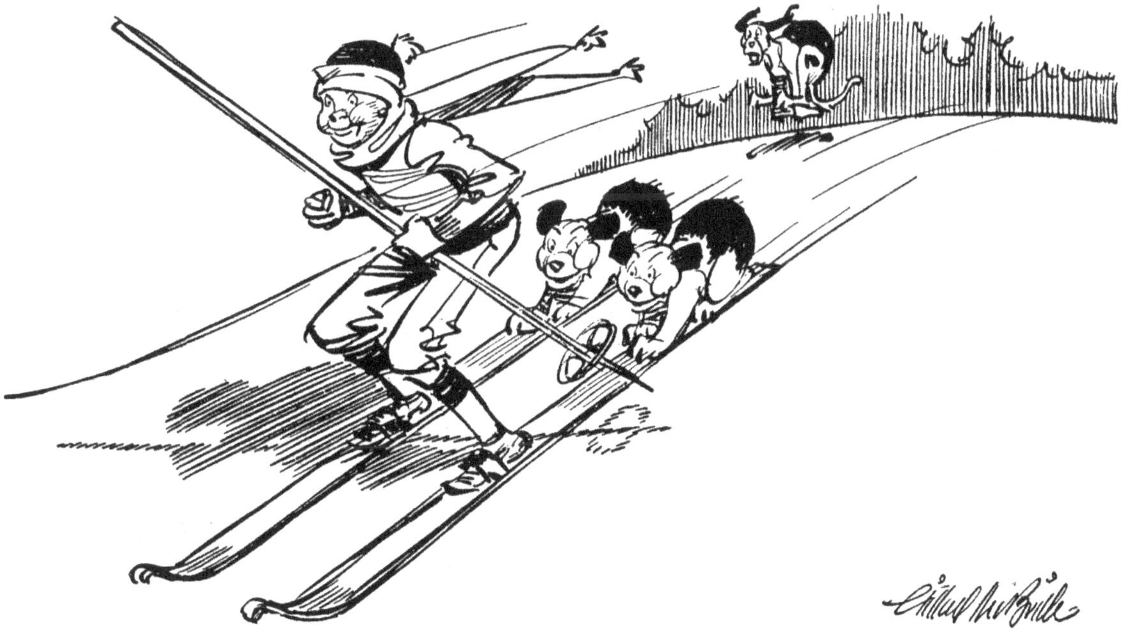

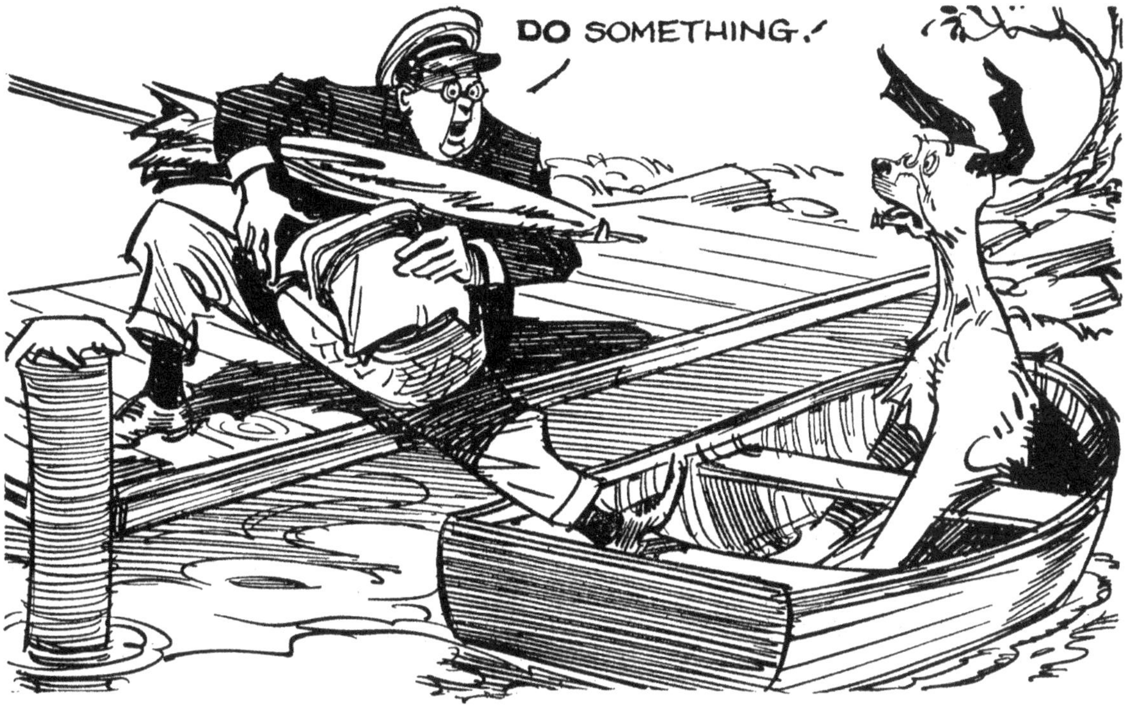
DO SOMETHING!

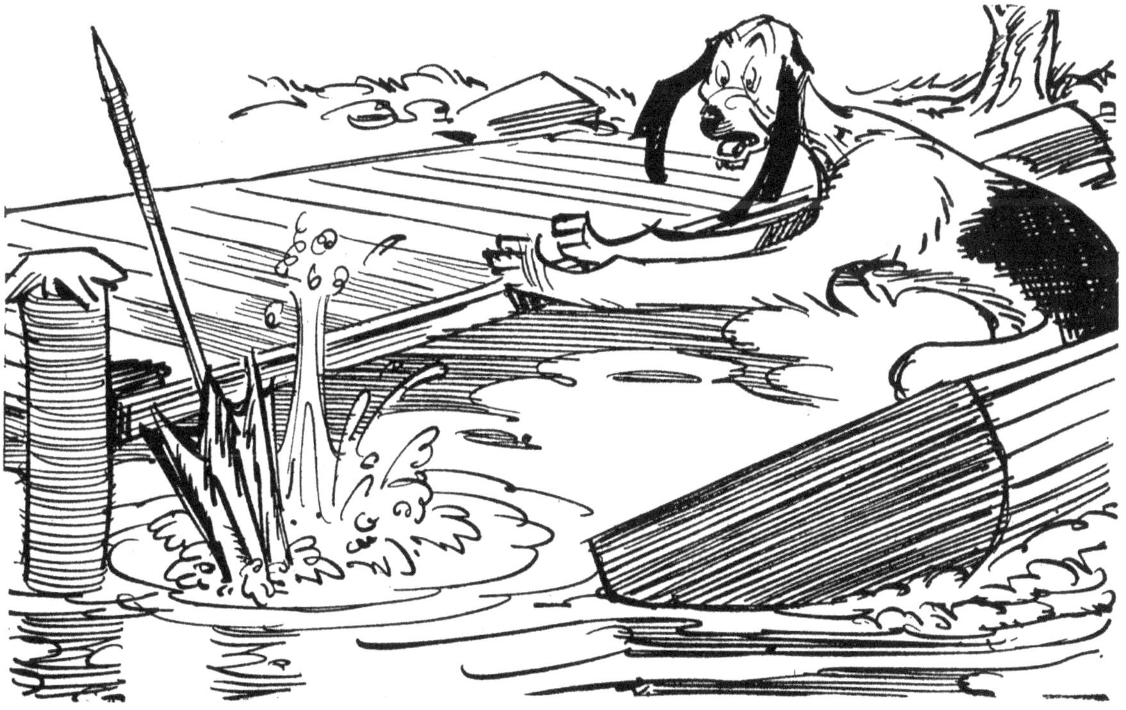

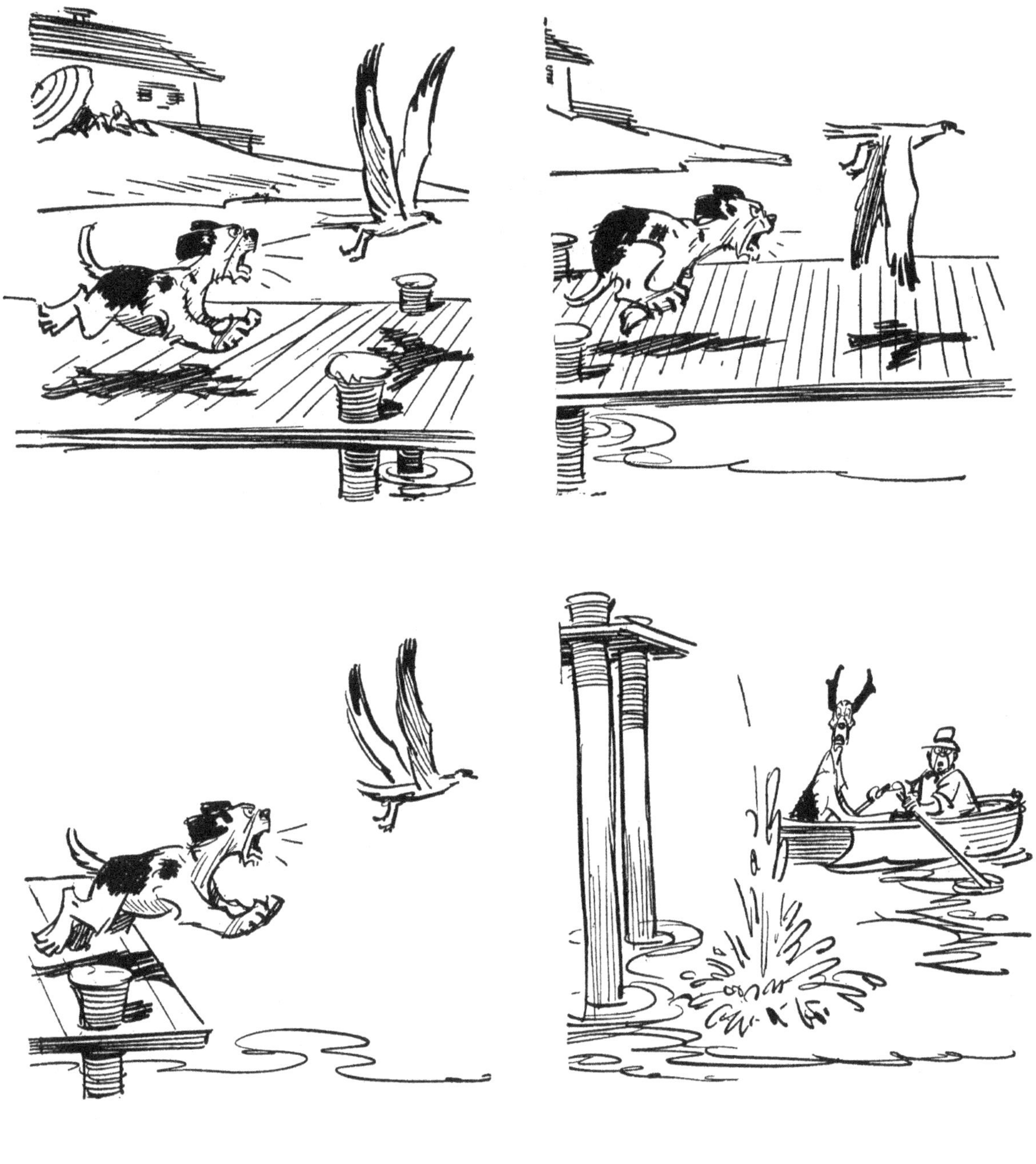

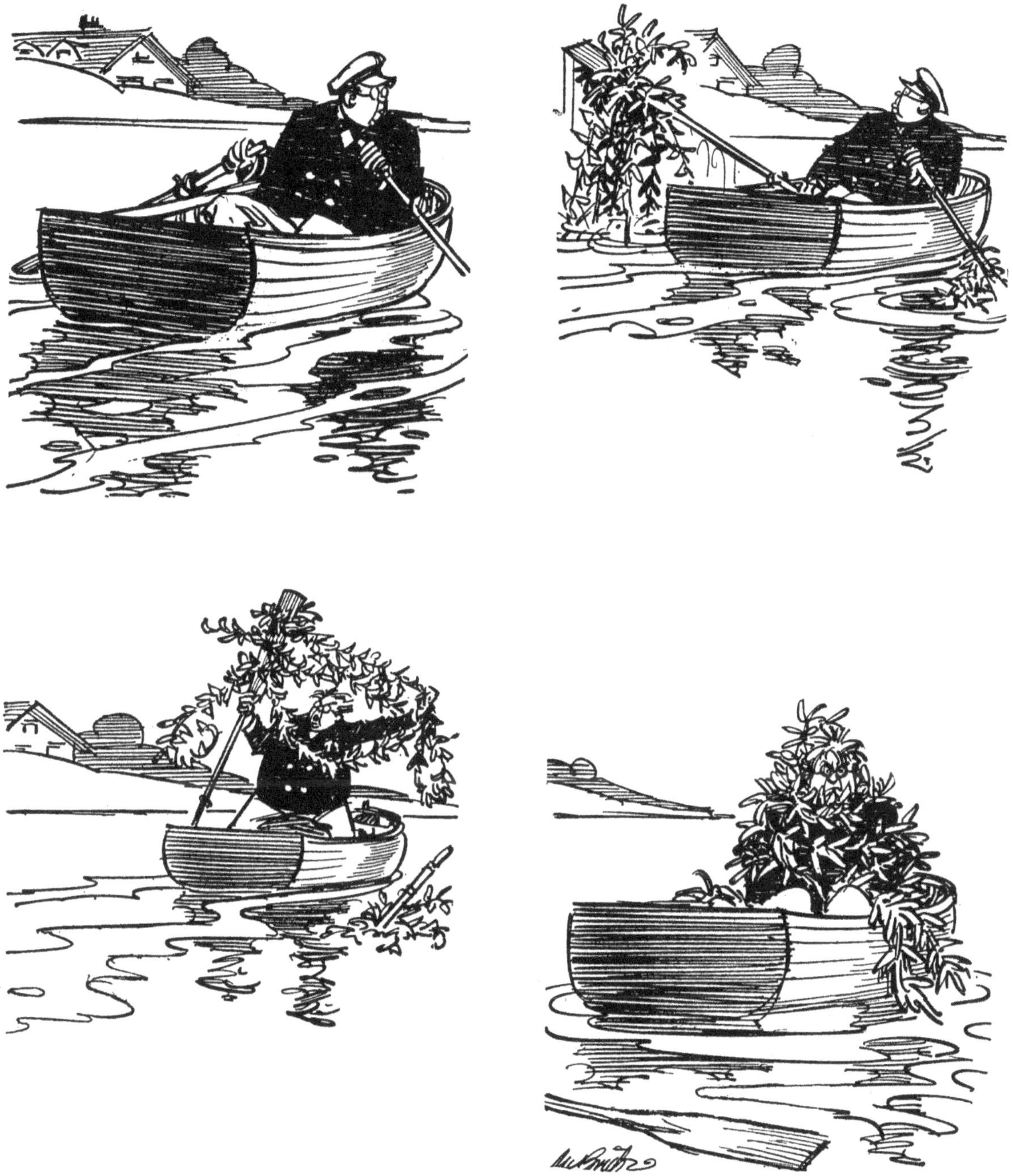

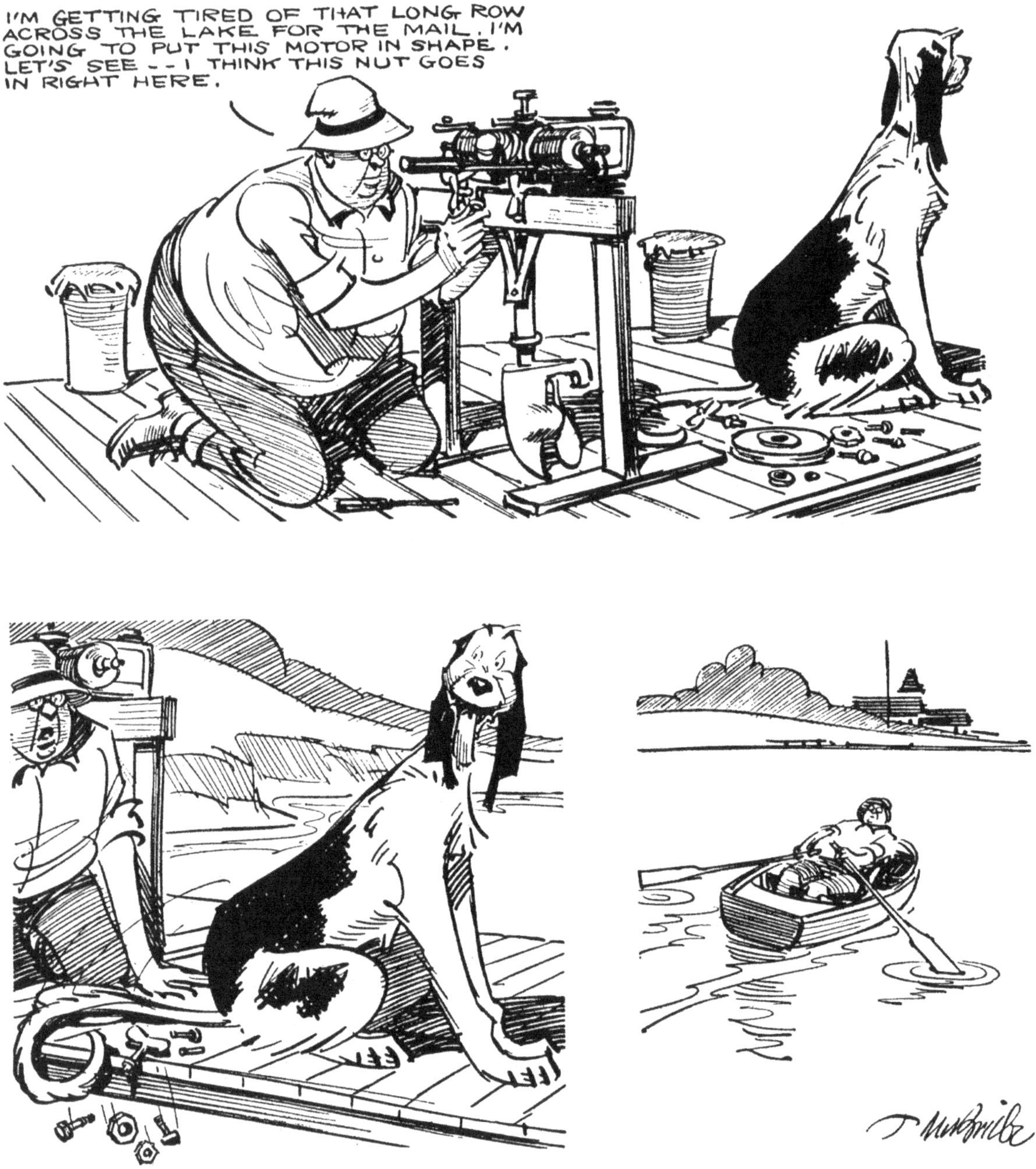
I'M GETTING TIRED OF THAT LONG ROW ACROSS THE LAKE FOR THE MAIL. I'M GOING TO PUT THIS MOTOR IN SHAPE. LET'S SEE - - I THINK THIS NUT GOES IN RIGHT HERE.

AND TH' INSTRUCTIONS SAY, "AFTER ROCKING TH' FLY-WHEEL A FEW TIMES TO PRIME TH' MOTOR, GRASP TH' STARTING CORD FIRMLY AND GIVE A STRONG QUICK PULL"!

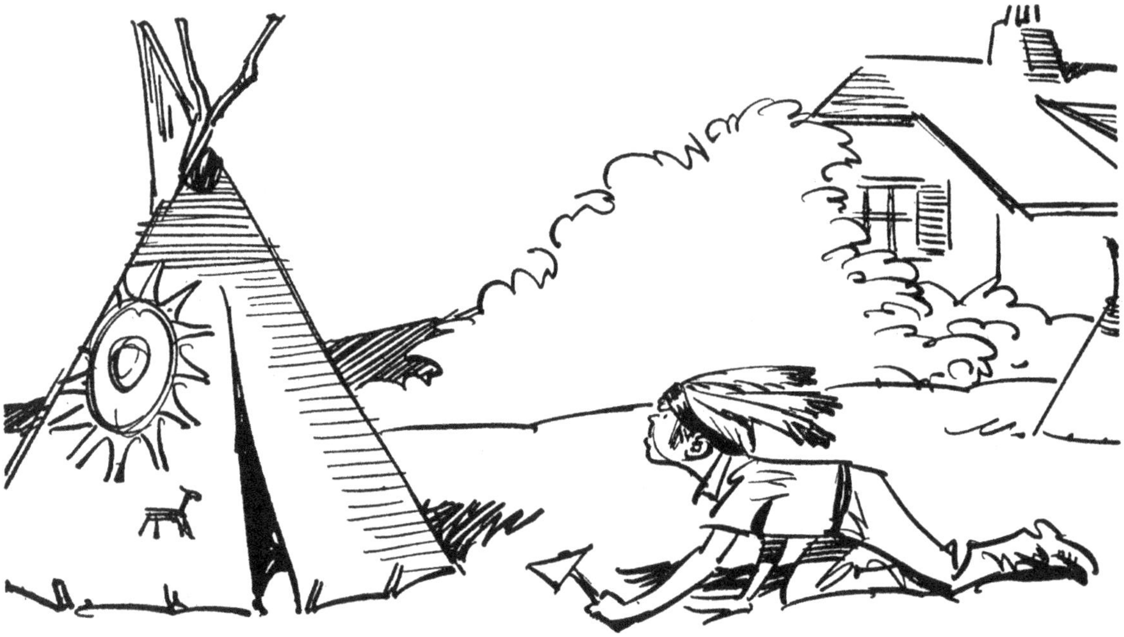

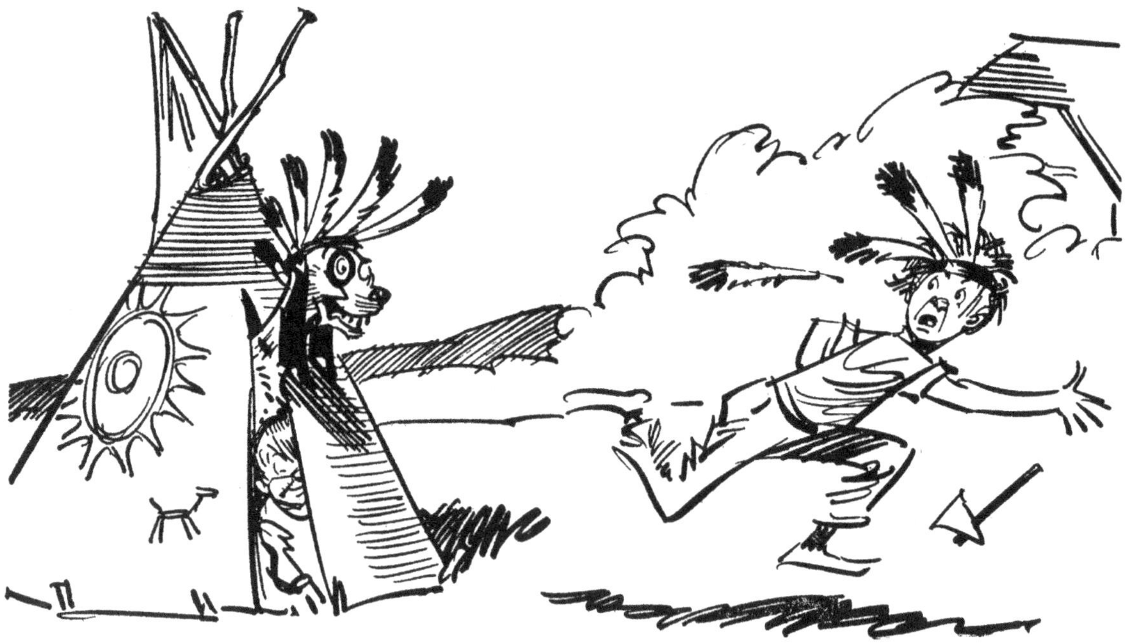

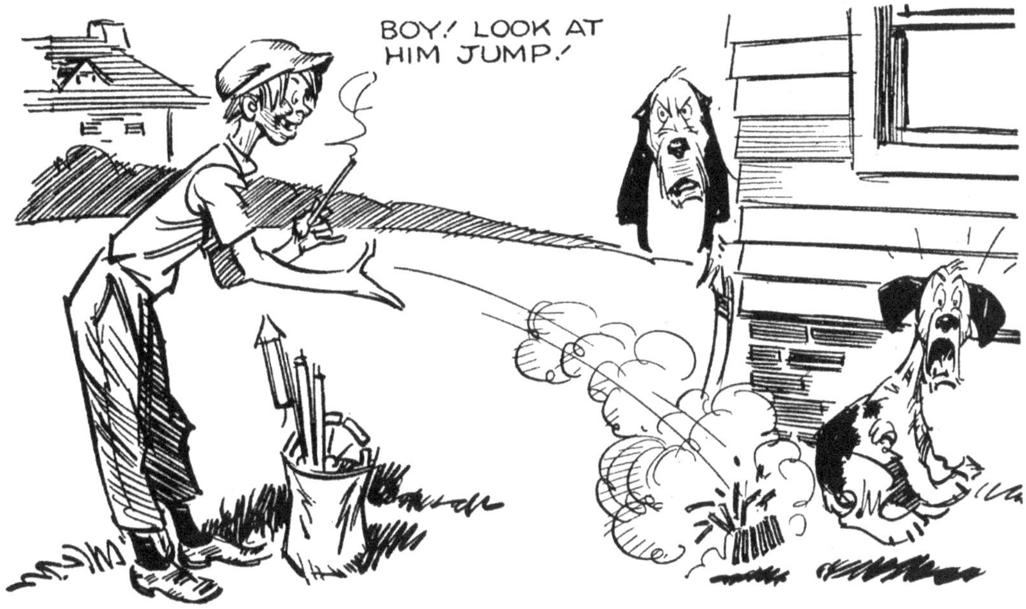
BOY! LOOK AT HIM JUMP!

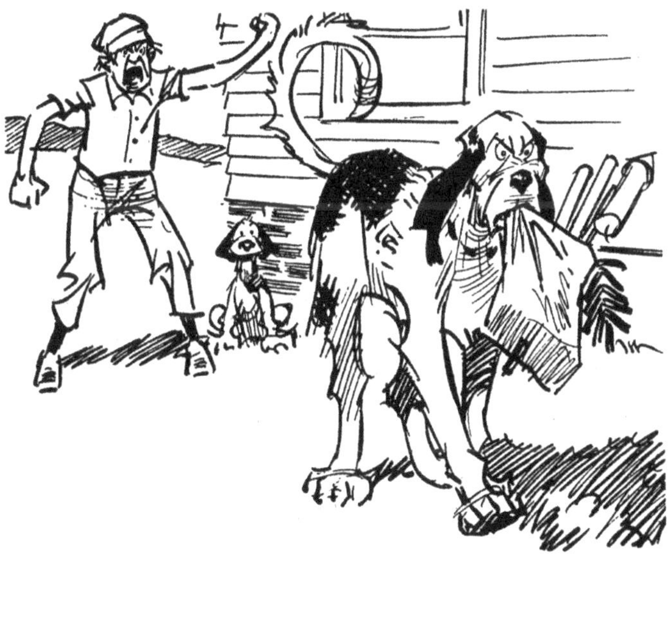

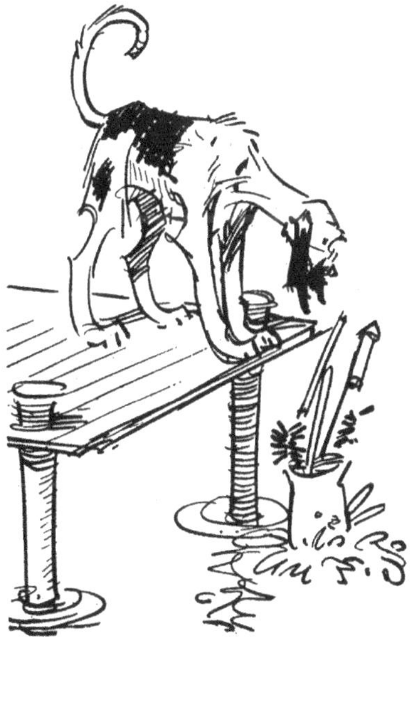

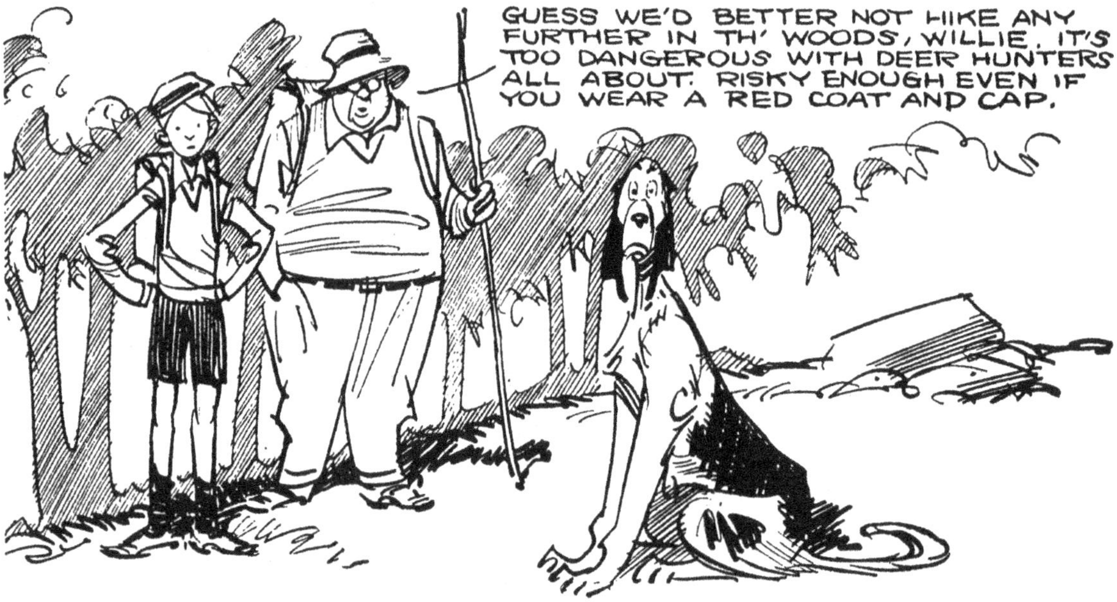
GUESS WE'D BETTER NOT HIKE ANY FURTHER IN TH' WOODS, WILLIE. IT'S TOO DANGEROUS WITH DEER HUNTERS ALL ABOUT. RISKY ENOUGH EVEN IF YOU WEAR A RED COAT AND CAP.

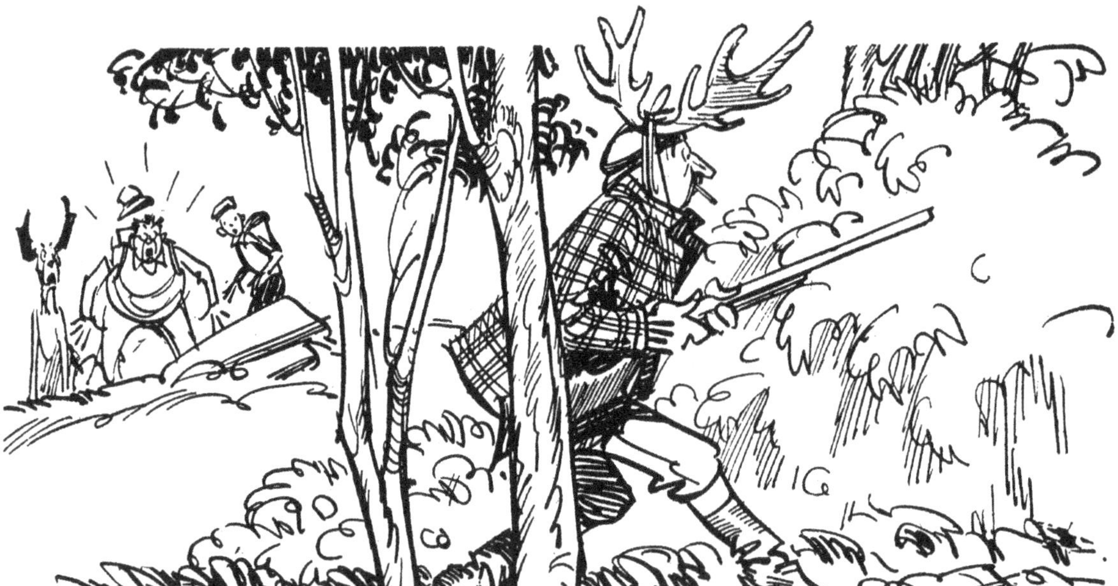

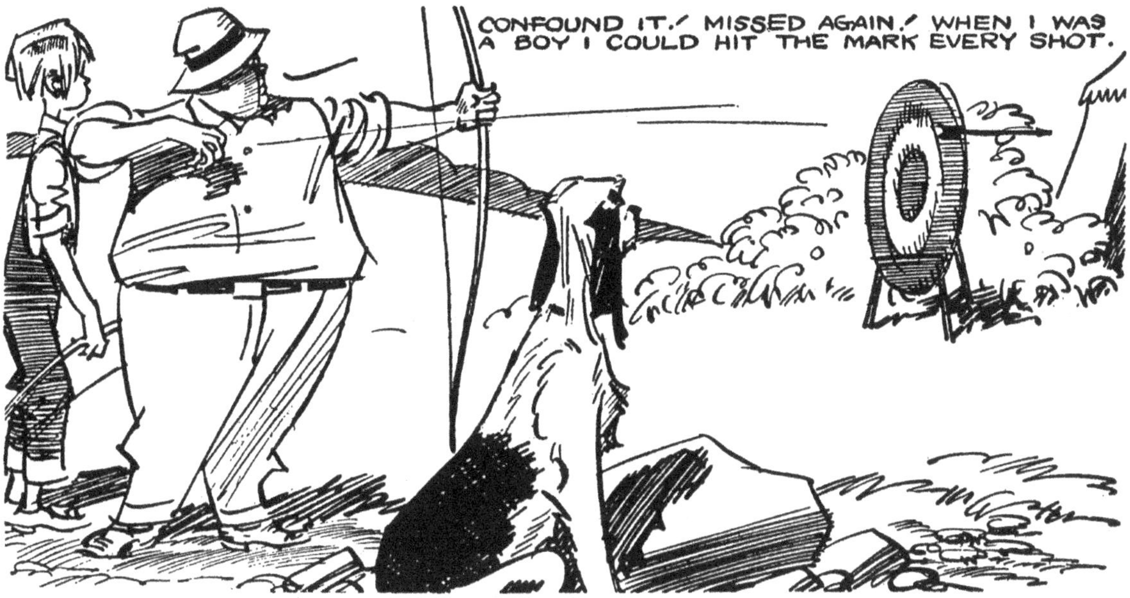
CONFOUND IT.! MISSED AGAIN.! WHEN I WAS A BOY I COULD HIT THE MARK EVERY SHOT.

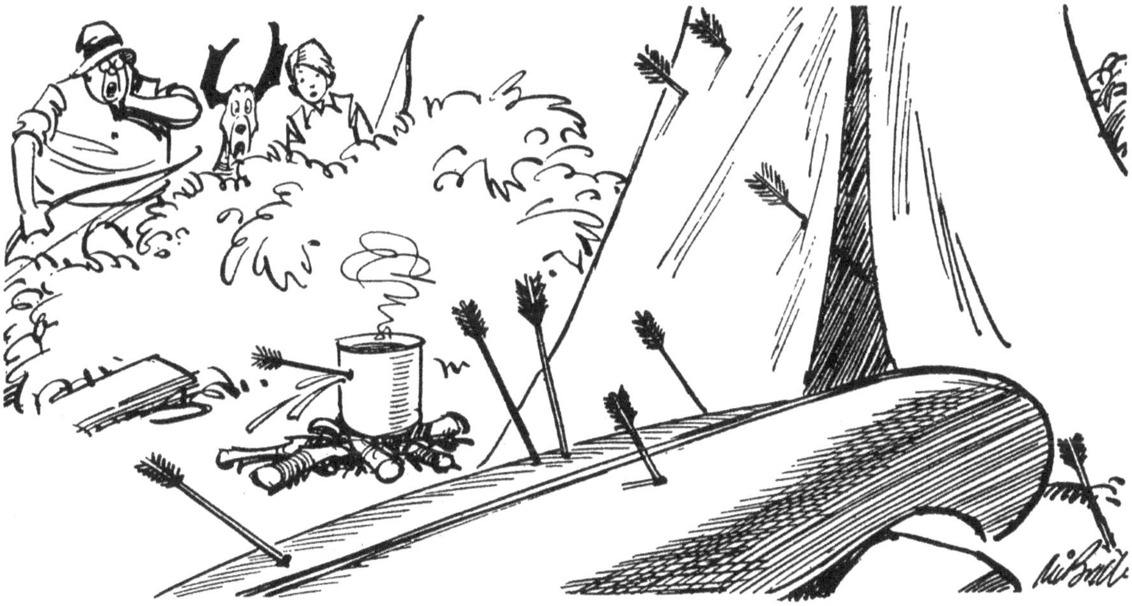

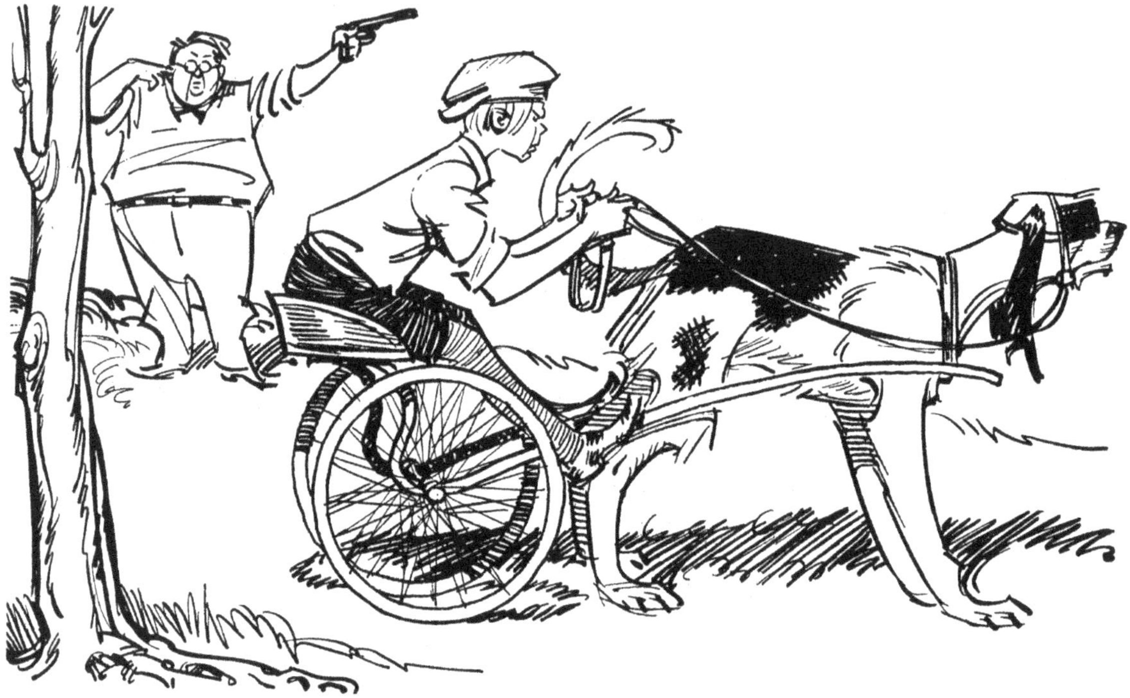

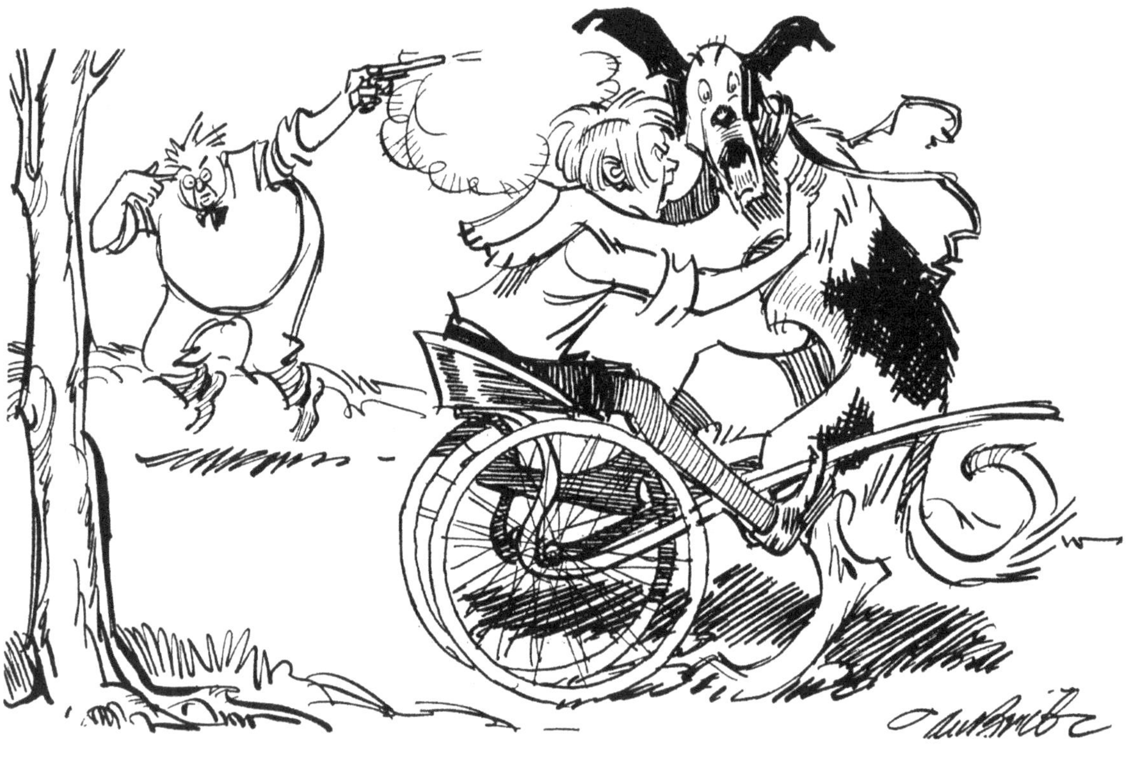

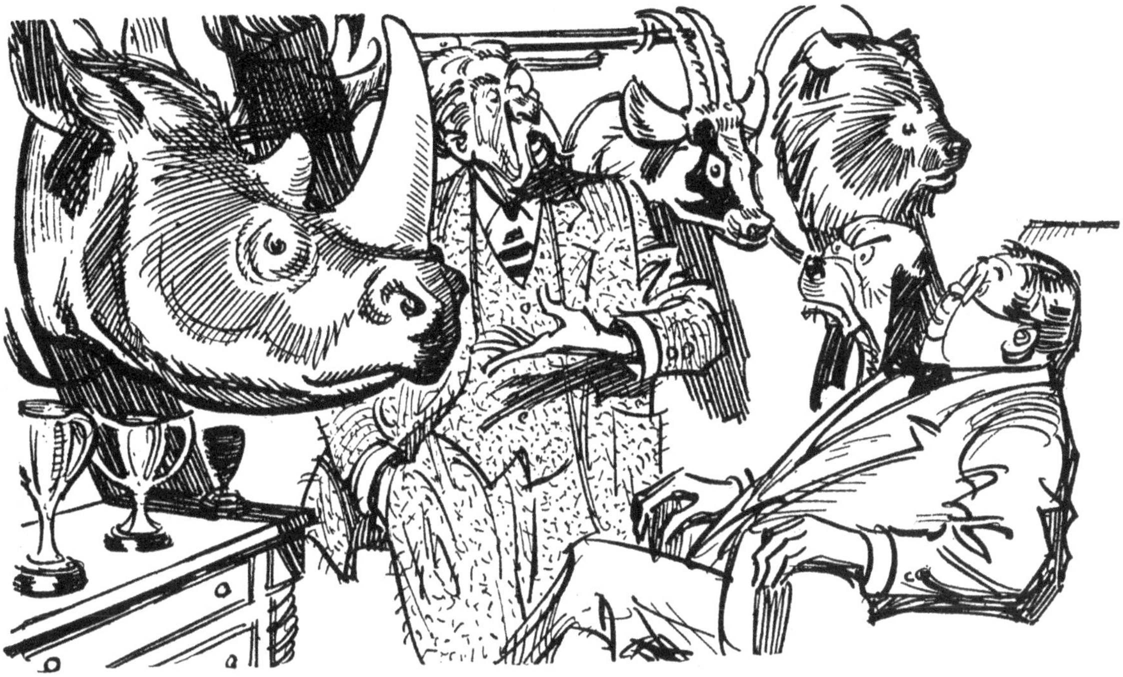

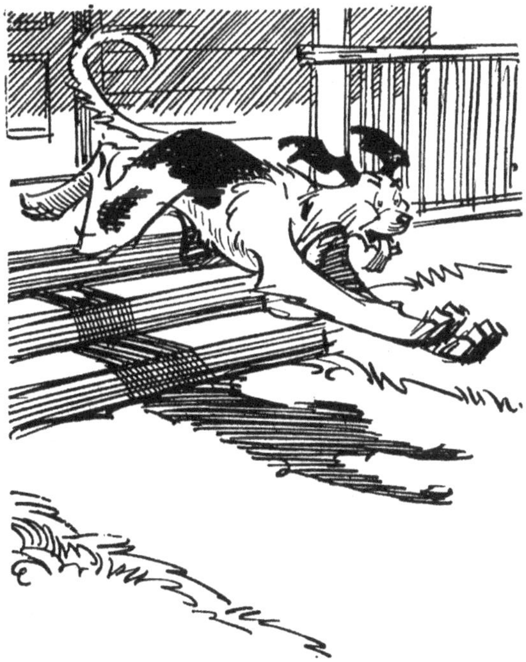

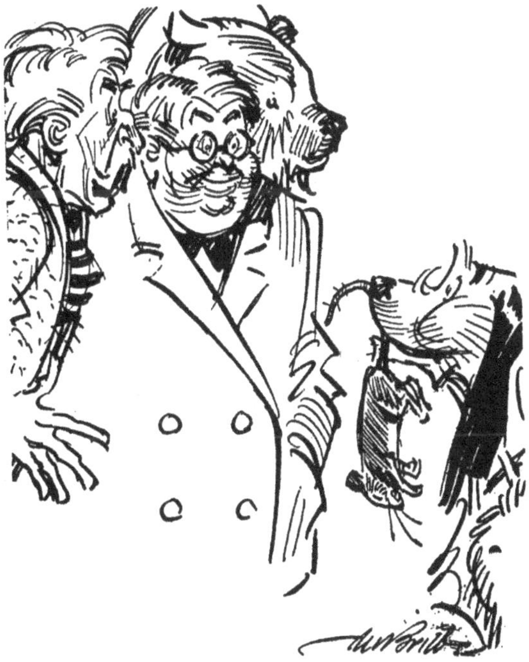

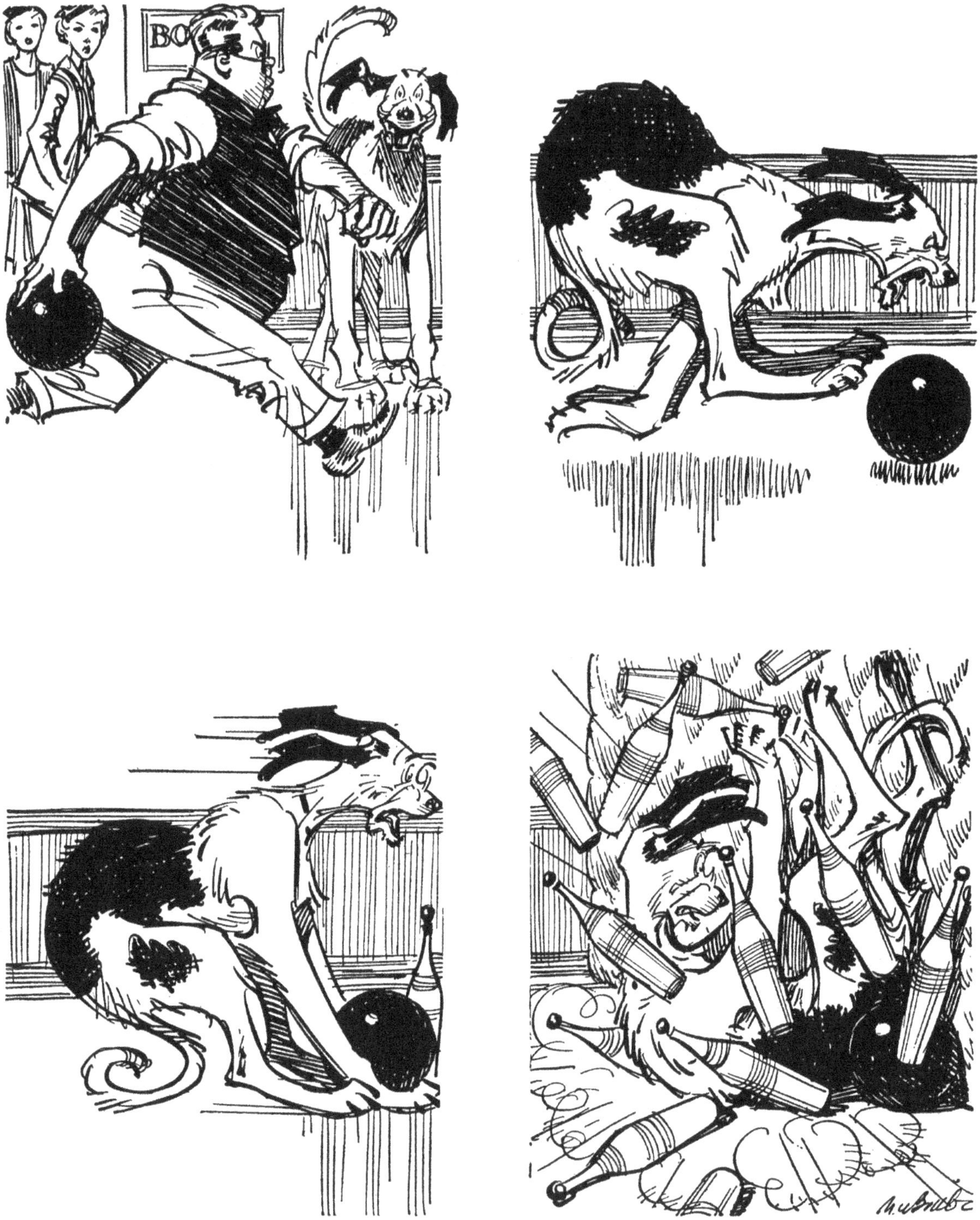
BO

127

THE END

More Vintage Comic Art and More at

CoachwhipBooks.com

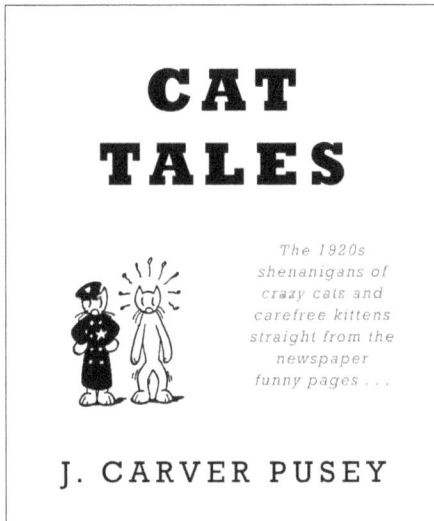

CAT TALES

The 1920s shenanigans of crazy cats and carefree kittens straight from the newspaper funny pages . . .

J. CARVER PUSEY

GUNNER and the DUMBO

Story by Lt. Dwight W. Follett, U.S.N.R.
Pictures by Don Nelson

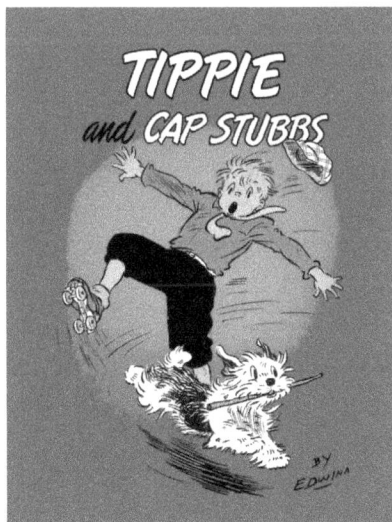

TIPPIE and CAP STUBBS

BY EDWINA

the CISCO KID

THE GOOD OLD DAYS
ERWIN L. HESS

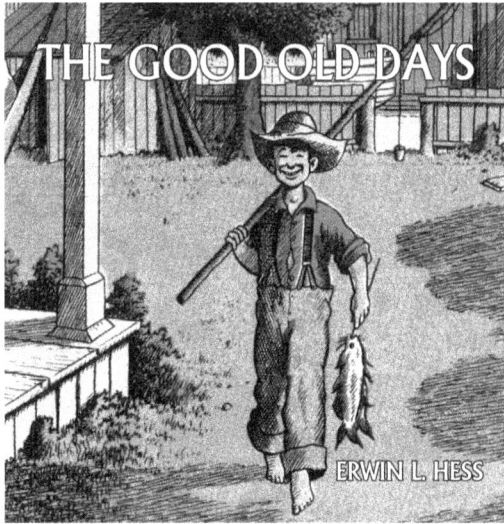

That Little Game
BERT LINK

KATZENJAMMER

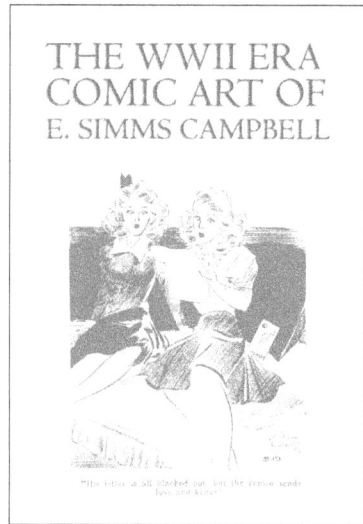

THE WWII ERA
COMIC ART OF
E. SIMMS CAMPBELL

SMITTY
MY MOTHER THANKS YOU MY FATHER THANKS YOU I THANK YOU
CUPPLES AND LEON CO.

JIMMY
HATLO
CARTOONS
PARKING FOR PATRONS

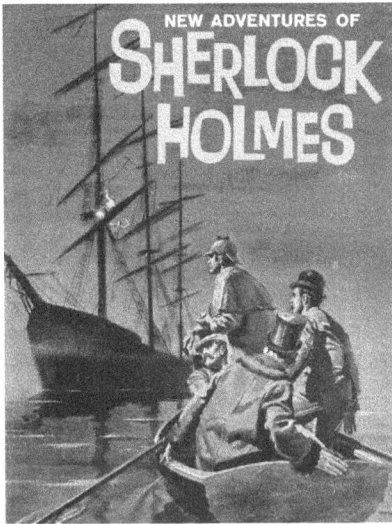

NEW ADVENTURES OF
SHERLOCK HOLMES

LARAMIE

Golf
by
BRIGGS

THE CLAN OF
MUNES
BY
FREDERICK J. WAUGH

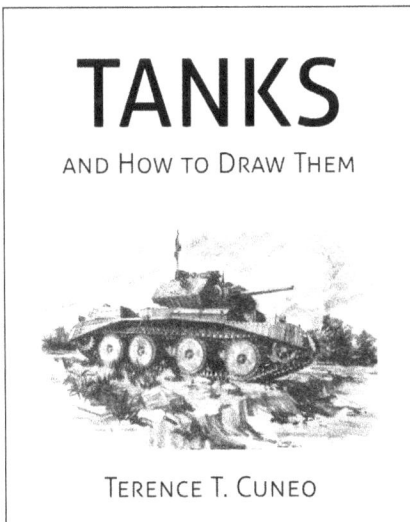

TANKS
AND HOW TO DRAW THEM

TERENCE T. CUNEO

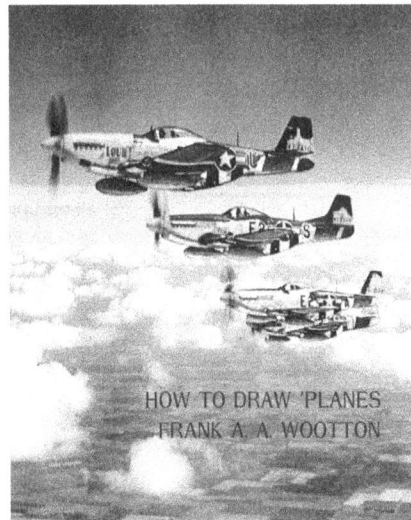

HOW TO DRAW 'PLANES
FRANK A. A. WOOTTON

www.ingramcontent.com/pod-product-compliance
Lightning Source LLC
Chambersburg PA
CBHW042047090426
42733CB00038B/2660